The Healthy Organization

A Revolutionary Approach to People & Management

Second Edition

Brian Dive

KoganPage

London Philadelphia New Delhi

Publisher's Note
Every possible effort has been made to ensure that the information contained in this book is accurate at the time of going to press, and the publishers and authors cannot accept responsibility for any errors or omissions, however caused. No responsibility for loss or damage occasioned to any person acting, or refraining from action, as a result of the material in this publication can be accepted by the editor, the publisher or any of the authors.

Indian Edition 2010

Kogan Page India Private Limited
4737/23 Ansari Road,
Daryaganj
New Delhi 110 002

This edition is for sale in the Indian subcontinent only. Not for export elsewhere.

ISBN : 978-81-7554-592-2

Published by Vinod Vasishtha for Kogan Page India Private Limited,
4737/23, Ansari Road, Daryaganj, New Delhi 110 002.

Printed and bound in India.

Contents

LIST OF STEPS TO A HEALTHY ORGANIZATION

Acknowledgements

The first edition of *The Healthy Organization*, in 2002, featured the implementation of the DMA Solution Set in Tesco and Unilever. It has therefore been applied in about 100 countries around the world. The key contributors were acknowledged in that edition.

Tesco has since extended the application into the areas of competencies and leadership development. These initiatives have been led by the HR Director, Clare Chapman, together with members of the board and top management. Max Weston, of the leadership consultancy Whitehead Mann, has helped the company benchmark externally 'best in class' management. Other key contributors included Tesco's Head of Learning Nicola Steele, Maxine Dolan and Rachel Howarth.

Amersham, the international healthcare company, piloted DMA in several areas and was considering global implementation when it was taken over by General Electric. The project was sponsored by the HR Director, George Battersby, and led by the Head of Compensation and Benefits, Malcolm Saffin.

The international DIY company B&Q, part of Kingfisher, applied the DMA Solution Set to help solve a number of organization design and succession issues. This was under the guidance of the CEO, Bill

Whiting and the HR Director, Mike Cutt, together with key members of his team such as Rob Barnet and Guy Eccles.

The approach has also been explored by Marks and Spencer. Those involved in the fieldwork included Karen Millar, Tim Jones, Trista Bennetts, and Mark Thomas.

Commander Lee Dawson has applied DMA ideas in helping to clarify strategic and governance accountabilities in the Second Sea Lord's organization within the Royal Navy.

Ani Lahiri, the CEO of ABP Publishing Company in India, has also applied DMA principles. He found 'The application of Work Levels has given us the basis for creating an organization design where empowered people drive superior performance.'

It has also been used in the analysis of the accountabilities of a secondary school. The latter is being used as the basis for the identification and development of potential secondary school principals.

These examples have been chosen to illustrate that the principles underpinning the DMA approach have had widespread application. They have been applied in many different cultures, in both the public and the private sectors, in organizations that are very large and complex and those that are not so large. These recent consulting assignments have also led to the addition of extra material in this edition. The importance of the differences between unskilled, semi-skilled and skilled work is explored as the basis for a sound approach to reward and job differentiation in level 1.

The emergence of 24 × 7 × 364/5 service operations in the 21st century, the issue of when to have support roles and the definition of their accountabilities are becoming more crucial. This has been examined in greater depth in Chapter 3.

The indicators of potential to move from one level to another are explored further in Chapter 7. This chapter also analyses the difference between values, skills and competencies, and gives evidence of how these are successfully handled in the DMA approach.

Common failings of traditional competency models are highlighted and a new approach to leadership development is laid out in Chapters 7 and 8.

Key organization design shortcomings, based on recent case studies, are set out in Chapter 3. The importance of 'context' established by applying the Levels of Accountability is explored in Chapters 3, 6 and 7.

A successful and new approach to the identification and development of general managers, based on work in an international company, is described in Chapter 8. The importance of 'boundary moves' is highlighted. This has led to some reworking of the original analysis conducted by Kate Phillips.

These developments have been used in the areas of organization design and development, individual and leadership development, career development and succession planning, reward, recruitment and one to one coaching. In short, the approach has been used in all areas relating to the management of people.

Finally, I am most grateful for the advice and help I received from Emily Steel and Catherine Gibbons at Kogan Page who ensured this edition successfully came to print. Any mistakes of substance or quality are those of the author.

1

The healthy organization

In the Foreword to Arie de Geus's *The Living Company*, Peter Senge (1997) commented: 'Most large, apparently successful corporations are profoundly unhealthy.' This is a remarkable statement because Senge is referring to successful, not unsuccessful, corporations and my own experience supports his contention. It seems that despite all the work of the behavioural scientists, the management gurus and management journalists in the 20th century, we still do not know how to build a healthy organization. As organizations have become larger and more complex, as a result of the pressures of globalization in the 1990s, this fundamental problem has become more acute. However, as I indicated at the International Cooperative Alliance Research Conference in Oslo, during August 2000, this is not just a problem of large organizations. Even small organizations, such as cooperatives, are apparently unhealthy, as they seem to be poor at individual and leadership development and are prone to succession crises in both the primary and secondary tiers.

WHAT IS MEANT BY ORGANIZATION?

Organization as used in this book was recently defined by Jay Galbraith (2000) as an aligned complex of structures, management processes, reward systems and human resource practices which must be aligned with each other and with strategy. The primary focus will be upon designing an optimal structure, since a healthy skeleton is the bedrock of a healthy body. Processes and their impact upon organization will be examined (Chapter 3) as will reward systems (Chapter 6) and human resource practices (Chapters 7 and 8). The strategic dimensions of growth and technology will be the subject of Chapter 10.

WHAT IS A HEALTHY ORGANIZATION?

For the past 20 years or so, I have been endeavouring to answer the question – What is a healthy organization? I have carried out assignments in over 70 countries trying to find answers to this conundrum, working in a number of different types of businesses, each of which has had its own unique properties. Some of these have been in consumer goods, some in the agricultural sector, the industrial sector, the chemical sector, the packaging sector and the retail industry. They have varied from research laboratories to the corporate centre of a global organization. The social, political, economic and cultural conditions in which they operate have varied widely. Some of them have been in a state of frenzied expansion, others facing almost certain decline. In this variety of organizational units there has been one overwhelming message: it is possible to develop ideas and tools which will assist managers and others concerned with the future of their organizations to develop healthy and effective organizations, despite the wide variety of settings and challenges.

In practice, managers still wrestle to find the answer to recurring questions, such as:

- How many people should there be in my organization?
- How many layers of hierarchy are necessary?
- What are the logical steps of personal development?

- What are the career paths which individuals should follow which will enable them to keep learning?
- How should I reward my employees?

A healthy organization is one that meets its mission and simultaneously enables inividuals to learn, grow and develop. There is also much talk of 'life beyond hierarchy', probably first introduced by Toffler (1970), which adds to the confusion. It is widely assumed that a flat organization is a healthy organization. But...

WHAT IS A FLAT ORGANIZATION?

The phrase 'flat organization' is now overworked and misunderstood. It is an oxymoron, a contradiction in terms. Any organization that exists for a purpose needs a spine of decision-making accountability. This applies to private corporations, public institutions, voluntary organizations and cooperatives. The theory is clear. The problem for managers is how to design it in practice. How many vertebrae should there be in this spine of accountability? What are the key jobs? How are they identified? What is the impact of removing a job from this spine? What impact will this have on the development and motivation of the incumbents? Surprisingly, at the beginning of the 21st century this is still an area of guesswork and fashion in most organizations.

WHY ARE ORGANIZATIONS UNHEALTHY?

There are a number of reasons. These can include:

- a faulty strategy;
- poor organization design;
- an unclear link to strategy;
- company culture;
- the quality of employees.

There are, in addition, two other pervasive reasons. Behavioural scientists (such as Mayo, Maslow, McGregor and Herzberg) give theoretical explanations of *what* motivates individuals and groups. But they do not always provide sufficient practical advice on *how* to achieve this. This is an ongoing challenge for managers of people.

On the other hand, practitioners, such as the re-engineering school, hack into organizations without a reliable theoretical framework to guide their actions. They set out to empower people but in reality they are often driven by a need or desire to cut costs in this more competitive age. But there is always scope for more cost reduction. The important thing to identify is when to stop before undermining the health of the people and the organization.

There is nothing as useful as a good theory, according to the old dictum. This book will provide a paradigm of *what* makes a healthy organization, together with practical advice on *how* to achieve it.

The salmon fallacy

There is a school of thought that believes that getting rid of 10–20 per cent of the worst performing employees automatically 'refreshes' the survivors, who become healthier. This is the salmon fallacy.

If 100 salmon are swimming slowly upstream, culling 10 will not enable the remaining 90 to swim any faster. The problem is the prevailing current, not the efforts and abilities of the salmon.

The salmon fallacy, explored more fully in Chapter 7, ignores the environment or organizational setting in which activity takes place. The focus is exclusively on the individual, to the exclusion of the context in which he or she is working. But talented individuals cannot contribute to their full potential in a cluttered, top-heavy organization which blurs accountability, and stifles initiative and achievement. No amount of training to improve skills and competencies will overcome this barrier. Just as 100 salmon will all swim faster downstream, so individuals will perform best in an optimally designed organization. The organizational setting and climate critically affect individual and group performance.

This book will focus on the former to enhance the latter. Much of the material is about the framework of the organization because of its critical impact upon the performance of people. However, paradoxical as it may seem, the core concern is always the individual. The healthy organization is the guarantor of the healthy individual. Or, in other words, salmon swim better downstream.

ACCOUNTABILITY IS THE KEY

The thesis of this book is that unhealthy features of both large and small organizations,whether private or public, voluntary or cooperative, all stem from the same source, namely a lack of true accountability. Organizations are unhealthy because they lack transparent **decision-making accountability (DMA)**. DMA is the genetic code of the healthy organization. The principal theme of this book is the discovery and mapping of DMA in a global consumer goods organization, Unilever, and its application to a growing international retail business, Tesco. The key principles will be explained together with insights into how to implement them.

DECISION-MAKING ACCOUNTABILITY

DMA is to the organization what DNA is to the human body. It is the genetic code of life. It maps the path to health and effectiveness. Excessive numbers of decision makers and channels for decision making clog the arteries of vitality, and slow down the speed of decision making and response to consumers and customers. A lack of well-defined and clear accountability leads to organizational sclerosis and inefficiency. An example is set out in Figure 1.1 on page 6, which shows a situation before and after DMA analysis in a distribution centre in the supply chain side of a business.

On the left it depicts a large distribution centre with too many layers of decision makers. On the right the DMA analysis demonstrates what is required for a healthy organization. The focus is upon the quality of decision making in the organization. Different types of decisions are required at different levels. In both Tesco and Unilever these were referred to as work levels (more detail about these different types of decisions will be provided in Chapter 3). Decision-making accountability focuses on the quality of the decisions taken, not simply the quantity of resources managed, when one is answerable to a higher authority for work, resources, service and results. This changing nature of decision making is summarized in Figure 1.2.

Integrated logic of decision-making accountability

The logic of DMA integrates everything needed to manage people successfully. Most traditional HR systems merely link the various

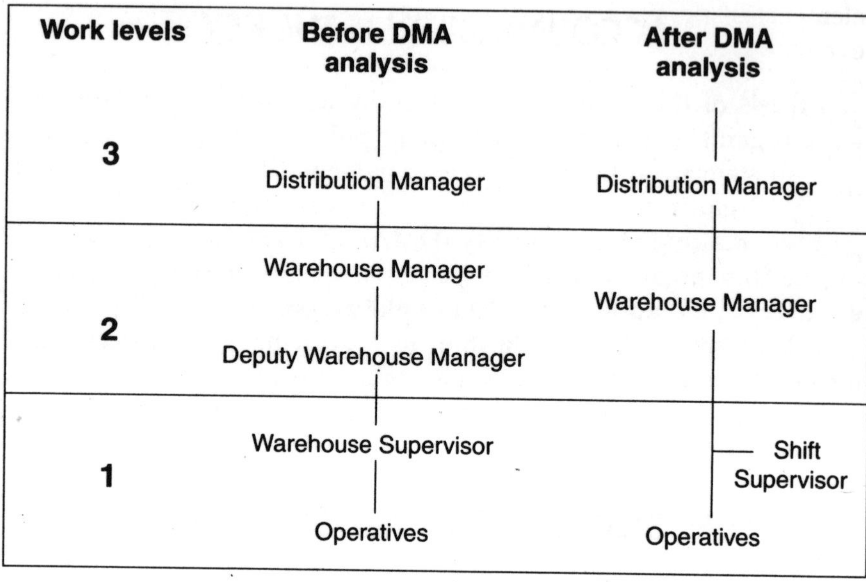

Supervisor is a support role – see Chapter 3

Figure 1.1 *DMA analysis of a distribution centre*

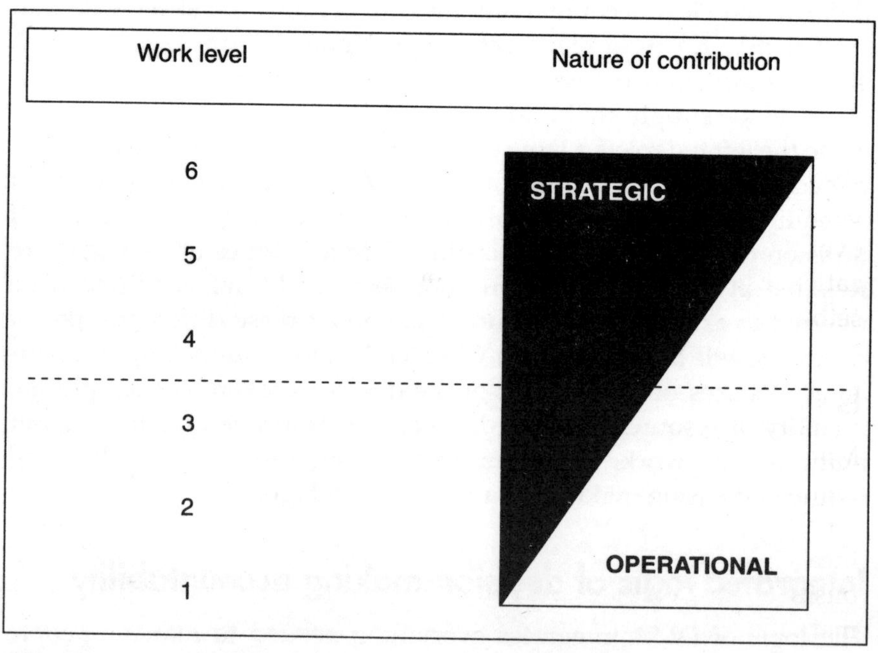

Figure 1.2 *Decision-making accountability*

elements of people management. For example, in a quantitative job evaluation system a grade is linked to pay, but it does not, indeed cannot, question whether the job adds value to the spine of accountability and, therefore, whether it deserves to exist in the organization. DMA, on the other hand, does answer such questions. It focuses on the quality of decisions taken, what they add to the work of others, while contributing to the unit's or organization's mission. It forms a conceptually integrated approach to:

- organization design;
- reward management;
- development of the individual;
- career planning;
- organization development.

This unique approach is summarized in Figure 1.3.

Pioneering research in Tesco and Unilever

This book will cover the extensive pioneering research undertaken globally over 10 years, which culminated in 1998 with the introduction of the DMA approach across 100 countries, affecting 20,000 managers in Unilever. It will also touch on the application of this approach in Tesco from 2000 and other organizations since then. The message is positive – these new ideas, tested and refined throughout the world over more than a decade, will ensure the building of a healthy organization. They are principles that can be applied in any organizational setting.

Is there a role for ratios?

Many organizations test and benchmark their effectiveness and organizational health in terms of ratios. Ratios are helpful but they are essentially limited, as Beaven noted in 1982. Yardsticks that measure the financial, marketing, sales and technical aspects of the business, such as return on assets, gross margin, market share, marketing appropriation, working capital, asset utilization, customer service ratings and quality, don't assess the softer areas of organiza-

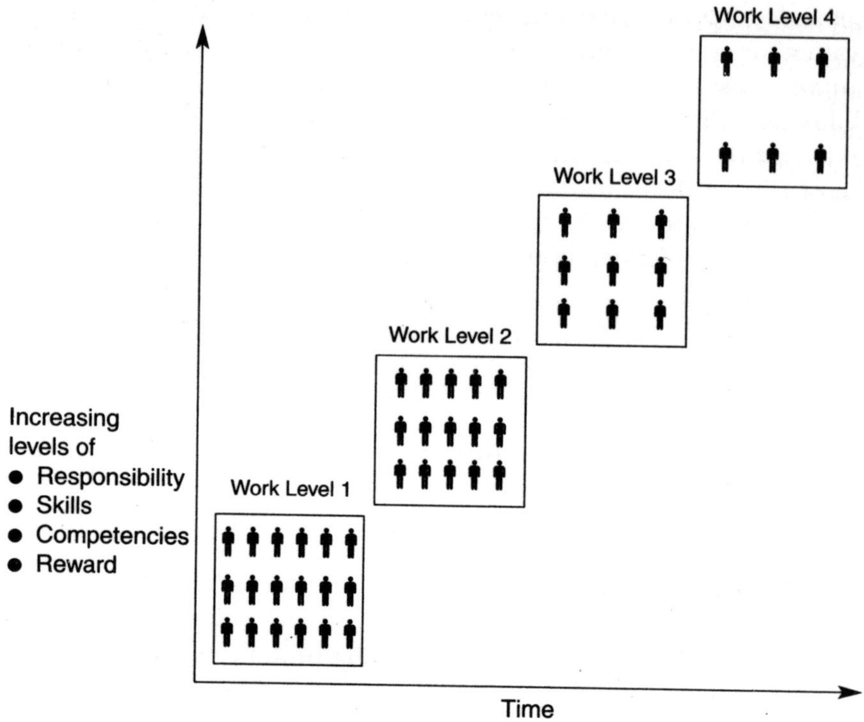

Figure 1.3 *The integrated logic of DMA*

tional performance. Volume ratios have major limitations. How do you compare an organization turning out litres of ice cream with one producing tonnes of chemicals? Indeed, what is the relevance of a tonne of detergent hard soap in India compared to the performance required to produce a tonne of liquid detergent in the United States? Similar problems bedevil financial ratios. No one currency spans the world; even purchasing power rates are controversial. There is no universal measure, which would give a reliable and valid mapping of the health of an organization whether in the public, private or voluntary sector.

No quick fix

There are no 'quick-fix' solutions for the reader. This is one of the major shortcomings of the management literature of the 1990s, which seems to offer immediate superficial solutions. This shortcoming has been well covered by people such as Hilmer and Donaldson (1996) and Micklethwait and Wooldridge (1996). Given the pressure of 'short-termism', managers today seek rapid solutions to their organizational problems; but I plan to offer the reader something more solid and systematic than the latest management fad or panacea. The type of audience I have in mind, therefore, is one that wants to avoid tomorrow's crisis. It wants to build an organization that continues to respond effectively to the needs and demands of:

- customers;
- employees;
- competitors;
- shareholders.

In an age when standards of customer service are constantly improving, employee demands for better learning opportunities are increasing, competition is more widespread and intense and the pressures for more growth and profit are unrelenting, the need for healthy, robust organizations has never been greater.

The knowledge age is now upon us. There are already impressive knowledge-rich companies (such as Microsoft, Cisco and Nokia) rapidly increasing their global reach. The best managers in companies such as these really do appreciate that knowledgeable people are their key resources and this is no longer simply a platitude to be read in the annual accounts. These are ambitious objectives, and it would be misleading to suggest that they can be achieved in a matter of days. The findings in this book have been based on extensive empirical study. Since 1988 over 3,000 hours of interviewing work have gone into establishing solutions to the problems outlined above. This work has spanned many cultures and all continents throughout the world. It has established that the principles set out in this book are capable of universal application. This is not a book about fads and labels.

HOW FLAT IS TOO FLAT?

In November 1991 (at a workshop in Amsterdam) Tom Peters

acknowledged that the reason why so many of the original 42 'excellent' companies were by then already off the list lay overwhelmingly in their shortcomings in structures and organization, not strategy, and not people. The view that hierarchies were too deep was widespread. Delayering, downsizing, rightsizing (some might say capsizing) was in vogue. The fact that organizations had to be flattened was clear. How they could be appropriately flattened was not at all clear. The key question was *'how flat is too flat?'* I tackled this issue in Dive (2003). Experience illustrates it is easy to damage an organization; to cut into the muscle rather than the fat.

Peters (1988) argued for not more than three layers 'in any facility'. Previously, Drucker (1954) had argued for six or seven. But by 1988 he believed that 'for a business of the size of General Motors, five might be appropriate'. Both quoted the Catholic Church as evidence to support their views but intriguingly they differed from each other in their enumeration of the hierarchical layers of the Church. In 1995 Johnson stated, 'The corporation of eight to twelve levels will implode to three to five.'

None of these or similar statements were supported with convincing analysis or evidence. They were simply statements of belief. The philosophy was unequivocal but empirical data was lacking. Indeed Drucker muddied the water even further in 1988 by comparing the hierarchy in modern organizations to that of an orchestra. But, as Elliott Jaques (1989) vigorously pointed out, associations (such as an orchestra) are not accountable hierarchies.

THE FORMULA FOR A HEALTHY ORGANIZATION: 'WORK LEVELS MINUS 1'

The DMA solution set outlined in Figure 3.2 on page 57 illustrates different levels of accountability (known as work levels in Tesco and Unilever). It will be demonstrated in Chapter 3 that only one layer of management is required in each level above the first. For example, in an organization with a frontline that starts at work level 1, and a top job in work level 5, only four layers of accountable hierarchy can be justified. Hence the formula for an optimal organization design is *'Work levels minus 1'*: in this example, 5 minus 1. See Figure 1.4.

Work levels	Before DMA analysis	After DMA analysis	Management layers
5	President	President	IV
4	Vice President	Vice President	III
3	General Sales Manager Regional Managers	Regional Managers	II
2	Area Managers District Managers	District Managers	I
1	Sales Supervisors Sales Representatives	Sales Supervisors Sales Representatives	

Figure 1.4 *DMA analysis of a field salesforce*

SHORTCOMINGS OF RE-ENGINEERING

As a result of the re-engineering movement during the same period, enthusiastic but ill-informed CEOs hacked into their organizations, often removing the wrong layers, severely traumatizing their hapless employees. This is a pervasive reason for the existence of so many unhealthy organizations. Most delayering initiatives were driven by short-term, bottom-line financial pressures. They were not really governed by the desire to build a healthy organization, establish real and challenging jobs, which would become the means of achieving genuine lasting empowerment – the buzzword of the 1990s.

Not surprisingly, thanks to the re-engineering movement, delayering has a totally negative connotation today.

Re-engineering had so many failures because it focuses only on the horizontal axis of an organization's structure. So-called 'functional (ie vertical) silos' were simply replaced with 'horizontal silos' of activities (processes), which lost sight of the need for accountable results. There was no paradigm to ensure the vertical axis was appropriately tall or short. A spine of accountability with one too few or one too many decision-making vertebrae is equally disadvantaged. Both situations leave traumatized employees in their wake.

THE CAUSES OF UNHEALTHY ORGANIZATIONS

Unclear accountability

Lack of clarity regarding accountability for work seems to be a widespread malaise in organizations. It is not a new problem. It is the fundamental issue addressed by this book. It is a well-publicized problem in governmental organizations. Europeans, for example, are increasingly disillusioned by the lack of efficiency, integrity and accountability of the EEC and the bureaucracy it is spawning. However, it is interesting that this appropriate focus on the shortcomings of the public sector organizations tends to divert attention from the widespread and chronic problems often found in the private sector, which is not subject to the same public scrutiny. My experience working with colleagues on the Council for International Management at the Conference Board has revealed that many global companies have had great problems in this area. This has often been clouded by the spate of mergers and takeover activities, which have often resulted in appalling organizational confusion such as the emergence of the 'straw boss', identified many years ago by Wilfred Brown (1971), or the 'clay layers' in Philips in the 1990s. DMA research indicates that when organizations suffer from clay layers or straw bosses a number of problems seem to correlate with this. These include:

- lack of vision or unclear vision;
- unclear priorities;
- inability to make quick (or even any) decisions;
- duplication of work;

- work missed and/or omitted;
- lack of true delegation;
- overstaffing;
- slow reaction to customers and competition;
- unclear career progression;
- difficulty of managing rapid growth;
- quality work not being done;
- managers dragged down to inappropriate levels of work;
- too many meetings;
- ineffective meetings;
- divided loyalties;
- under-utilization of individual capacity;
- loss of creativity;
- loss of good people;
- long and stressful hours of work;
- excessive numbers of authorization steps;
- poor shop floor relations – 'them and us' mentality.

These are all problems which have emerged from empirical work since 1988.

Anticipating future growth

In periods of fast growth, past trends tend to be simply extrapolated into future plans. But when a downturn occurs managers sometimes try to 'grow their way out of trouble' rather than tackle the immediate problems. The dilemma posed by the role of structure is then quite acute. On the one hand it is argued that if resources are not provided growth will not follow. On the other, if too many resources are provided too soon the initiative will collapse under the burden of the early costs.

One such case occurred in Australia. The CEO at the time suspected the business was top heavy. A colleague, Roger Roes, and I confirmed this after an extensive investigation and recommended that the eight business units be gradually streamlined into two. Just as the programme was to get under way, a new director was given responsibility for East Asia Pacific.' In a mature and saturated market, he decided to grow his way out of the problem. This strategy failed. Following his tenure, the business was structured into two companies and business acquired during the 'growth phase' was sold.

The arrogance of profit

'Nothing fails like success' (Arnold Toynbee)

The assumption here is that once a company is very profitable it is automatically perfect in all aspects of its organization. Otherwise it wouldn't be successful, runs the argument. This thinking blinds organizations to their own deficiencies.

For over 30 years, T J Lipton in the United States grew continuously in both sales and profits. It developed an unparalleled record unmatched by any other company in the Fortune 500 list at the time.

Yet, at the end of the period, it had an average span of control of about five and many instances of a least eight layers of hierarchy across the organization. It was demonstrably unhealthy. Only when the bubble finally burst was there a serious attempt to redress the unhealthy organization, which had emerged in the meantime. Similar examples could be quoted from Germany, South Africa and the UK during the same period.

The argument here is not that all profitable companies become unhealthy. It is that those making good profits can be lulled into thinking that every aspect of the business is equally impressive. Good short-term profits can blind leaders to shortcomings in the wider performance of the organization. There are good examples of well-led, highly profitable companies reorganizing sensitively and successfully over a longish time frame, to maintain their success. Brooke Bond in the UK, led by Peter Johnson, ably supported by Ian Watson, is a good case in point. But experience suggests that this example is more the exception than the rule.

Impact of job evaluation systems and administrative promotions

The growth of formal systems to assess jobs, such as job analysis, job ranking, job grading and job evaluation, accompanied the growth of bureaucracies in the 20th century. Most global companies and large governmental institutions either developed their own grading systems or purchased one from a consultant. These systems were quantitatively based and did not assess the quality of decisions taken or whether they added value to the organization.

The linking of rewards with job evaluation has led to its distorting impact upon the structure of organizations. Movements from one grade to another have become known as 'promotions' which deliver more money, status and 'progress'. These administrative promotions were often achieved by adding more layers in the organization as the way to obtain more budget, assets and subordinates, which were the touchstones of the job evaluation measuring system. This tendency to over-layer was compounded by the desire of multinational companies to correlate their systems to facilitate the measurement of market pay rates. Thus, prior to 1998, job class 20 in Unilever would be aligned to job grade 52 in IBM, 40 in Kodak, 5 in Shell and M1 in Tesco. In this way the disease of over-layering was easily spread. Job evaluation came to drive organization design. DMA reverses that process. The large numbers of ranks in the military and the police seem to have the same effect.

Some years ago I was involved with a project team assessing the effectiveness of the organization of one of the world's largest metropolitan police forces. The 'Cornerstone problems' were identified as:

- no unity of purpose;
- organization too self-sustaining (rank obsession)
- ill-defined roles/boundaries;
- Head office strangled the organization.

The 'hypothesis of root cause' was identified as:

- order/disorder struggles;
- illusion of order;
- system upon system;
- rule-bound bureaucratic dependency structure.

The project team then made some radical recommendations – too radical, it would seem, as this police force still attracts public criticism. But the key point is this: the presence of a well-defined job evaluation or system of ranks does not guarantee a healthy organization.

Designing top-down

If the span of control of a CEO is unduly narrow there is an inbuilt tendency to build unnecessary layers into the organization. When one organizes top-down it is very difficult to establish where value added decision making is really taking place. The temptation is to insert 'span-breakers' (jobs present for the comfort of the superior but adding nothing of value to the lower echelons) near the top of the organization. It is like looking at a tapestry. Top management see a nice pattern and design from above but their subordinates see the loose, untidy stitches from below.

Another fault, which seems to stem from the tendency to organize top-down, is the desire to build new structures and jobs around the existing people in the organization. Although, obviously, people are the critical component in the new organization, a planned structure should abstract from needs of the current people in the design stage. It may well be that the design is subsequently modified on account of the availability, shortage or ability of people. Then the variance can be noted and corrected over time.

When Unilever planned its first pan-European structures, it had many fine objectives about being close to the customer, speeding up innovation, decision making and communications. But then, bearing in mind the people available, top management initially proposed a structure of eight or nine layers, which undermined the effectiveness of the proposed objectives.

Impact of titles

The desire to motivate individuals by having an elaborate array of different titles invariably seems to correlate with unhealthy organizations. Titles can have the same impact as job evaluation systems as outlined above. Over-reliance on titles in the United States has led to a number of organizational problems. The problems of differentiating between the accountabilities of CEOs and COOs are well documented by Bennis (1989) and Harman (1996). There is also the tendency, having established the title of President, to underpin that role with a Senior Vice President and/or an Executive Vice President, then a Vice President, then a Director followed by varying layers of management. This proliferation of titles in the United States has contributed directly to over-layering and unhealthy organizations. A clear example was the marketing arm of a fragrance business run out of the USA. Under the President there was an Executive VP, whose subordinate was a VP, who in turn managed Directors of Global Marketing who in their turn supervised various Brand Managers and their assistants. The titles were grand; the individuals in the department were all highly competent and well educated, but the excessive number of titles contributed to over-layering and blurred accountabilities, which resulted in frustration and demotivation.

Emphasis on control

Historically, one of the factors that has contributed to unnecessary layers has been the emphasis on control. This arose initially because over 100 years ago those at the frontline of the organization were illiterate or unskilled. In the 21st century this is increasingly not the case. However, in the developing world there is still a tendency to believe that less educated subordinates require greater supervision. This in turn leads to the insertion of unnecessary layers. There is plenty of evidence to show that inexperienced or unskilled workers in undeveloped countries will be better trained and will learn more quickly by reporting directly to a genuine boss rather than being a 'bag carrier' for a straw boss.

The UK government is confusing the issues of accountability and control. Baroness O'Neill made this clear in her 2002 Reith lectures on Trust in the Public Services: 'New conceptions of accountability which superimpose targets… burdening, even paralyzing, many of those who have to comply'. This is not empowerment (see Chapter 5) but a desire for control.

Promotion from within

As Collins and Porras pointed out in 1994, those companies which have been successful and have survived for over 100 years tend to have a policy of growing their own talent. The danger with this philosophy is that in an effort to create jobs for 'promotion' or for 'training', new posts and layers of hierarchy are created. These new jobs are often non-jobs and do not really achieve the aims for which they were designed. This shortcoming invariably stems from confusing rank (job class, grade or job points), status and pay with notions of accountability. Contributing factors have already been referred to, such as the tendency to build top-down. Although the result of a positive philosophy, it can be corrupted if there is not a rigorous mental framework of principles to act as a safeguard. Grade drift or inflation cannot occur in the DMA model (see the 'principles' set out in Chapter 3.)

Provincial thinking

Many organizations try to justify their unhealthy structures, when challenged, on the basis of their unique local circumstances. In a world of increasing globalization this merely reflects provincial thinking within present or accepted boundaries.

In the United States, presidents and CEOs are apt to argue that because of the geographical spread of the country it is impossible to have fewer layers, as indicated by the DMA model. In India the argument is likely to be based on the large number of employees requiring supervision in their labour-intensive activities, while in South Africa managers argue that the problems of managing a Third World work force with First World technology requires more hierarchy than is the norm elsewhere. In Central and Eastern Europe and China, the lack of understanding of the market economy is cited as a reason justifying deeper structures than would be accepted in the West because more training is required. Experience to date indicates that these and similar arguments are equally spurious rationalizations once examined against the requirements of the DMA approach.

Horizontal overload

Any organization can be examined on two axes: one vertical and one horizontal, covering the spread of resources being managed. These axes mutually interact. Undue horizontal loading generates undue numbers of vertical layers, just as too few layers can lead to horizontal overload. The key is to achieve a balanced equilibrium. Horizontal overload can occur, for example, when there is excessive functional specialization.

A classical example of this was the craft basis to British trade unions. In the 1970s, when these unions reached their zenith, it was quite common to enter a factory and find numerous demarcations of 'engineers' who in turn had their separate foremen, supervisors and managers. Comparable continental European, North American or Latin American factories in the same industries could be found with both lower totals of engineers and less complex superstructures.

When there is a genuine request for an extra layer to be placed in the structure, one should start by examining the horizontal reach of the proposed organization. Frequently it is assumed that one unit can manage another without another layer being required. This might work, if there are widespread synergies between the two, but often there are not and an unnecessary non-value-adding layer emerges as a result. This occurred in the United States when Unilever acquired Breyers, the largest national ice cream company in the world. Initially it was placed within the T J Lipton company since it ran a small ice cream division, called Good Humour. However, there were insufficient synergies between these two businesses and the result was horizontal overload for the President of Liptons. This was resolved by splitting off Breyers into a separate self-sufficient unit that included Good Humour.

Confusion between line and support jobs

Confusion between line and support (or lead jobs as they are referred to in Tesco) jobs frequently leads to excessive layers of management, and an unhealthy organization. This is an issue that will receive fuller treatment in Chapter 3 on the DMA model. Suffice it to say at this stage that this confusion leads to support jobs being incorrectly placed on the spine of accountability. This is frequently a situation where management accountabilities are not clear, which creates confusion, for example on shift work.

CAN AN ORGANIZATION BE TOO FLAT?

There are some cases where the cause of distortion is a tendency to have **too few layers**.

Among the most typical causes are the following.

'Down with hierarchy'

One of the principal causes of dangerously flat organizations is the faddish belief that hierarchy is something bad in itself. As indicated above, there is no shortage of management journalists who advocate flatter structures as a good end in itself.

Hilmer and Donaldson (1996) have highlighted four myths that underpin the desire to flatten organizations:

1. The orchestra model for organizations. (This myth seems to have originated with an article by Peter Drucker in the 1988 *Harvard Business Review*. But 10 years later he seems to have modified his views: 'One hears a great deal today about the end of hierarchy. This is blatant nonsense. In an institution there has to be a final authority, that is a boss.')

2. Management by walking around.

3. Bloated overheads (the theory here being that hierarchy only inflates cost).

4. The inverted pyramid (the so-called inverted organization with customers and frontline workers at the top and the CEO at the bottom), which confuses symbolism with substance.

Excessive cost reduction

Cost reductions are often excessive when they are based on delayering by decree or inspection. The most common and simplistic approach is cost reduction by a fixed percentage. This falls into two traps. Some divisions are cut too deeply and others insufficiently. The cosmetic across the board percentage is invariably incorrect for every division for different reasons. It is usually the result of a political decision and is the last refuge of weak leadership. The big problem with reductions driven by cost is knowing when or why to stop.

Guesswork

Closely related to the previous cause. Most managers will recognize a unit which has too many layers of management, but when asked which job or jobs should be removed the fun really starts, as they really don't have a clue and most solutions seem to be based on ignorance and guesswork. Organizations that have moved from 'functional silos' to the tyranny of 'horizontal processes' are typically prone to errors of this type, as they have no fix on the vertical axis.

I recently worked with a major business in Europe and another in the United States, both previously advised by two different consultant organizations, which in their zeal to set up flat process structures produced organizations out of kilter with the need for transparent accountability.

Teamwork

Teamwork is the mythical antidote to all the evils of excessively tall organizations, which arose in the 20th century. Flatter organizations rely on effective teamwork but teamwork does not supersede the need for accountability. It is important to build effective teams but the process is not helped by vague or flawed definitions of teamwork as provided by Boehm and Phipps (1996) when they argued that 'a horizontal organization is focussed on meeting customer needs and built around natural flows instead of conventional functions like marketing and sales'. This superficial relabelling implies that sales departments previously did not focus on their customers or that marketers ignored their consumers. Arguing that horizontal organizational principles 'transform management roles from "command and control" to "process leadership"' and 'make teams the basic organization building block, within and across processes', as they do, is fashionable but unhelpful. An obsession with (central) processes can lead to the breaking up of a natural team, eg in a factory. Higgs and Rowland (undated) are more convincing:

> ... while many management writers are extolling the virtues of teams and teamworking, we, as management development practitioners, are witnessing the strains and stresses this entails in implementation. We believe this is because there is a failure to examine the four following assumptions:
>
> - That teams and team working are necessarily appropriate for every area of work design and practice.
> - That 'team' exists only as a singular concept, and that there are not different types of team.
> - That team working attitudes and behaviours can easily and practically be developed within all areas of the organization.

- That industrial democracy and employee empowerment will necessarily be achieved through team working ('all pigs are equal').

Teamwork is not the panacea for all ills (and lack of accountability) as David Brown seemed to think when he wrote in 1998 that 'Teamwork replaces the Chain of Command', but gave no evidence even to support the contention, let alone prove it. He stated that 'information is fed up and down the supply chain' which is similar to Rao (1997), who claimed that the 'growing use of computers is killing the middle management job'. Computerized information flows along the supply chain. It may collapse interfaces between jobs on part of the horizontal axis, but middle management as such is not disappearing. It cannot, any more than a healthy vertebra is unnecessary in the healthy spine. The truncating of numbers in a lateral team does not do away with the need for vertical teams, which is hierarchy by another name. A successful retail business recently 'flattened its structure to promote teamwork'. Senior managers often had anything between 30 to 70 direct reports. Within a year many of these managers were overloaded with people issues. As a result, a number of them introduced 'soft hierarchies' of informal reporting links to ensure their subordinates were being managed because 'the flat team structure was not working'. Subsequent analysis demonstrated that a level of accountability was missing.

A final word on this topic from Higgs and Rowland: 'It is therefore misguided to assume the introduction of team working will automatically create a flat, egalitarian, organization culture.' Teamwork can enhance accountability, but not replace it.

Impact of IT

S L Rao is one of those who think that middle management accountability is disappearing because of the computer. The introduction of IT (and the Internet) has already tempted some executives to compress their structures partly in an effort to justify the additional expense and partly because IT has been heralded as the gateway to organizations beyond hierarchy. Working online in real time, in 'eco structures', does not supplant the need for accountability, even if the frontline of some of these organizations is being automated (more will be said on this topic in Chapter 10).

The introduction of IT does not help if work is ineffectively organized and structures are badly designed. The CEO of a multinational in Germany who was considering delayering his company because the 'computer could now provide him with data on yesterday's sales in Buenos Aires' was in danger of operating in the wrong level of accountability. In which case he would be neglecting his strategic accountabilities.

The principles of DMA have been applied in a fast-growing dot.com company to ensure their accountabilities were clear and understood by all those affected.

The problem of rapid growth

Sometimes when a business is growing quickly there comes a point where it probably moves into a higher level of accountability. Thus the head of the business unit finds the work has lifted into a higher strategic domain while at the same time a number of the subordinates will be confronted with more complex decisions which move them into longer and more critical planning horizons.

While it was pointed out above that the anticipation of planned growth can lead to over-layering, it is also possible to unduly delay the addition of key resources to meet the increasing work and accountability. This is sometimes caused by the desire to increase productivity. The work of J B Quinn (1992) has demonstrated that productivity dramatically increases with growth in size and the maximizing of economies of scale and administration. But there inevitably comes a time with significant growth, for the addition of key resources into the hierarchy.

TOO FLAT OR TOO TALL – THE SAME CONSEQUENCES

As Hilmer and Donaldson (1996) have pointed out:

> It is ironic that making a structure too flat or too tall produces similar problems. In a too-tall structure, the numerous levels frustrate communication between the CEO and the frontline. Similarly, when the structure is too flat the overloaded supervisor cannot cope with all the communications and decisions. Reports from the subordinates languish on the desk. News from upper

> management cannot get through the supervisor to the subordinates, because the supervisor is too busy with other things. Communications both up and down the hierarchy are choked in a bottleneck. Thus, a too-flat structure is as much a barrier to communications and decision making as is a too-tall structure.

Farnham (1999) came to a similar conclusion: 'Flattened organizations end up with the precise problems they were meant to solve.'

OUTLINE OF THE BOOK

There are therefore many reasons why organizations might be unhealthy. The remainder of the book will concentrate on the reasons that contribute positively to an optimal and healthy organization. DMA will be at the core of this story.

Chapter 2 will outline the convincing empirical credentials of this story.

Chapter 3 will outline the DMA solution set, covering the key principles, the seven elements, and the critical contribution of line and support jobs.

Chapter 4 will describe the unfolding of DMA based on extensive empirical testing across two large, complex, international organizations, Tesco and Unilever. Insight will be provided into the identifying of value-adding levels of accountability.

Chapter 5 will demonstrate how DMA drives an integrated approach to the management of people, firstly by ensuring effective organization design, which in turn empowers individuals and teams, which in turn stimulates more innovative work.

Chapter 6 focuses on the second critical stage in the establishment of a truly integrated approach to the management of people, namely reward management. The most common new reward solution of the 1990s, broadbanding of money, will be analysed. Its stated advantages will be explored and shown to be illusory. DMA will demonstrate that need not be the case.

Chapter 7 will focus on the third phase of the integrated DMA model, the development of the individual. The importance of the organization context and its impact on performance will be explored. Six new competencies will be described and aligned to the seven elements of DMA. These can guide progression through the levels of accountability in a way that overcomes the **salmon fallacy**. The value of the **leadership log** and its role in mentoring those transitioning different levels of accountability will be explained.

Chapter 8 will move on to the fourth stage in the development of a healthy organization, demonstrating how the accountability levels of DMA facilitate leadership development and career planning. The concept of more predictive **career tracking** and the research underpinning it will be introduced. New findings about **boundary moves** will be outlined.

Chapter 9 will illustrate the major challenge of introducing a change of DMA's all-encompassing nature in 100 countries and will outline the critical five-phase communication model utilized to mobilize change.

Finally, Chapter 10 will move the focus to the 21st century and pose the question 'how will DMA cope with the demands of the future?' The challenges of sustained growth and the dot.com revolution will be examined. A new idea, **time in accountability level**, will be introduced. This will link back to the new findings of Chapter 8, which will complete the case for DMA as the genetic code for a healthy organization, whatever its mission, size or complexity. By which stage it will be apparent that successful companies do not have to be 'profoundly unhealthy'.

THE VISION OF A HEALTHY ORGANIZATION

This book will outline the path to achieving the vision of a healthy organization. That vision can be summarized as follows: It is an organization with the optimal number of layers of leadership, which demonstrably add value to the work of others. This includes the design and delivery of mission and strategy. The conundrum of how to provide space and challenge for individuals to achieve, continue to learn, grow and enjoy their work and be duly rewarded for their performance, will be solved. It will become clear how to ensure the right number of jobs as the basis for a cost-effective organization. It will be demonstrated that the identification of talent is easier, as is the planning of relevant development opportunities to meet the needs and objectives of both the individual and the organization.

In short, the DMA model will turn claims about 'flatter structures, faster communication, quicker decision making, better innovation, being closer to the customer with a highly motivated workforce' from the realm of fantasy and platitudes to that of reality.

2

The empirical evidence

The last quarter of the 20th century saw the emergence of a clear consensus on the critical drivers of a competitive business. I will briefly outline these key business drivers as they are the criteria against which any approach to the management of the organization and its people must be judged.

The origins of what developed into the DMA model will be touched upon in this chapter. The reasons why first Unilever and then Tesco had to change will be explained. I will also describe the field tests undertaken which led to the refinement and validation of the model in Asia and Africa. It will then be critiqued against the business drivers to demonstrate how it enhances competitiveness.

THE DRIVERS OF BUSINESS SUCCESS

HR initiatives must align with business strategy and contribute to competitive performance. DMA had to meet these twin challenges. It had to improve the following features of successful business practice.

1. Focus on quality

The story of how the Americans began to preach total quality to the Japanese, without practising it themselves, and how the Japanese subsequently 'shot to the fore' as a competitive force in the 1970s, is now both well understood and documented. This led to the temporary preoccupation with 'Japanese management' – see Pascale and Athos (1981). The examples of the Fords and IBMs realigning their corporate objectives to stress the importance of quality in order to re-compete in the marketplace have helped to spur the spread of the commitment to total quality management in many Western organizations since. Many of the current quality councils and prizes for quality arose as a result of this learning.

The effect of these initiatives has meant that quality is now a commodity, something that is taken for granted in today's fast-moving, more competitive, global world. It no longer guarantees a competitive edge. If everybody is excellent you can't afford not to be in the same category. The organization that does not have top quality products, processes, people and structure cannot expect to compete with the best players in the marketplace.

2. Responsiveness to the customer/consumer

One of the surprisingly simple facts of the excellence movement in the 1980s was that it rediscovered 'the customer is always right'. Spending time with actual customers has always been a good idea; it is not a new idea. But the reawakening of this neglected realization unleashed a widespread desire to get close to the customer. But how do we get close to the customer? The first answer lies with structure. A deeply layered organization is prone to be preoccupied with internal problems. It is unlikely to be sensitive to its environment, let alone its customers or consumers. Some companies, such as SAS and Nordstrom, even drew their organization charts upside down, with the frontline at the top next to the customer to stress the importance of this philosophy.

Tesco is fanatical about the importance of customers. So much so, that when communicating the DMA model customer supremacy was enshrined in the logo used in the training sessions and in the workbook outlining the descriptions of work and accountability at each of the different levels. See Figure 2.1.

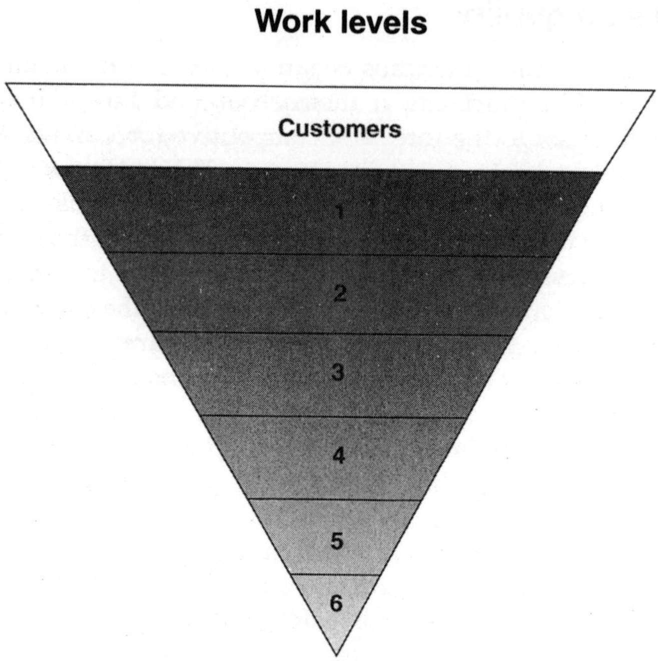

Figure 2.1 *The Tesco approach*

Even an 'upside-down organization' with the wrong depth of structure would not be effective. Some companies seem to think decentralization necessarily guarantees better customer focus. But decentralization willy-nilly is not the answer, since it is apt to correlate with duplicated cost, fragmented effort and a dilution of core services. The British electronics industry, for example, was ultimately undermined in the 1980s by excessive decentralization, which weakened its competitiveness. Thus we have a paradox: in attempting to get close to the customer, wholesale restructuring, delayering and decentralization can lead ultimately to an ineffective customer service and therefore failure. This process needs a guiding hand: a paradigm or a framework to ensure it is successful.

3. Cost effectiveness

Few would argue that a healthy organization must have an appropriately competitive cost base. One of the key driving components of any cost base is the organization structure. This is a sensitive issue since too often many top executives only view their structure in terms of costs. Unfortunately, many major restructurings are cost driven in a search for short-term results, often driven by the need to satisfy the investment analysts. Takeovers and corporate break-ups often have the same motivation. Cost reduction, not corporate health, is the name of the game, led by predators who seemingly understand neither the essence of corporate value-added activities nor the principles of organizational health.

The most common cause of expensive organizations is a misconception about the nature of hierarchy. This is often linked to issues relating to excessive emphasis upon control (this is most focused in terms of tight financial controls), as was pointed out by G G Fisch over 30 years ago: 'Control from the top means narrow spans of control and few levels, which is mutually inconsistent in a large organization.' There is a trade-off to be achieved between avoiding an unnecessarily deep vertical structure (typically centralized) and an unnecessarily wide horizontal structure (typically decentralized) giving rise to excessive support functions and unnecessary duplication of activities. Most organizations seem to compound their problems on both axes. It is very rare to come across a large multinational organization with the correct depth of structure, yet many pride themselves on their perceived decentralization. The end result is frequently excessive cost and organizational ill health.

4. Innovation

Competitive pressures in recent years have placed a premium on the need to innovate for success. This ability has been well described by Abbeglen and Stalk (1985) who illustrated how a Honda could out-innovate first Yamaha and then General Motors and Ford. The world's largest companies spend millions of dollars on their research and development divisions – anything between 3 and 14 per cent of sales, depending upon their industry. My investigations have indicated that deep and diffuse structures militate against the ability to innovate. Unfortunately, this is neither a new nor isolated experience. Burns and Stalker (1961) first highlighted this negative impact of organization with their reference to 'mechanistic structures'. In 1985 Rosabeth Moss Kanter pointed out that 'less innovating companies are dominated by tall structures'. One analysis (Dive, 1989) of layers of management in a number of different units in the Netherlands revealed that the most heavily structured sections were in research and development.

Managements are sometimes concerned that scanty structures in their laboratories may overload their scientists and stifle innovation. The obvious response to this is 'show me a large laboratory with a tall hierarchy that has a successful record of innovation, let alone invention'. Inaccurate thinking about the frontline work of the research laboratory, development department or marketing department has led to sub-optimal organizations, which tend to eliminate the facilitators of innovation. The logic of DMA provides answers to these problems, as will be demonstrated in Chapter 5.

5. Speed of response

Many of the factors that make up a healthy organization are interlinked and build on one another. In 1988 George Stalk pointed out that 'Time is the Next Source of Competitive Advantage', alerting Western management that once again the Japanese were then in the process of moving the competitive goalposts of international competition. He had also touched on this earlier, in 1985, when he and his colleague James Abbeglen had pointed out that they 'repeatedly find that the Kaisha are able to move products from development through production into the marketplace at a much more rapid rate than our Western client companies. The speed of response of the best Kaisha to the marketplace opportunities appears to be unusually rapid.'

It was becoming obvious that it was no longer enough to deliver total quality. To be in touch with customers and consumers and to be at the forefront of innovation, it had to be done faster than anyone else. Marketers have long preached the virtues of being first in the marketplace. Competitive pressures and greater use of technology are ever shortening the time from concept to market. The first glaring successes were scored by the speed of companies such as Honda and Toyota in producing superior new models to those of the then flat-footed US companies, General Motors, Ford and Chrysler. The same happened in the field of computers, semiconductors, robots, office automation, electronics and opto-electronics.

Furthermore, both Japanese and Western companies discovered the need to go on innovating and improving their products and keep delivering superior quality, or lose market share. The examples of this intensifying speed to market are many. When Procter & Gamble introduced Pampers into the Japanese market, after initially enjoying great success, they lost their huge market share within a couple of years to a superior Japanese product. In the era of the Internet time has become the equivalent of money, productivity, quality and even innovation. Use of time is on the cutting edge of competitive advantage and it is also evident that a cumbersome, diffuse, poorly designed organization becomes a forbidding obstacle to short-term delivery, contributing ultimately to medium-term failure if that shortcoming is not quickly addressed.

6. Good communications

The need for fast, accurate, clear communications in a large organization is self-evident. But as Moss Kanter (1984) has pointed out: 'The information pathologies of overly hierarchical, overly specialized organizations are well known.' In the 1950s Peter Drucker noted that 'each additional management layer in a company tends to cut in half the possibility that information is correctly transmitted, while it doubles the noise'. Even if Drucker is only half right it helps explain why so many people in the middle and lower echelons of large organizations often do not know what is going on. When reviewing the arguments for and against tall structures, John Child (1977) stated: 'tall structures involving many levels of management can lead to communication problems and a dilution of top management control. They make it difficult to distinguish between duties at different levels in the organization. And hence have a deleterious effect on motivation.'

Leading executives have also recognized that undue hierarchy quickly has a detrimental effect on communication networks. According to Don Petersen (Petersen and Hilkirk, 1991), a previous Ford President, 'You don't need all those layers. Doing without some of them will be good. You greatly reduce the chances for errors in communication as a subject is passed up the ladder. Fewer steps, fewer errors.' But once again the tantalising questions about which layers should be removed, and why, is not addressed by Petersen. The consensus between the theorists and the practitioners is clear. There is rock-solid agreement that too many hierarchical layers distort communications but that safe, reliable, practical remedies and solutions seem to be few and far between. DMA is one proven remedy.

7. Dedicated people

In the now classic 1968 article 'One More Time: How do you motivate employees?' Frederick Herzberg highlighted the importance of 'responsibility, recognition, growth, achievement and challenge' as sources of motivation or 'enrichment'. By and large, his work focused on the needs of the so-called knowledge worker. By the end of the 1980s the concept was extended to all employees, under the heading of 'Empowerment'. The extended theme was consistent with the work of early behavioural scientists. Generally people seek space in their work to undertake worthwhile tasks, which give them a sense of achievement and purpose, which enables recognition of their inherent worth and ability, providing satisfaction as a result. Clearly this cannot happen on a widespread basis in an organization that is choked with excessive vertical layers and horizontal specialists. Job responsibilities are then necessarily diluted and opportunities for achievement evaporate in the ensuing bureaucratic inertia. It is extremely difficult to recruit and retain dedicated employees in an over-managed organization. Frequently the most talented become diverted from the main purpose of the business and undue attention is diverted to peripheral or non-productive tasks. The tendency is for relations to build up among specialists and their internal customers rather than with external customers to determine how much work, and which work, needs to be done. Form takes precedence over purpose.

8. Teamwork

The other key dimension of a dedicated workforce is the influence of the team. Volvo is one company that did pioneering work in this field. As a result they have established very flat organizations in their factories. When studying his Japanese competition, Don Petersen at Ford recognized the importance of teamwork in achieving a dedicated workforce. His views on the contribution of a flat structure to enhance this process have already been alluded to above. In fact, most companies that have reduced their hierarchies in recent years have discovered that the first critical step involves developing a multi-skilled frontline to the organization (ie the team), which becomes the bedrock for successful organizational change. This in turn enables the establishment of comparable team structures in middle management leading in consequence to what Peter Drucker calls 'The Twilight of the First Line Supervisor'. This will be covered in some detail in Chapter 5, where the focus will be on the successful empowerment of a personal products factory in Jefferson City in the United States. The contention will be that a correctly layered organization is the most effective first step towards achieving and maintaining a dedicated workforce. Then dedicated people have the opportunity to exercise their talent if, and only if, they are held clearly accountable for specific tasks and assignments.

But flat structures do not cause teamwork. In the late 1990s, a head office department flattened its structure 'to create better teamwork'. The subsequent DMA analysis revealed that a key value-adding layer had been removed. A layer was missing. This created a number of unexpected problems. As a result, 'soft hierarchy' re-emerged as a common-sense but informal solution for top managers overburdened by an organization that had become too flat.

A critical element of the unfolding DMA story is the significance of the work undertaken in Unilever in the 10 years between 1988 and 1998, and in Tesco during 2000–2001.

EARLY DEVELOPMENTS

From 1988 I was working with colleagues trying to find the answer to the organization design question posed in Chapter 1, namely how to recognize when an organization is too flat. As part of an environmental scan of other companies and available research I came across the analytical study of Rowbottom and Billis (1987) on the contribution of work levels to organization design.

This study built on the seminal work both of Jaques and Brown, who had first identified different strata of work, based upon the time it takes to complete key tasks (time span of discretion), which had become known as Stratified Systems Theory. Rowbottom and Billis moved away from reliance on time measures. Their key idea was the expected work of a role, what it was meant to achieve, what distinguished it from other levels of work. But their analysis was heavily slanted towards large social welfare enterprises (such as the Health Service), and was limited to jobs up to work level 5 in the UK. Furthermore, the ideas had not been implemented across a significantly complex or large organization. The major challenge was to find whether these initial ideas could be adapted to a global organization.

IMPLEMENTATION AT UNILEVER AND TESCO

The twin stimuli of the collapse of the Berlin Wall and the increased openness of Western European markets post-1992 saw Unilever embark on a period of rapid expansion. A number of new businesses were set up in Central and Eastern Europe. With the opening up of a number of developing countries significant investments were made in Arabia, Egypt, Morocco, Russia, China and Vietnam. During this period, Unilever was faced with more business opportunities than it had resources to match. This was particularly the case in the area of Human Resources.

A small team of operating business unit heads was asked to review the concern's then personnel policies and practices and examine whether they would be appropriate as the business moved into the 21st century. Not surprisingly, this team concluded that radical change was called for. One of their major concerns was evidence that pointed to the erosion of key business skills in Unilever compared to key competitors. As they probed further for reasons that might explain this demise, they discovered that a major contributing factor was the fact that many young high-flyers changed jobs every one to two years. Further examination of this phenomenon revealed that a key driver of this process was what became known 'the job class obsession'.

During the 1990s Tesco transformed its business. It assumed market leadership in the UK food retail industry, displacing the previously much-vaunted Sainsbury. By 1999 it was voted the UK's 'most admired company' and had embarked on an international expansion programme. A key element of its strategy is getting closer to customers and each other. But its people management systems were fragmented, designed for a UK-only business. This was recognized as a potential drag on the expansion plan.

Administrative promotions

For some 25 years Unilever had operated an international job evaluation scheme for its management across the world. This system consisted of 17 different job classes. Although at the time the company had a policy of openness in relation to the development of an individual and his or her career plan, in fact in many cultures this desired openness was not practised. The result was that the only way young managers, in particular, could gain concrete feedback on their progress was reflected in progression through the job classes. Thus the job class system had become the talisman of management development success – an objective for which it was not designed. Thus in order to ensure rapid administrative promotions, it was important to change jobs frequently in an effort to drive job classes ever higher.

Job classes had become the lingua franca of the international management group and were the one public item that people were prepared to share with their colleagues in their efforts to establish themselves in their respective pecking orders. This obsession with administrative promotions was beginning to obstruct the smooth running of the business. It was recognized that the existing systems had to be replaced.

Tesco had similar problems, in that it had a multiplicity of grades and evaluation systems. This was compounded by its rapid growth as it pursued new business opportunities. The CEO, Terry Leahy, sought a solution that would be like the electrical wiring beneath the floor. Everyone knows it is there but it is taken for granted. 'I want an approach that is robust, transparent, fair, understood and taken for granted so that it does not distract people from serving the customer.'

Too many job classes or grades tended to generate a tall hierarchy, which was increasingly inappropriate in the international scramble for markets during the 1990s. It was evident that a new approach to measuring responsibilities needed to be found that would be consistent with the drive towards flatter infrastructures, portfolio careers and the greater competition for the best talent. By the end of the 20th century it was also emerging that the very notion of a job with fixed, defined, unchanging boundaries was under siege. Ironically the concern about short job tenure, which was prevalent at the outset of the 1990s, was already becoming dated by the end of the decade.

If there were to be fewer categories of responsibilities, which were commonly accepted, then they had to be designed in a way that also facilitated the development of individuals influenced by the thinking of the 'new employment contract'. This meant more focus on skill acquisition and the development of key competencies, which would more readily enable people to achieve real, as opposed to administrative, promotions.

In response to these developments, I initially proposed an 'Integrated Approach to Personnel Management' in Unilever based on the logic of what is now the DMA model. Herwig Kressler, Head of Global Remuneration, and the then Personnel Director, Clive Butler, were in favour, and Clive set about ensuring that the board supported this new approach. The board decided that it was necessary to reduce administrative promotions, and to devolve responsibility for implementation as far down into the business as possible. Furthermore, any new policies and practices were to be totally transparent, made available to all affected by them, and were to be managed and owned by line management. It was agreed in principle to replace job classes with work levels.

The DMA outline for a solution to the future needs of the management of people, relevant to the 21st century, had been agreed. But the proposed approach was unique and had not been applied anywhere else on a global basis. Therefore, the next two important steps were: 1) obtain more empirical evidence to determine exactly how many accountable decision-making levels operated across the concern, worldwide; 2) assess whether this new model conflicted with any of the prevailing ideas underpinning business success.

FIELD 'STRESS TESTS'

Now let us return to the challenge of testing both the embryonic ideas of DMA and their contribution to drivers of business success. It was clear that a culturally demanding test in a totally different type of environment was needed. The initial choice was India where Unilever had a large successful set of businesses with about 40,000 employees, led by Hindustan Lever (HLL).

The HLL case study

The Chairman of HLL in 1988 was Dr Ashok Ganguly, who later became the Research Director of Unilever. He was an impressive man with an open mind, always prepared to experiment in the search for a more effective organization and improved business performance. Fortunately the Personnel Director at the time, Keki Dediseth (also later to become a highly successful Chairman of HLL and Director of Unilever in 2000), was equally supportive. Experiments such as this must have the support of the top of the business if they are to have any chance of success.

The case study would reveal that although the earlier models of 'strata' and 'work levels' developed prior to 1988 were still incomplete and needed radical improvement and extension, the approach was already quite helpful in diagnosing an organization's bill of health.

The approach

David Billis and Natarajan Sundar from HLL assisted me in this project. The approach adopted was as follows. We met with the Chairman who gave us a broad brief. One of his concerns was that he knew the business was able to recruit very talented individuals from some of the best universities in India. It was also evident to him that they were working hard, and indeed many of them worked over the weekend. Yet despite this talent and dedication to work, there were cases where the business was being beaten in the marketplace. The most dramatic of these was the continuing growth of a low-cost competitor, Nirma, which had managed to carve out a business approaching half a million tons of low-cost detergents. This was eating into the HLL market share.

We then undertook to conduct a series of probes into different areas of the business, such as manufacturing, sales, marketing and commercial, including finance. We interviewed over 50 people in these areas of the business. Typically we would interview up the spine of accountability (the reporting line) in each of these areas, starting with the frontline and working right back up to the top of the business. During these individual interviews, which could take up to two hours each, we would focus on the expected work of the individual's role, the resources managed, and who they worked with both inside and outside the business, and which planning cycles they influenced or were involved with, what decisions were taken and what results were achieved. We would look for factual backup and clear examples, which could then be cross-referenced to others in the organization. This was particularly important if we found more than one person claiming to do the same work, which is not uncommon in unhealthy organizations.

Key finding

The key finding was that indeed the DMA approach worked and was verified as a powerful, albeit imperfect at that stage, instrument for revealing the organizational behaviour, decision-making patterns and culture within the company. It also revealed that there were some sub-optimal elements in the structure and organization of HLL.

Before discussing these findings in detail, it is important to note that HLL was and is a very successful company. During this period it was voted India's best company on more than one occasion by India's *Business Magazine*. But even excellent companies have areas for improvement and, as history shows, they can fall into decline if complacency sets in.

Evidence of over-management

The study established that HLL was over-managed, and therefore had too many layers across many parts of the business examined. The historical impact of a previous broad-banded management grade system had also created structural distortions. Key salary ranges and benefits were aligned to the management grades. But there was at least one more grade available than the number of value-adding levels of decision making, which therefore invariably led to over-layering. There was confusion between operational and strategic work: for example, in some areas there could be weekly 'strategic meetings' with up to four layers of decision-making management present to discuss 'last week's results'. There was therefore a tendency to have too many meetings, occupying, in some cases, 50 per cent of middle management's time. Blurred accountabilities, overlapping responsibilities and duplication of work were present. There were too many approval steps in the budget and planning process. Monetary differences in authority limits were too narrow. Each layer had to be seen to be doing something. Activity meant work. Response times were slow. Too many people were doing the work available. The culture seemed to be not how could more be done with less, but how could more be done with more. A major cause of much of the overlaying stemmed from a belief that in many parts of the business, for example sales, it was not possible to supervise and manage more than six direct subordinates. Consequently the very large sales force had twice as many sales supervisors as it needed and two unnecessary layers of management. See Figure 2.2.

This in turn bedevilled personal development and career planning. Inevitably an over-managed structure has a high cost base. Hindustan Lever had always benchmarked its costs against other Unilever businesses across the world. As a low-cost country it always compared very favourably. The problem was that they had not benchmarked their local competitors who invariably worked off a lower cost base than HLL.

Impact on talented individuals

Largely as a result of the above, it was more difficult to identify personal contribution and performance (good or bad). Morale in some

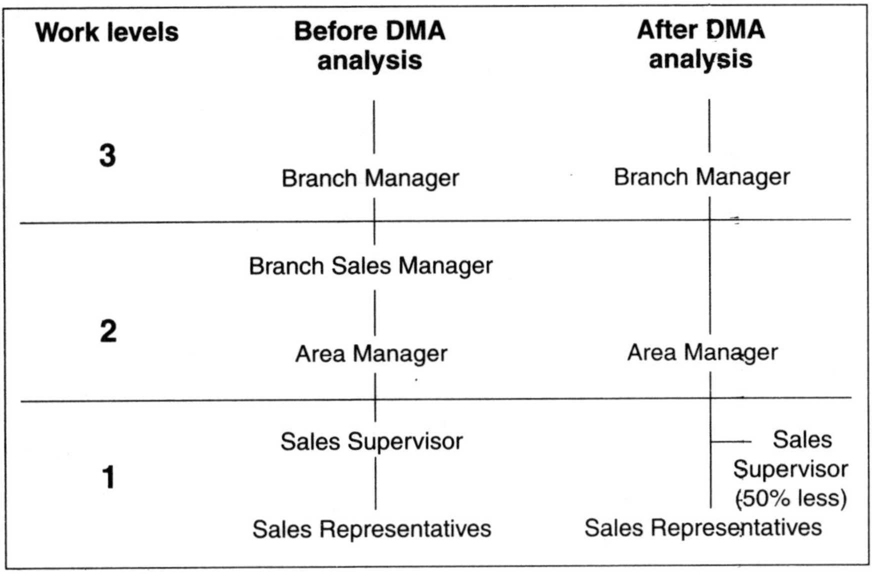

Supervisor is a support role – see Chapter 3

Figure 2.2 *DMA analysis of sales organization*

areas tended to be brittle. The culture was to talk results, but the work ethic was often about effort and activity. On balance the management of the business was more inwardly than outwardly focused. The huge administrative machine, in a huge country with, at that time, a backward telecommunications infrastructure, took long hours of work to maintain. The rudimentary availability of IT and general technology contributed to an enormous manual workload.

Highly educated managers in this sort of environment can be prone to analysis paralysis. If it is not clear who can make decisions, debate becomes the last refuge of management. Middle management increasingly tends to spend more time in meetings and discussion with each other.

In the middle of this project an unexpected event dramatically heightened the credence of these findings. A highly respected senior high-flying manager tendered his resignation. As it happened, we had just completed interviewing his section of the business where it had emerged that he was in a non-value-adding layer of the hierarchy. There was compelling evidence to verify the reasons for his dissatisfaction. His job was in the same work level as his boss. They were expected to make essentially the same decisions about the same resources within the same planning cycles. There is always a danger in an over-managed business that the most talented are the first to be demotivated. As they are invariably the most marketable, they can easily leave, with the less talented remaining, which only serves to compound the above problems. They are the quickest to resent micro-management and close supervision from their superiors. Significantly, at about the same time, *Business Week India* did a lead article on why HLL was losing larger numbers than usual of its talented management.

Working in the wrong level

Two other factors were found, which seem to be associated with rich structures. Top managers often work too far down into the organization (work in the wrong work level) for too much of their time, which means that on balance their real strategic work is neglected. The urgent short-term work drives out the important longer-term work. Companies are particularly prone to this when bottom-line results start to slip. The other surprising feature is that despite all the overlap and doubling up combined with long hours of hard work some important tasks are neglected or omitted. This is another consequence of blurred accountability. (The loss of trust inside many public services has occurred because professionals are required to do too much work at the wrong – lower – level.)

This first major DMA analysis in Unilever graphically illustrated why sometimes capable and hardworking employees do not always achieve the best results, even in a successful company. Sub-optimal organization design generates an inevitable sequence of people management issues and problems. These findings were summarized in 'Competitive Structure for the 1990s', which was then widely distributed throughout Unilever.

Further evidence

We then set out to see if it was possible to replicate these findings in other parts of the concern. Using the same approach, we studied small and large companies in Europe and North America, growing businesses, profitable and less profitable ones. We moved into developing countries where it was argued that more management was needed for the training of indigenous employees. We undertook major studies in Kenya and Nigeria. The Nigerian case provided a further dimension since we conducted work-level probes in a brewery, which at the time Unilever ran in partnership with Heineken.

In all these cases, of which the vast majority were successful operations, the rudimentary DMA analysis revealed that there were areas in these businesses that were over-managed and sub-optimally organized, with a number of unhealthy features that needed to be rectified. Often unnecessary layers of management were identified. Figure 2.3 illustrates the case in relation to one of the breweries.

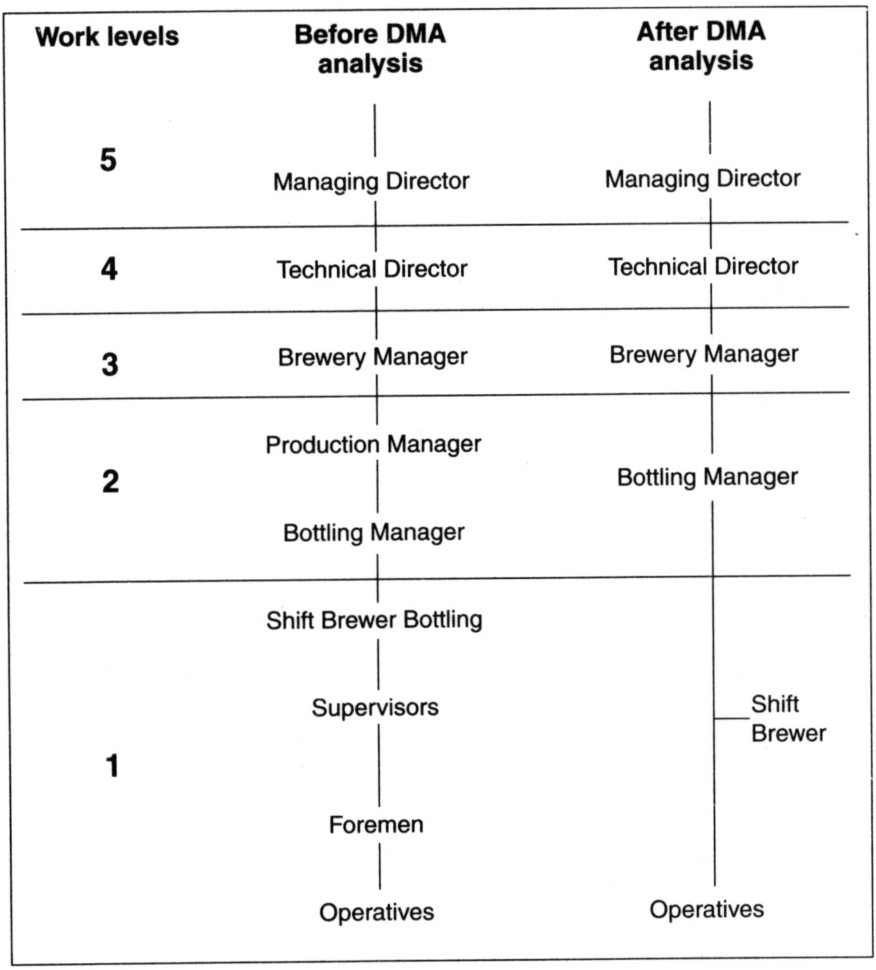

Shift Brewer is a support role – see Chapter 3

Figure 2.3 *DMA analysis of a brewery*

The efficacy of the case for the global application of DMA was strengthening with each investigation. Whenever someone said: 'Ah... yes, but it will not work here because we are different', it provided another challenge to test the emerging model. As a result, the model was continuously being refined and improved to ensure that it was indeed a universal set of principles, capable of worldwide application.

If one accepts that competitive advantage stems from being able to generate better products, services and results faster than others in the market, then the DMA model was emerging as a powerful source of competitive advantage as it was a robust blueprint for continuing to streamline the business without falling into the 'slash and burn' mentality of the process re-engineering school.

Knowledge work

The final piece in the jigsaw was to meet the challenge of assessing knowledge workers in the research laboratories and the International Head Office. The scientists were particularly sceptical of a 'system for factory workers, salesmen and administrators' being applied to knowledge work.

In these cases probes were again carried out into numerous sections of the three principal Unilever research laboratories in Port Sunlight and Colworth in the UK and Vlaardingen in the Netherlands. As mentioned above, people such as Burns and Stalker (1961), French and Bell (1973) and Moss Kanter (1985) had written about the need for creative and innovative work to be carried out in dynamic organizations with uncluttered hierarchies. Yet once again fieldwork revealed that the organization of work in the laboratories was not always optimal. Quite a few structures were unduly deep and over-managed with virtually all the unhealthy symptoms we had detected elsewhere. The work-level laser unerringly exposed areas of concern, which explained why, over a number of years, so much attention had drifted towards input and internal bureaucracy rather than output and the innovation of new products. In fact the analysis seemed to be even more powerful in the domain of knowledge workers and opened up some fundamental issues about the role of the science in the laboratories and the management of key projects. The umbrella term 'innovation' tended to mask the difference between development and research, whether applied or pure. Was the main purpose of the work in the laboratories meant to be development or research? The DMA analysis threw this issue into high relief and uncovered ambiguous accountabilities, which not surprisingly was also discomforting as it helped to explain some of the role confusion, overlap and duplication of effort. This obviously impacted the motivation, individual development and career paths of scientists.

Project work

The management of projects was a problem area in both the laboratories and the Head Office. There was some confusion about the difference between tasks, ongoing work and projects. There was also unclear accountability for the roles of sponsorship, ownership and leadership of projects. There was not always a learning mechanism in place to study the outcomes and lessons of previous projects. Finally, the nature of project work at different management levels was not defined. Definitions were vague and undiscriminating. The DMA approach was able to help resolve these issues, as will be outlined in Chapter 10.

Suffice it to say at this juncture that nothing emerged from these analyses which contradicted earlier findings elsewhere. In fact they were strongly reinforced.

THE DIVERSITY OF THE EVIDENCE

At the time of this study Unilever was in effect a diverse conglomerate operating on the ground in 100 countries, with its products available in about twice that number. The cultural spread covering every continent in the world in some depth is probably unrivalled among even the largest multinationals. Furthermore, the firm's management is genuinely multinational, with over 60 nationalities working outside their home country. Ninety per cent of the top 200 managers have worked outside their own country at least once.

Unilever is essentially a consumer goods company majoring in home and personal care products and food products. At the time of this research it ran major labour-intensive operations such as tea estates and palm plantations, while in contrast it also ran a number of capital-intensive chemicals companies around the world. In addition, there was a large trading company, United Africa Company International, which contributed about a third of Unilever's total profits in the early 1980s, while running textile, retail businesses, electrical goods distributorships, breweries (in conjunction with Heineken and Guinness), timber businesses and Caterpillar agencies involved in construction, road building and mining. For a while it also ran the world's largest ranch as a result of the Brooke Bond takeover in 1985.

In addition to the above, Unilever maintained an extensive number of research laboratories across the United States, the UK, the Netherlands and India. These were knowledge-intensive organizations working with budgets totalling some hundreds of millions of pounds. Similar levels of knowledge work were also a feature of the International Head Office. This blend of cultural and business diversity, coupled with extensive geographical spread, was unique. Only a few years later, many of these contrasting businesses had been divested as part of the strategy to focus on consumer goods. The DMA research took place when the company was 'optimally diverse', providing a uniquely rich seedbed for industrial and social research on a global basis. Such an unrivalled blend of data established the basis for the claim that the DMA principles can be applied anywhere to any organization with a clear purpose or mission.

The fieldwork with Tesco demonstrated that the approach works equally well in the retail industry. The work was undertaken at the outset together with David Billis and Maya Brown, Richard Dodd, and then with Nicola Steele. It is important to stress that initially I could not be sure about the number of decision-making levels. But by this stage, having developed the full DMA model (outlined in Chapter 3), it was quite a straightforward exercise. We initially probed the people-intensive elements in the company such as stores, distribution and one of the major head office departments, commercial (buying). We interviewed bottom-up, from the frontline up to and including the CEO. This established the total number of value-adding levels of accountability. As in the HLL case already cited, we uncovered sub-optimal structures with cases of both too many and too few layers, as the overall picture unfolded.

CONCLUSION

The field tests established conclusively that DMA directly enhanced all but one of the eight drivers of business success.

Focus on *customers* is the core ethic in Tesco. The DMA model demonstrated how to build a healthy organization that was closer to the customer. Their logo (see Figure 2.1), set by the board, was designed to reinforce this aspect of the Tesco values. In both Tesco and Unilever a number of examples (see Figures 2.2 and 2.3) were given, showing scope for improved *cost effectiveness*. The scope for improved *innovation* and more effective deployment of projects was established, and will be covered more extensively in Chapters 5 and 10 respectively. The early examples of work in HLL in India and NBL in Nigeria illustrated how more healthy organization design could *speed up response times* and lead to *more effective communications*. Evidence was given in HLL of how talent could be released once unwieldy structures were uncluttered, leading to *more motivated* employees. Finally, it was shown, in the Tesco work, that the DMA analysis could lead to more *effective teamwork*. Perhaps the one exception is *focus on quality* where the influence was mostly indirect. On balance, there was overwhelming evidence to prove that DMA could improve both business competitiveness and organizational health.

The fieldwork in Unilever had enabled me to improve the model and ensure that it could be implemented across the world. The five added elements made it more effective. More account was being taken of *resources*, especially knowledge, being managed and the type of *decisions* that needed to be taken. There was better recognition of the challenges of *change* management and the impact of *teamwork* and networks across the organization. Finally, the critical importance of customers, consumers and the key external *environmental factors* such as competition were being assessed. The work in Tesco further confirmed its robustness and reliability in another industry. Since then the DMA principles have been used in a number of complex organizations in both the private and the public sector.

The next chapter will outline the DMA solution set, with definitions of the different work levels and some concrete examples of their application in different parts of Unilever and Tesco.

3

The decision-making accountability solution set

This chapter is the fulcrum of this book. It outlines the conceptual basis of the DMA solution set, and describes how the DMA logic integrates everything involving the management of people. It is a 'solution set' where the answer can vary according to the needs of a particular situation.

The focus is on the individual. The approach outlined is a blueprint for the development and leadership of people. It is holistic, not fragmented, as is the case with traditional approaches to human resource management. Most classic approaches, such as job evaluation, are quantitatively based with points awarded for size of budget, turnover and number of subordinates. DMA has a qualitative focus. It concentrates on the added value of decisions taken and how they differ from those of subordinates and superiors. It questions whether a job should exist if it does not add to the mission of the organization and the growth of an individual.

Accountability is defined. The vital difference between operational and strategic accountability is set out. The confusion between line jobs and support jobs is clarified. The contribution of processes, process organizations and their linkage with the DMA solution set is touched upon.

Finally, it becomes clear that this is a flexible, dynamic model. It is not static and fixed. The principles can be applied to organizations that are small or large, established or starting up, growing or not, publicly or privately owned, voluntary and/or cooperative, bricks and mortar or clicks and mortar. In short, any organization with a mission.

LINK TO BUSINESS STRATEGY

Effective people development programmes reinforce the organization's purpose and strategy. Once the organization's *mission* has been established, measurable *critical success factors* (CSFs) can be identified which in turn call for key *values*, the critical behaviours that make a difference. This is reflected in *skills* and differentiating *competencies* – the former reinforcing performance, the latter serving as indicators for leadership development and career planning. Training in skills and the identification of competencies is needed together with programmes for continuous improvement. This is outlined in Figure 3.1.

DECISION-MAKING ACCOUNTABILITY

Decision-making accountability (DMA) is the genetic code of a healthy organization. It is the lifeblood of any goal-oriented organization. It provides the genetic programme that shapes and determines how an

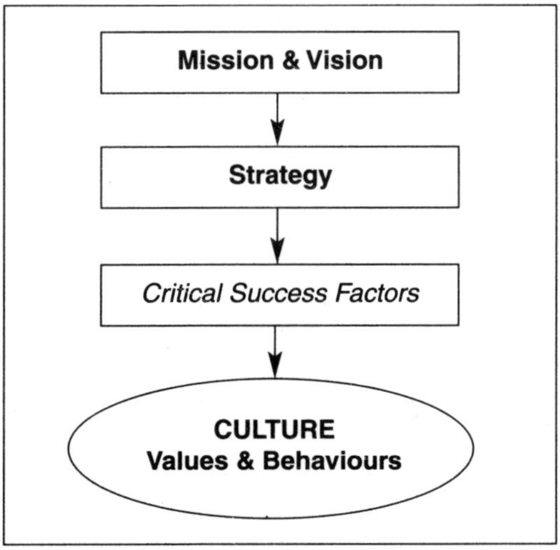

Figure 3.1 *Linking people to business strategy*

organization will function, or indeed malfunction. This genetic programme is mapped by examining the levels of decision making in an organization. These have variously been labelled: Strata, Levels of Work and Work Levels. Other terms could be Contribution Levels or Accountability Levels. The label is not important so long as the underlying principles or *elements* are not compromised.

DMA is a powerful X-ray, which reveals the inner workings of an organization, whatever its age, size or mission. It is one thing to know that organizations depend on their DMA, but it is quite another to detect that it is in perfect working order. In most organizations I have encountered, the determining of organizational health is still an area of speculation. The DMA approach plots how the organization behaves and makes decisions. In the case of Unilever, this is encapsulated in an application of the model which entails eight work levels in total. Tesco, which has less geographical reach and complexity, has fewer. That could change in future if the organization continues its path of international expansion. The principles of DMA are adaptable to the context of the organization.

Decision-making accountability defined

First, some basic definitions of the essential DMA concepts:

- A *decision* is a considered act in response to a demand or need, to progress a process, change a state of affairs, or solve a problem.

- *Accountability* occurs when one is answerable to a higher authority for work, resources and results. Results could involve service.

- *Work* is goal-oriented behaviour. Role incumbents can be rewarded or sanctioned for their performance in pursuit of agreed goals.

Klatt, Murphy and Irvine (1999) have established a practical theory of accountability:

- 'Accountability is a statement of personal promise, both to yourself and the people around you, to deliver specific defined results.

- Accountability for results means activities are not enough.

- Accountability for results requires room for personal judgement and decision making.

- Accountability is neither shared nor conditional.
- Accountability is meaningless without consequences (rewards, sanctions).
- Accountability applies to individuals.'

Kraines (2001) distinguishes between accountabilities for employees and those for managers. Those for employees entail Commitment and Adherence:

> *Commitment:* employees must fulfil the output commitments exactly, in terms of quantity, quality, and time parameters, as defined in the assignments, projects, services and other deliverables – unless the manager agrees to alter them. Under no circumstances can the employee surprise the manager at the due date with changes.
>
> *Adherence:* employees must simultaneously observe and work within defined resource constraints – that is the rules and limits set by policies, procedures, contracts, law and managerial guidelines.

In addition, 'managers have to be clear with their subordinates about what (quantity and quality of output) they are expected to deliver, when. They are also accountable for providing the relevant resources.'

Accountability is concerned with expectations, obligations, commitments and adding value. It encompasses rights *and* responsibilities.

Teams and shared accountability

Popular wisdom has it that teamwork is shared accountability. Teamwork is shared endeavour, not shared accountability. A team is led by an individual who is personally accountable for the team results. Current management fashion encourages CEOs to talk of 'we', 'the team' and 'consensus decision making'. Autocratic styles are out these days, democratic leadership is in. But no matter what the language, no one doubts who is the boss. This is clearest when a crisis occurs, even the dot.com threat, as discussed in Chapter 10. It is also clearly the reason, when businesses don't perform, why some of the mighty CEOs have fallen at IBM, General Motors, BP, Marks & Spencer, Barclays Bank and the New York Stock Exchange, to mention but a few. It is equally clear in the cases of malpractice when key individuals are cited, depending on the nature of the case: for example, in the Guinness affair when the CEO and the Finance Director were in the legal limelight with subsequent imprisonment for the CEO. Likewise the CEO at Enron.

It is also worth noting that Katzenbach (1997) has pointed out that CEOs and their executives rarely even function as teams, let alone share accountability. Board members are expected to take a corporate and balanced perspective but this is not strictly shared accountability.

'Collective responsibility' is not shared accountability either. It is a form of discipline where, especially in politics, individuals are required to toe the party line. Neither DMA principles, nor many others it seems, apply to politicians.

Accountability assumes a proactive and conscious commitment to the purpose of an organization by an individual. It also presupposes clarity, transparency and participation, which enable contribution to that purpose. Single point reporting enables the ultimate enhancement of the individual. Interestingly, or perhaps significantly, current writers on the well-being and health of civil society, such as Gifford (1998), see factors such as transparency, accountability, participation and focus on the individual as the very fundaments of democracy. Putnam (2000) is equally adamant that they are the basis of a healthy community.

Accountability and responsibility

The terms accountability and responsibility are totally synonymous. When referring to dictionaries in different languages, they are defined in terms of each other: for example, 'Accountable... to be responsible for'; 'Responsible... to be accountable for.' Yet, for some reason, people like to think the words represent different concepts.

At the beginning of the 1990s Unilever set up a global Foods Executive matrix structure where the executives at headquarters were 'profit accountable' and the country managers around the world were 'profit responsible'. This was not a helpful distinction, and only added confusion.

Responsibility refers to personal maturity and reliability. In Gerry Kraines' terms it amounts to 'what an individual demands of himself or herself. It has to do with one's conscience, aspirations, and internal standards.' Thus one can be responsible without having the authority to be accountable. This is a common flaw of unhealthy organizations.

I have also come across two separate and different consulting organizations (one in the United States and the other in Europe), which peddle an 'RACI' approach to clarify roles where:

R = Person responsible for getting work done (the operational owner)
A = Person accountable for results (the process owner)
C = Person to be consulted
I = Person to be informed.

Both companies are selling 'process organizations' as the latest panacea for organization design.

As it happens, I have worked with two of their different clients, one in the United States and the other in Europe. Both had unhealthy structures (both were over-layered and under-layered as well) in different parts of their organizations. RACI definitions did not guarantee clear and healthy solutions. This is because focus on horizontal processes alone neglects the vital vertical components of structure. It is necessary to take both the horizontal and vertical axes into account to achieve an effective balance. Intriguingly, employees focused on who 'had the A' and did not really refer to who 'had the R' for their work. The application of levels of accountability helped sharpen 'who had the A' and of what it consisted.

In this book, for accountability read responsibility and vice versa.

As Klatt, Murphy and Irvine (1999) have pointed out, focusing on processes is 'allowing employees to stay stuck in activities rather than outcomes... it's limiting, self-defeating, and disempowering'. Accountability is not about activities and control. That is the path to bureaucracy and the limiting of decisions to the top of the organization. As will be demonstrated in Chapter 5, DMA is about pushing the right decisions down to the lowest competent level. It will also be shown later in this chapter that processes are limited to operational levels of accountability, which restricts their effectiveness as an organizing principle in large, complex organizations.

Managerial accountability

Managerial accountability can be viewed from two perspectives. The first is from above. This takes on board the commitments a manager has made to the level above. The second is from below. This takes into account the manager's commitment to subordinates: the work and results that have to be achieved, together with their learning and development.

If managers cannot decide who comes into their team they cannot be held accountable for the team's performance. This is a fundamental tenet of management accountability, and it was astounding to see the 2003 Higgs report on governance in the UK suggest otherwise in a bid to satisfy certain political constituents.

A line manager must be accountable for the following:

- deciding (or at least having a veto over) who comes into the team;
- defining the work that needs to be done and establishing goals in terms of quality, quantity and time;
- deciding who will work where and when;
- securing employee commitment to attain the relevant goals;
- providing the authorities and resources subordinates need to deliver their goals;
- ensuring the members of the team meet all their obligations, and if necessary changing the goals, obligations or team members bearing in mind the overall situation;
- calling team members to account if they fail to meet their commitments;
- giving constructive feedback and appraising individuals' performance, agreeing their training and development needs and ensuring these are acted upon;
- deciding appropriate rewards on the basis of performance and contribution against the agreed commitments;
- coaching subordinates to improve their performance and fulfil their potential, and deciding whom to recommend for promotion.

These are the 10 key accountabilities of a manager, adding value in a spine of accountability. If all these accountabilities are not present, then the job in question is either not adding value or it is a support role (see Chapter 4) to the spine of accountability.

Accountability and health

The secret of individual and collective health in an organization is accountable achievement and learning. Doing worthwhile things motivates people, and knowledge workers in particular enjoy learning how to do more worthwhile things. This is the basis of the desire for 'achievement, self-actualization and recognition' identified by behavioural scientists in the 20th century. True leadership cannot be learnt or experienced without accountability to make decisions to move forward (add value) the work of others.

The absence of true accountability stifles the development of leadership. Accountable decision making cannot reside in top-heavy hierarchies. This is why large global companies are often rich in managers but bereft of leaders.

Clear examples in the early 1990s were Philips, Ford and IBM, each of which went into serious decline for a period. Latterly one of Unilever's major strategic thrusts has been to build an enterprise culture in direct response to the inertia and absence of accountable decision making redolent of its leaden organization structures of the same era.

There is a tendency to forget that someone like Jack Welch was initially referred to as Neutron Jack in the 1980s as he set about the then over-layered and top-heavy General Electric Company. Many managers at the time argued vehemently that GE's spans of control of 10 and more would break people. At the time, executives in Unilever had an average span of control of just over two managers. Although the company prided itself as a marketing company, it was in fact driven by a philosophy of control, mostly financial.

Jack Welch has shown that to be a good soft manager you must first be an effective hard manager. Organizational spinal curvature damages the central nervous decision-making system. When it occurs it must be remedied. Revitalizing an over-managed, rich and bureaucratic organization is hard work. It requires difficult people and organization decisions, taken by a leader with vision, determination and a sense of humanity. Too often it seems, CEOs take reactive 'tough' decisions after they have fallen into the trap of first advocating boundaryless behaviour and soft management styles before ensuring that there are clear and well-determined levels of accountability in the organization. Instead, lacking a blueprint of a healthy organization, they blunder into the world of fads and fashion.

THE DMA SOLUTION SET – A BLUEPRINT FOR THE LEADERSHIP AND DEVELOPMENT OF PEOPLE

The key premise of the DMA approach is that jobholders must take decisions that cannot be taken at a lower level and which need not be taken at a higher level. In other words, they must add value or enrich the decision-making process on the spine of accountability. Subordinates cannot make these decisions, not because they're not permitted to, but because they do not have the relevant knowledge or experience. Similarly, if a subordinate and the immediate superior are both working in the same decision-making zone, then one of them is superfluous. The application of DMA logic enables the integrated management and development of people. The model sets out a set of principles, which govern:

- how work is organized;
- how the organization is designed;
- how work is rewarded;
- how individuals can be fulfilled in their work;
- how performance and potential can be assessed;
- how individuals can grow and develop;
- how challenging future assignments can be planned.

In short, a blueprint for the leadership and development of people.

We have already seen that the early work done by Jaques and his colleagues was based on the fundamental proposition that there is a universal, underlying stratification of managerial levels in all employment organizations. This, he argued, reflected the distribution or work capacities of human beings. Later work, such as that of Rowbottom and Billis, moved the focus of attention away from individual capacity to focus on the work that needs to be done. The extended work undertaken at Unilever, Tesco and elsewhere takes as a starting point the organization and the work that is to be achieved by the employees in the organization to meet the needs of consumers and customers. The premise is that the hierarchical levels in an organization emerge from complexity in work rather than discontinuities in mental functioning of individuals as envisaged by Jaques. Nevertheless, as will be demonstrated in Chapter 8, there seem to be identifiable patterns of development in individuals whose careers clearly reflect their innate abilities, developed over time.

DMA principles

The DMA approach is based on **three fundamental principles**:

1. All organized work, managerial or non-managerial, falls into a hierarchy of discrete levels or strata. At each successive level the objective to be achieved and the decisions which therefore have to be taken become broader in nature; the range of environmental circumstances to be taken into account become more complex, extensive and change in quality; the discretion and authority required correspondingly increase; and more time is required to assess the impact of these decisions.

2. The second key principle is that for any assigned work level, the balance of major tasks falls into a single level. A good indication of this balance or 'burden' of accountability is to identify which tasks take the most time.

   However, in some cases work will be spread over more than one level. For example, an executive who is accountable for strategic decisions may also need to spend some time on less challenging administrative matters, ensuring that subordinates are carrying out key responsibilities. But if the major portion of the superior's time is spent on discrete, lower-level tasks, then this will lead to organization development problems.

3. The third principle has identified that each accountability level above the first requires one and only one layer of management. This is the *Golden Rule of DMA*. (*Hence* the formula: *Work levels minus 1 = an optimum structure*, referred to in Chapter 1.)

   A layer of management is required only where the boss really is accountable for making decisions that cannot be taken by subordinates. The fundamental reason why reporting relationships in the same level do not work is that a genuine boss must have the authority to make decisions that take into account and integrate a genuinely broader and more complex area of work than their subordinates.

It will not be enough if the boss is just doing more of the same sort of work as a subordinate. If the boss and subordinate are accountable for identical planning cycles, such as the annual plan, this is usually a sure indication that they are operating in the same work level. The inevitable consequences are organizational problems and personal unhappiness – see the list of symptoms of an unhealthy organization in Chapter 1. It seems that the main cause of confusion about work within an accountability level stems from unclear authority. If a superior is to have full accountability for his or her work, then he or she must have the commensurate authority to ensure that the right people can achieve the work in the right order, in the right way and in the right time frame. I will cover this issue in more detail later in this chapter under the section 'Line and support jobs'.

The key ideas of the DMA solution set covering organization design and development, the varying nature of accountability, and the contribution to identifying, developing and rewarding of talent are summarized in Figure 3.2.

UNDERSTANDING THE DMA SOLUTION SET

The special feature of the DMA solution set is its *conceptually integrated logic*, which underpins everything that needs to be mastered in the management of people. The components of other HR models are at best only administratively integrated. Their job evaluation systems, for example, are not able to demonstrate that a job is not required, is not an appropriate vehicle for personal development and therefore is an unnecessary cost for the organization because it is not adding value to its mission.

As Figure 3.2 illustrates, the same guiding principles:

- identify the type and level of work to be carried out;
- identify the number of organizational layers required to add value to the decision-making spine of accountability (the Golden Rule);
- provide insight into the development and growth of individuals, which in due course can impact on their career development and career planning for the organization as a whole;

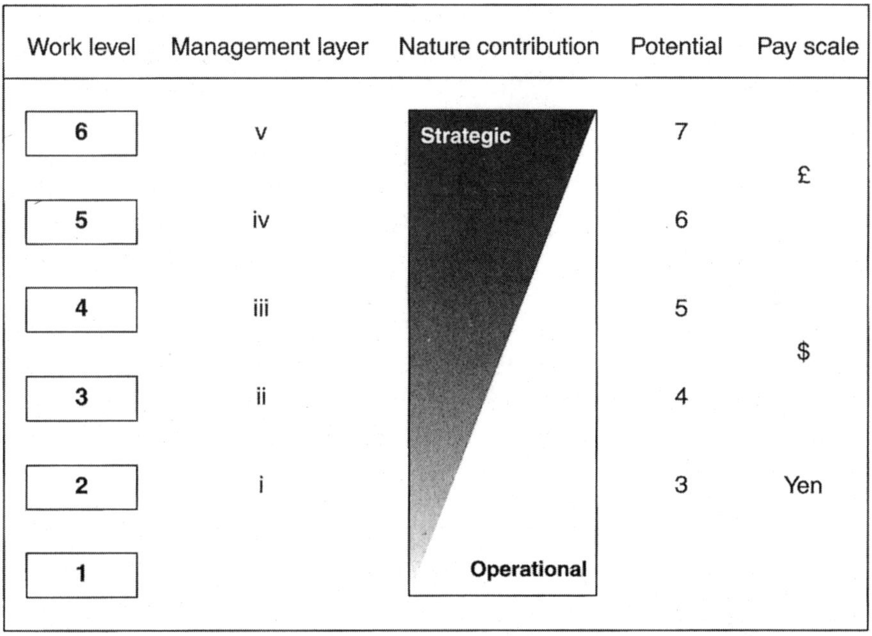

Figure 3.2 *The DMA solution set*

- can help establish how people should be paid by linking the level of work or responsibility to a national or industry market.

Nature of contribution

In the model there is reference to the *nature of contribution*. Empirical work has demonstrated that all jobs seem to have elements of work related to operational tasks and strategic tasks. The key point, though, is that up to work level 3, accountability for work is essentially operational. *Operational work* involves accountability for existing resources, whether they are physical assets, systems, ideas, money, people or services to be delivered. By the time people reach level 3, they are being held accountable for the improved performance or productivity of existing assets. They have very clear plans to meet, which are often specified in terms of volume, quality and time. They are not held accountable for reconfiguration of these existing resources.

From work levels 4 to 6, the balance of accountable work is *strategic*. At the strategic levels, the constraints of operational work are removed. In other words, now the jobholder must make authoritative (based on his or her competence) recommendations for change, based upon analysis of gaps in the availability and performance of key resources, product portfolios, systems and technology, knowledge (eg science), services and people. The key accountability here is identifying opportunities and constraints and initiating the introduction of new resources as well as the withdrawal of old ones. An important point that I will return to throughout the book is that strategic accountability does not necessarily mean that all the best strategic ideas come only from the jobholders in level 4 and above. This is the mistaken identification of accountability with control. Often, subordinates will suggest new ideas for promotions, products, and new developments. The key accountability of the boss is to set the framework of priorities, to recognize which new initiatives should have support and extra resource to ensure that the unit or company objectives are met. Thus, the strategic manager frequently has to assess and trade off ideas for new directions or developments, given that inevitably the resources available are not unlimited.

Potential

It is important to identify what qualities individuals need to exhibit before moving up to the next level. The column on potential in Figure 3.2 refers to how the DMA logic can drive individual development. This will be covered in considerable detail in Chapter 7, where a competency model will be outlined to help guide personal development. It is evident, though, that with only six levels to traverse in a career, the time spent in each level is considerable – about six to seven years on average.

The importance of appropriate 'dwell time' in work levels 3 and 5 (both often involving different types of general management responsibilities) will be further demonstrated in Chapter 8.

Link to market

Once the levels of accountability have been established, one can then decide the appropriate market pay per level. This can apply around the world, which is not to say pay per level would be identical. Thus, pay for work level 3 in Australia would differ from that in Zimbabwe. The presence of a consistent measure of responsibility makes identification of fair and relevant expatriate packages easier to determine. This is a valuable benefit in an international organization wanting to build a multicultural workforce.

In the DMA model, organization design drives job evaluation and pay, not the other way round. This overcomes the weakness of traditional systems, which have led to the building of unhealthy and cluttered bureaucracies.

THE ELEMENTS OF DMA

The early work of Brown and Jaques indicated that it was possible to analyse the work of an organization and conclude that it required fewer managerial layers than were described on the organization chart. However, as Rowbottom and Billis had shown, it was not clear what the difference was in the nature of work at each managerial level. But they had not provided a complete solution nor shown that it would work in practice. As more empirical work was conducted within Unilever, I came to the conclusion (as indicated in Chapter 2) that more was required to demonstrate the differences in the accountability of work at the different levels across the concern.

The earlier work was extended in Unilever, as a result of over 3,000 man-hours of fieldwork, to include seven separate *elements*, namely:

Expected work
Resources
Problem solving
Change
Lateral teams
Environment
Task horizon

The headings for these elements were modified in Tesco, although the integrity of the concepts was retained, as shown in Figure 3.3.

These elements will now be described in more detail, because a job is assigned to a specific accountability level by taking into account these seven elements. Chapter 4 will go into more detail to demonstrate how the seven elements help identify work at the different levels.

1. Nature of work

The work expected of a role, not an individual. It focuses on the core reason for the existence of a particular job and where it differs in

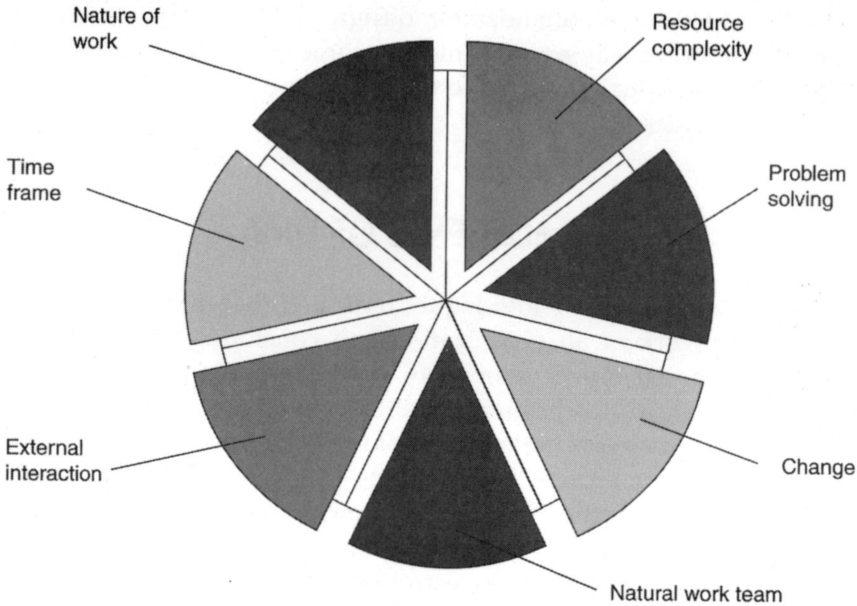

Figure 3.3 *The DMA elements*

essence from those below and above. It therefore looks primarily at the nature of the work, which becomes more complex at each successive work level.

One of the key issues in this whole process is: how do we distinguish between the person and the job? Clearly, people are more or less capable, and matching an individual's skills and competencies to a job remains a fundamental challenge for managers. This element refers to what the organization expects and sanctions the individual to do (his or her role). It defines the nature of his or her accountability for a distinct area of work. A higher level of authority therefore sanctions the work expected of an individual or team. If this is not clear, it is extremely difficult to identify the performance expected of the incumbent.

2. Resource complexity

This element defines accountability for resources: people, technology, budgets and know-how or knowledge. Given the onset of the knowledge age, know-how is rapidly becoming the critical resource. It is manifest in the worldwide recognition of the importance of skills and competencies in delivering sustainable, competitive advantage.

Roles in ascending levels are accountable for an increasingly extensive and complex array of resources. At work levels 1, 2 and 3, the balance of physical resources is given. For example, the manager of a margarine factory cannot decide to make ice cream. The challenge is to maximize performance as set out in the appropriate plan. Thus, a production manager of one product or department within a factory has a more straightforward allocation of resources than, say, the factory manager who has a number of departments and technologies to manage. The latter will have specified productivity targets for the factory as a whole, together with clear accountability for volume, quality and overall performance. Such expectations are innately more difficult and complex than subordinate accountabilities in accountability levels 1 and 2.

At work levels 4, 5 and 6, gaps in resources (for example, factory capacity) or opportunities in a given market have to be identified. This entails planning and negotiating relevant resources since these are rarely available in either sufficient or unlimited quantities. Jobholders are expected to make authoritative recommendations to add/delete resources within their specific area of accountability. Thus, at work level 4 a supply chain director, for example, would be expected to draw up a plan to add to existing manufacturing capacity, output and efficiency, or by rebalancing production between a number of different factories. At level 5, the resource configuration within Unilever would often be a company or a national business unit outside the UK, accountable for a complete value chain of activities as defined by M E Porter (1980).

At work level 4, a resource issue which identified a gap in an existing product range, given a new market opportunity, would require a modification to the existing marketing strategy. At level 5, the company-wide implications, for example in the supply chain, company budgets and profit position of such a change in the product portfolio, would need to be assessed and managed. The job at this level is therefore accountable for resource reconfigurations and boundary changes within a self-sustaining business unit or service. This is the distinguishing difference from resource management in the infrastructure of work levels 1 to 5.

At level 6, on the other hand, the resource infrastructure is a network of such self-sustaining entities, frequently spanning more than one country in the context of an international or global business. At this level, the boundaries of previously self-sustaining business units may themselves be reconfigured as part of the more comprehensive level 6 network.

One of the key resources that needs to be managed is people. Accountability for people can be a critical factor in determining a job's position in the spine of accountability within an organization. There is an important distinction here to be made between line jobs and support jobs. This will be covered in the last section of this chapter. The critical difference between a support job in work level 1, such as a night shift supervisor and a manager in work level 2, is accountability for people and budgets.

3. Problem solving

The nature of the problems to be solved changes at each successive level of accountability. At work levels 1, 2 and 3, problems are concrete and operational in nature. The type of thinking that different tasks require influences the problem-solving element. Wilfred Brown (1971) referred to different levels of abstraction that he aligned to the respective work levels. The first level of abstraction he referred to as Perceptual Concrete – the object of the task must be physically present. At the second level of abstraction (Imaginal Concrete), physical or visual contact isn't necessary, so long as sufficient contact has occurred in the past. At the third level of abstraction (Conceptual Concrete) the jobholder must be able to deal with the future in mental models based on models of tasks in concrete terms, based on past experience. For the fourth level of abstraction (Abstract Modelling) the jobholder must have capacity to discard past experience and think afresh.

This is the first level at which breakthrough 'thinking outside the box' occurs. Jaques and Cason (1994) also outlined 'categories of complexity of mental processing' aligned to different levels of work. Although we did not try to establish strict alignment of reasoning ability with work levels in Unilever and Tesco, nevertheless it has become very apparent over the years, from interviews with jobholders, that people with potential to operate at, or already operating at, strategic levels of accountability clearly think in different ways and even use different language to describe the challenges they face. When establishing a work level, therefore, it is very important to focus on the nature of the problems being confronted and the extent of the decisions required.

Accountability for solving problems of a strategic nature, which emerges from level 4, requires abstract and conceptual analysis to identify problems and assess potential solutions, including new formulae, products, technology, systems or policies. Tomorrow's solutions may not yet physically exist and therefore have to be conceptualized. This modelling process entails identifying the causes of patterns and linkages in consumer or customer behaviour and the performance and capacity of plant, people and systems.

4. Change

This element is concerned with accountability for driving market/technological change, often referred to as innovation. While creativity can exist at all levels in an organization, not all levels are accountable for ensuring that innovation takes place or that creative ideas are implemented. Levels 1 to 3 work with existing technology, systems, products and services. The work in levels 1 to 3 is essentially development, modifying, or improving, something that already exists.

From work levels 4 to 6 there is a need to discover or invent new solutions. At level 4, for example, the jobholder is accountable for establishing new linkages among existing bodies of knowledge or ideas. This can lead to totally new products or services performing differently as a result of the new knowledge, rather than simply adaptations of existing ones. Tomorrow's requirements are as important as today's. Whereas at levels 1 to 3 the balance of requirements is upon today, or the short term, accountability for true research emerges at the fourth level of accountability. The jobholder spots gaps in received wisdom and discovers ways and means of closing those gaps. It is then level 5 accountability to manage the integration of the resources to ensure that the identified needs and solutions are successfully implemented. The typical example of change at level 5 is organizational change, where the chief executive of a national business unit would be accountable for boundary reconfiguration of the company, whereas at work level 6 the boundary reconfiguration would automatically involve a number of companies and/or countries.

5. Natural work team

The work of lateral teams does not refer to boss–subordinate relationships – that would be vertical teamwork. This element refers to the lateral interaction or collaboration with peers across the total organization, which is needed to complete common tasks. These are the colleagues with whom one must work to achieve one's own accountabilities. This collaboration involves more than simply contacting colleagues. In the lower levels, teams are accountable for outputs that tend to be localized; in the higher levels teams have outputs that are international and even global. Again it's important to stress that the key is accountability. Being a member of an international team contributing, for example, to the development of a new product does not necessarily mean that the individual warrants a higher work level. Nevertheless, plotting the natural peer's of common roles within the organization is a very powerful indicator to the nature of the work required, in other words the accountability level. These levels reinforce one another so that it would be unlikely for work to be established or to be assessed as being at level 3 in *nature of work* and resources and yet only at level 2 in terms of *natural work team*. As already indicated in Chapter 2, there is a tendency to confuse the existence of teams and the need for hierarchy. Perhaps the last word should be given to Katzenbach and Smith (1994): 'Contrary to some popular opinion, teams do not imply the destruction of hierarchy. Indeed quite the reverse. Teams and hierarchy make each other perform better because structure and hierarchy generate performance within well defined boundaries that teams, in turn, productively bridge in order to delivery yet more and higher performance.'

Thus, at work level 1, a team may be limited to a production line in a factory, the workbench in a laboratory, a checkout location in a store or a workstation in an office. But at level 4 and above, natural work teams typically involve membership of a network, which enables jobholders to collaborate with colleagues beyond their accountable operating environment. This collaboration requires a wide knowledge of the relevant company resources or key individuals, able to contribute to the identified tasks, which often takes many years to establish.

6. External interaction

The previous element, *natural work team,* covers lateral interaction within the organization. External interaction, where consumers, customers and suppliers are part of the lifeblood of a company, is covered by this element. The increasing global competition of the 1990s has intensified the external challenge of doing business. Many public sector agencies or organizations that have been privatized have now been transformed by the need to respond to and cope with competition. The importance of the customer has been reflected in the emergence of the so-called process organization. Total quality initiatives, supplier partnerships, more powerful trade groupings and increasing numbers of strategic alliances, not to mention the increasingly active non-governmental organizations (NGOs), have added to the external pressures on organizations over and above the traditional institutions such as governments, the media, financial institutions and trade unions. Many jobs in a large multinational are accountable for achieving results in the external domain.

In a business like Unilever, the prime focus is upon the consumer, but the interface with customers and suppliers is a critical area of accountability. Tesco is a customer for Unilever. In Tesco, on the other hand, the prime focus is on the customer coming into the store. Unilever is one of Tesco's suppliers. External management and collaboration are becoming more complex, more difficult and therefore more critical for overall success.

In the operational levels 1 to 3, roles have clearly defined customers and/or suppliers, for example, with whom they work. At level 3, external contacts could be at the national headquarter level, where tailor-made solutions or responses might be required to maximize the performance of a network of customers or suppliers.

At level 4, the environment is likely to involve national government and similar institutions. Supply networks are likely to be international and similar customer developments are quickly emerging around the world. In the grocery industry a number of major retailers such as Wal-Mart, Carrefour, Promodores, Arholt and Tesco are currently expanding on the international stage. This process has been fuelled by other external pressures, for example recent developments within the EEC, which have led to the establishment of pan-European organizations and structures. This means that the external network is widening and there is a greater need for strategic and proactive collaboration with more and more external organizations.

At work levels 1 to 3, these external contacts tend to focus on one area affecting the value chain. While this still largely is the case at level 4, there is a greater need to be proactive and positively influence external developments in line with the company's assessment of gaps, opportunities and threats in the marketplace. By level 5 the manager has to reconfigure elements of the internal organization to reflect significant external developments while at the same time managing the environment, which at times may work against the aims and interests of the organization. At level 5, in self-sustaining operating units, this is apt to be in a national context whereas at level 6 the external reach would be international and would affect business results in a number of countries. A clear example of this is the emergence of international customer bases, which wish to negotiate across more than one country. The response would require orchestration from level 6. The network could include international finance and political institutions such as the World Bank or the European Commission, or a pressure group such as Greenpeace.

7. Time frame

The focus is upon *the average time it takes to complete the balance of tasks for which a person is held accountable*. This is not a diluted form of the time span of discretion. In 1987 Rowbottom and Billis had already concluded that 'time measures are not, in our experience, easy ones to use in detailed organization design or problem solving'.

But the concept of task completion and accountability within a certain time frame is logical and is a factor in the assessment of accountability. However, the original time sequences suggested by Brown and Jaques seem to be increasingly ethereal above work level 4 and are not universally reliable or sensible. For example, it does not make sense to assess the level of a heart surgeon's accountability solely on the time it takes to complete an operation. They seem to confuse the longevity of the task or assignment with accountability for its completion. Jaques (1989) argues for time spans between 10 and 20 years at work level 6 and between 20 and 50 at work level 7. But an accountable time span of 50 years is of no practical help to any organization trying to assess accountability. Perhaps most tellingly, Jaques has provided no evidence to support his spans of discretion theory above level 4, even though in *Requisite Organization* he seems to envisage businesses going up to, and including, work level 8.

The work in Unilever is based on actual time horizons of accountable value-adding tasks observable at the different levels of accountability. This has been derived from empirical work. The work done with Tesco revealed that the retail industry has shorter planning horizons than consumer goods companies, principally in the operational levels. Maybe oil companies are different again. Focusing on work done, rather than individuals' theoretical innate capacities, suggests that industries work with different decision-making time frames. This is consistent with the earlier work of Goold and Campbell (1987) on strategy and styles.

Time scales drive large organizations. Factories' activities are divided into shifts, production plans into days, weeks and months. Sales results in supermarkets and hypermarkets are monitored on a daily, weekly and monthly basis. Management accounts mirror these same reporting periods. Statutory accounts are available quarterly and consolidated on a yearly basis. These are usually referred to as budgets or short-term plans. Longer-term, or strategic, plans are often up to three years on a country basis. Regional plans, affecting capital investment, are more typically up to five years and global planning tends to take a somewhat longer perspective.

Although technology, for example fax, e-mail, the Internet and computer simulation, is compressing time available for decision making, accountable tasks clearly fit into time frames and business planning cycles. Thus roles at work level 2 operate within the boundaries of the annual plan. Managers at level 3 are, in addition, accountable for contributions to the policy and substance of the following one-year plan. By level 4, an accountable contribution to the next strategic plan (ie up to three years) is expected. At level 5, one would be expected to deliver the current strategic plan and play a key role in establishing the following strategic or long-term plan while ensuring that all interim plans and results are achieved. This typically requires a planning horizon up to five years. At level 6 this time frame stretches a little further as an authoritative contribution to the long-term global plan as a whole is also required.

Time frames are prone to inflationary claims once individuals know that they influence their work levels and therefore their remuneration. It is important, therefore, to establish the true balance of task accountability. This is particularly important where individuals are working in teams and/or research assignments. Identifying budgeted milestones usually helps provide realistic answers to these conundrums. Thus, to take an extreme case: a worker planting palm trees on a plantation, which have a planned life cycle of 25 years, does not have an accountable time frame of 25 years. The task of successfully planting a sapling can be assessed within a couple of days, by which time the plant is either thriving or has already died. Accountable time frames, therefore, can extend from minutes in some frontline jobs to many years at the higher levels. Accountable completion times for tasks are normally set by the boss and sometimes approved by even higher authorities.

LINE AND SUPPORT JOBS

Careful assessment of the above seven elements will establish the appropriate accountability level for a given job. There is one other factor that should be taken into account when deciding whether or not a job should be placed on the vertical spine of decision-making accountability, and that is consideration of whether the job is a line or support role. (See Figure 3.4.)

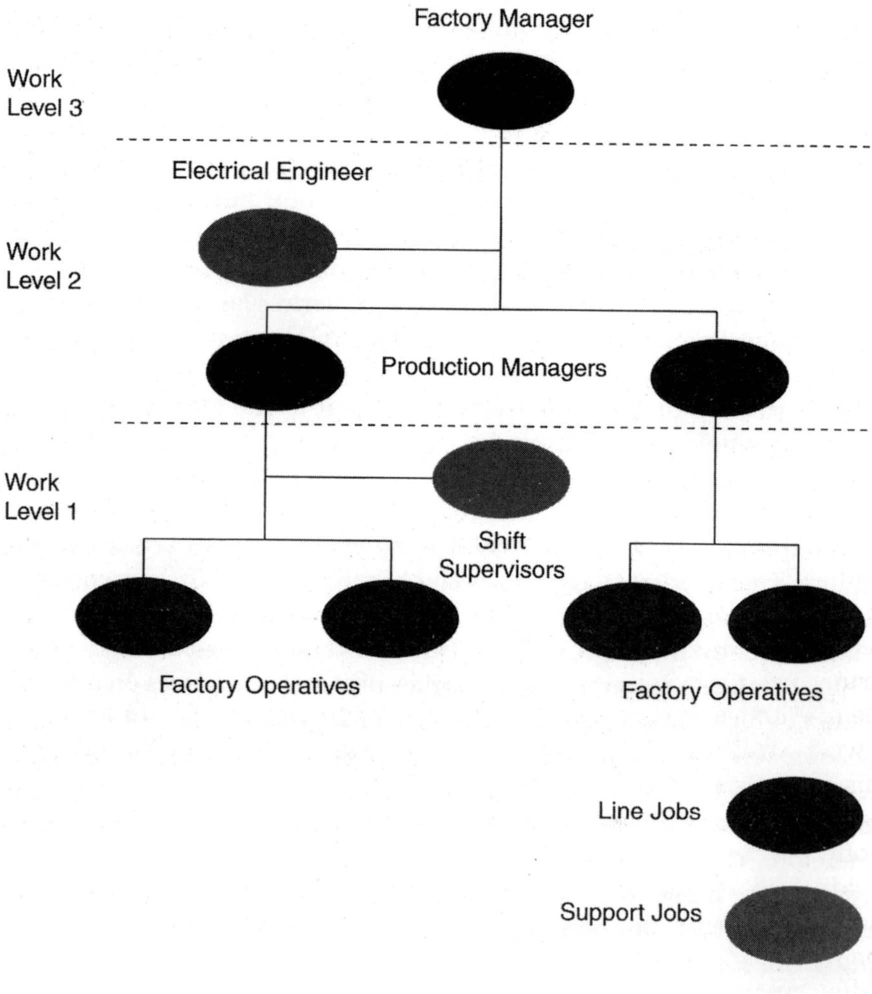

Figure 3.4 *Line and support jobs*

As already indicated in principle 3 above, there is only one line or core job per accountability level in a given chain of command. The line jobholder is 'the boss' who is individually accountable for the performance of subordinates in lower work levels and has the authority to select staff and assign tasks; set objectives and task horizons; appraise performance and change plans, responsibilities and, if necessary, staff. A boss may ask others to contribute to the appraisal of subordinates, typically a task of supervisors, but in the end it is the boss who is accountable for the total department or unit. It is the line job, or boss, which is justified as a value-adding layer on the spine of accountability.

Other jobs, which add value but do not form part of the chain of command or accountability, are termed support jobs. Support jobs are required when, for example:

- there are exceptionally large numbers of subordinates to be supervised;
- there are widely dispersed subordinates to be supervised;
- there are multi-shift operations requiring continuous supervision;
- there is an absence of essential, specialist know-how in the lower work level(s).

In short, support jobs are only required to help manage large numbers, time (shifts) or provide necessary expertise that otherwise does not reside elsewhere in the team. Line and support jobs were found in all Unilever and Tesco activities (although in Tesco support jobs were labelled lead jobs) and at all levels of accountability. One of the clearest examples of a critical support job in work level 1 is often the role of supervisor. There is often some confusion about the assigning of work levels to these jobs, particularly when shift work is involved. This is invariably because the actual accountabilities are not clear. Usually night shift managers (supervisors, superintendents – the title is often varied) are not accountable for the hiring and firing of staff, deciding merit increases, drawing up operating plans for weeks and months ahead, deciding personal development plans, eg promotion and managing budgets. In such cases they are invariably value-adding support roles at the top of work level 1.

Support roles at level 1

Key accountabilities of the support roles as the top of level 1 in a large retail outlet would typically involve all or most of the following:

- Ensures the product is effectively displayed in accordance with existing guidelines.
- Monitors customer preferences and recommends (to someone at level 2 as a rule) changes to display and presentation plans to help maximize sales.
- Trains frontline staff in the relevant display and customer service guidelines and policies.
- Tracks ratios and contributes to statistical reports on sales, waste, cost/expenditure versus estimates and plans on a daily and weekly basis.
- Acts as a role model for frontline staff and trains them in ways of working to help ensure best practice prevails.
- Possesses 'expert' knowledge, know-how and skills on the various frontline roles.
- Carries out or organizes induction, training and coaching of front-line staff.
- Audits and checks the performance of frontline staff based on manuals and guidelines.
- Can discipline staff and is usually the first step in the grievance procedure.
- Recommends performance improvements and helps supervise their implementation.
- Ensures frontline staff are in the right place (such as on tills during peak periods) at the right time.
- Is capable of frontline skill cover for absences to maintain customer service.

- Monitors frontline performance, attendance and management of holiday patterns within policy guidelines.
- Often contributes to the recruitment and appraisal process.
- May serve as a deputy for the manager in level 2, when the latter is absent.

It is difficult to give guidelines for optimal spans of control for support roles such as the above. (For more on this subject see Chapter 4.) Ratios of 1:35 or 1:50 are quite feasible, depending on the nature of the work, the clarity of the tasks and the quality of the training. The key to the effectiveness of such spans depends upon the quality of the operating processes (such as the Tesco 'Routines'), which ensure consistency and reliability of behaviour and performance. These are the essential precondition for empowerment at the frontline.

Work at level 1 can be categorized as unskilled, semi-skilled and skilled. The trick is to define the differences accurately. All too often empowerment is bedevilled in level 1 by too many grades or ranks, which only serve to introduce politics and self-serving bureaucracy.

As already indicated, support roles can be identified at any level in an organization, except the top line.

Finally, there are some apparently confusing situations where certain jobs are support roles with direct subordinates, ie line responsibilities. The key point here is to examine the seven elements, which will help determine the support activities. But if, when examining the element of resource complexity, the job under review is responsible for subordinates, then it can still be a support role to a boss on the main spine of accountability while also functioning as a boss of a small off-line department. An example would be an HR manager supporting the manager of a large factory (who was not therefore the boss of the production managers and the factory engineer) but who in turn was the boss of the factory HR department.

WORK LEVELS AND PROCESSES

The advent of re-engineering led to the emergence of 'processes' and 'process organizations'. Michael Porter claimed at Harrogate in 1997 that they are merely the relabelling of his value chain.

A process, as defined by Kumar (1994), is 'a set of linked activities that take an input and transform it to create an output'. Processes, it is argued, break down functional silos because they focus on a customer. Robert Kramer (1995) would argue, based on his analysis of Hewlett-Packard, that they should also help reduce cycle times, cut variance costs, and increase efficiency and productivity. (But these should be outcomes of any effective oganization.)

Observation would suggest that processes actually build horizontal silos, dilute professionalism and specialist know-how and break up natural teams – not a very helpful development in an age where knowledge and learning are seen to be the sources of competitive advantage.

Shortcomings of process organizations

The process organization seems to be a misnomer. Structures built on processes at the frontline are invariably subsumed into functions at the top of an organization. Relabelling has blurred this reality. Thus, Personnel Directors are now HR Directors, former Sales Directors and Marketing Directors are Customer Service Directors and Category Directors, and so on. These changes are mostly children of fashion.

The major shortcoming of the process organization stems from the fact that processes do not naturally align with the strategic levels of accountability in large, complex organizations. The application of DMA logic reveals that processes relate to the operational levels. But effective principles of organization design ensure the seamless integration of both operational and strategic accountabilities.

Processes are operational

Processes meet customer needs. In organizations such as Tesco and Unilever this interface is invariably at work level 1. The processes involved are concrete, repeatable, mechanistic and measurable.

Processes in Tesco

In Tesco processes being used at work level 1 are known as 'routines'. These routines are prescribed methods of service provision, which are standardized, for example, across about 1,000 stores. They cannot be altered without reference to someone in a higher level, typically work level 2. Routines are owned at work level 2 and delivered at work level 1.

Work level 3 is accountable for delivering continuous improvement. An incumbent is expected to ensure that the process is still relevant and better meeting a customer need. Total redesign or introduction of new processes resides at work level 4. The level 4 role is required to ensure the process is meeting both an organizational need and the identified customer need. Thus the process owners in an organization exist from this level. Various processes are then coalesced at work level 5 and above into functions, depending on the complexity and geographical reach.

The natural level of accountability for processes is level 4. This is where operational and strategic needs are fused together. Accountability at this level calls for matrix thinking. At this level the need (resource gap, service or market opportunity) is defined and met with a concrete solution. The process in question is then introduced or modified at the relevant operational frontline.

At the fifth level of accountability the challenge is to integrate and balance a series of needs. The common boundary of these needs has to be identified so that they can be dovetailed with the organization's mission, goals and purpose. Roles at this level tend to be general and umbrella many different processes.

At level 6 the concern shifts more towards values, philosophy and vision. These set the context and ensure that individual processes are aligned, coherent and work for the good of the organization as a whole. For example, in Tesco, any changes to one process must meet the group's mantra of 'better, simpler, cheaper' for the company and its customers. This is a core set of values, which ensure that operational processes do not become horizontal silos damaging some part of the business–customer interface. Thus a buyer would not be sanctioned to purchase a product simply because it was cheaper if it added complexity to the supply chain. This would not be simpler and better and therefore would actually add indirect cost to the business.

Contribution of process to organization design

The strengths and weaknesses of processes are now clear. They make a major contribution to establishing the operational levels of the organization, provided they are synchronized for the benefit of the whole. When aligned to role accountabilities at each work level, they will help design an optimal structure. When used in isolation there is no such guarantee.

But process owners naturally reside at level 4. This is because processes are concrete activities related to service, product or system enhancement and operational problem solving. Processes do not help resolve the conceptual and increasingly abstract problem solving called for in levels 5 and above. 'If you give a man a hammer, he will see all his problems as nails.'

This also means that 'organizing by process' is best suited to small organizations or units within larger organizations. It is of limited value for huge, complex, international organizations which have to balance the potentially conflicting goals of business lines, geography and world-class specialization. Organizing by process alone will not provide them with a workable solution.

THE DMA SOLUTION SET AND YOUR ORGANIZATION

Having read thus far, you are now probably wondering whether your organization is really healthy, and if not, what could be done to improve the situation. The following questions might help determine the relevance of DMA to your organization. Consider the following:

- Do you know exactly how many value-adding decision-making levels there are in your organization?
- How would you find out?
- How many should there be?
- Do you have the optimal number of layers in the spine of accountability?
- Are responsibilities for people (recruitment, performance management, deciding rewards, training development and promotion, setting of objectives and deadlines, tasks to be achieved) unequivocally clear?
- Which are the support roles in your organization?
- Do you have too many or too few?
- Is career planning in your organization based on a series of administrative (grade driven) or real promotions?
- What objective factors identify talent for promotion?

- If you have broad bands, is the basis money or accountability?
- What is the basis that drives individual learning in your organization?
- Is pay progression transparent and understood or simply driven by cost factors?
- Is the competitiveness of your reward programme validly and reliably linked to the market?
- Is the basis of deciding international assignments in your organization fair, objective and consistent, adding real value to both the individual and the organization, or is it based on head office nationality?

If you cannot answer all of these questions quickly your organization could be 'profoundly unhealthy'. The rest of this book provides an approach that will enable you to answer these questions, and sets out a number of steps that could lead to the establishment of a healthy organization.

SUMMARY REVIEW

This chapter set out to define the key concepts of the DMA solution set and demonstrate how they are integrated. This involved clarifying the confusion between the use of the words accountability and responsibility. The link between accountability and organizational health was explained, as were the seven critical elements based on the work done at Unilever and Tesco. The distinction between line and support jobs was made clear in relation to the establishing of the spine of accountability first mentioned in Chapter 2. The role of processes and their link with DMA were outlined.

Finally, an insight into how this might be relevant to your organization was provided.

There are two decision areas, which help decide the level of accountability: 1) the analysis of the seven elements and 2), in conjunction with the first, identifying whether the job is in a line or support role. The next chapter plots how this was done in Unilever and Tesco and suggests how it might be done in your organization.

4

How to develop a healthy organization

This chapter has three objectives. It will describe the process of field testing which led to the development of the *seven elements* of DMA. The levels of accountability will be described in some detail, with examples of typical jobs from each level, in both Tesco and Unilever. They will be divided into operational (levels 1–3), strategic (levels 4–6) and governance (levels 7–8) accountabilities. A number of key steps will emerge that suggest how the DMA model can be applied.

FLEXIBLE APPROACH OF DMA

The DMA approach is flexible and can be applied to organizations of different sizes, complexity and stages of growth. Unilever, for example, has more levels in total than Tesco. The family corner store may be a level 2 organization (that is, the top role would be at work level 2). There will be some strategic and governance work, but the balance of work (see principle 2 in the previous chapter) will be operational. Other family or private firms could be variously work-level 3, 4, 5 organizations and so on. US oil milling company Cargill, the largest private company in the world, would arguably be more comparable to a Unilever than a corner store.

Similarly, not all organizations have the frontline at level 1. This is one of the reasons why some high-tech and dot.com organizations justify flat structures. Their frontline might start at level 2 or 3. These different organizational types are illustrated in Figure 4.1.

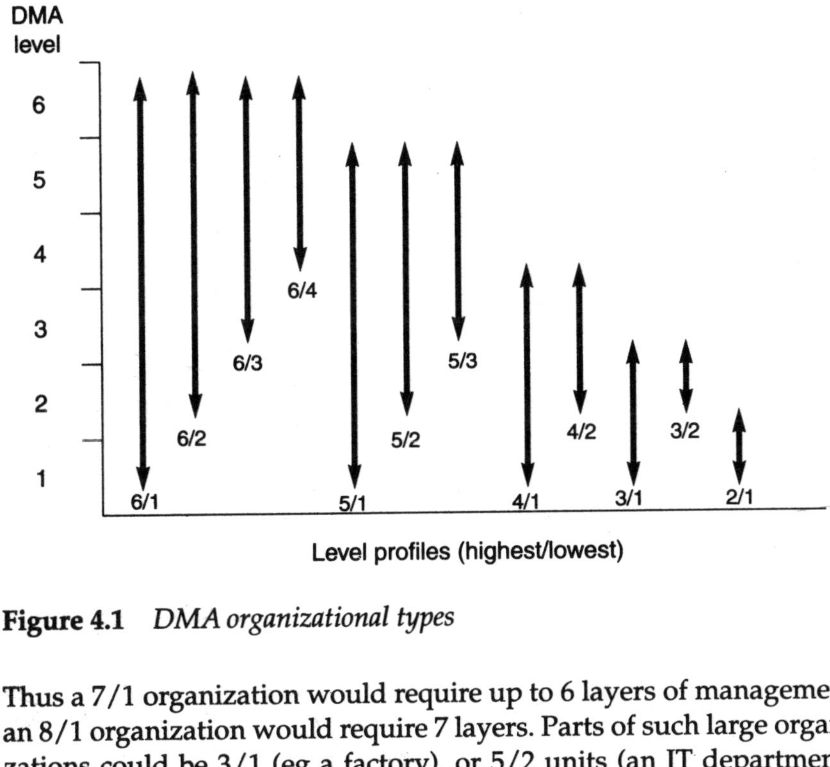

Figure 4.1 *DMA organizational types*

Thus a 7/1 organization would require up to 6 layers of management, an 8/1 organization would require 7 layers. Parts of such large organizations could be 3/1 (eg a factory), or 5/2 units (an IT department), and so on.

The importance of bottom-up analysis

As indicated in Chapter 1, the most reliable way to establish value-added decision making is to verify how decisions are made from the lowest to the highest roles in a spine of accountability. This means starting with the frontline and pursuing the chain up to the CEO. Each incumbent is interviewed and the decision-making process is mapped against the seven elements of DMA. This process is called a *probe*.

PILOT PROBES AT UNILEVER AND TESCO

It was important to prepare for implementation by first undertaking fieldwork to establish precisely which key jobs fell in which work levels. This also revealed the total number of accountable levels in the total organization. This is the critical first step.

Step 1

Fieldwork is needed to verify the true levels of accountability.

Three main pilot studies were undertaken at both Unilever and Tesco. The first, at Unilever, involved Lever Europe (LE), the detergents company, which had two main advantages. Firstly, as it was the concern's initial attempt at a pan-European organization covering 15 countries in Western Europe, many of the jobs were new. This meant there was less history and political baggage, which was an excellent test-bed for the new approach. Secondly, the sponsor of the pilot study was Niall Fitzgerald, at that time responsible for detergents and Chairman Elect of Unilever plc. His unequivocal public support was a great asset in the early stages of the project.

The second pilot study was Personal Products Europe (PPE), another new pan-European business, but with a different structure and modus operandi than Lever Europe. Antony Burgmans, who was later to become Chairman of Unilever NV, had set it up.

The third pilot study took place in the highly successful Chesebrough-Ponds business in the United States. We carefully chose this case because the company had an excellent Vice President of HR, Jim McCall, and an outstanding Compensation Manager, the late Kathie Cunningham. Together they championed the cause in the United States and were instrumental in ensuring that their country was the first to implement.

When the work started at Tesco, I could not be sure of the levels required, even though by that time the Unilever work had been completed. Fieldwork was needed to establish the answer. This was done in 2000 by completing probes in key areas of the business. In distribution, a very people-intensive activity, interviews commenced with those at the frontline. The decision making of the line of bosses (the spine of accountability) as set out on the formal organization chart was carefully mapped. Interviewing upwards through a distribution centre to the Regional Director, the National Director, the Director on the main Tesco board and ultimately the CEO, did this. Once this process had been replicated in other key areas of the business such as commercial (buying), a sample of specialist departments was similarly studied. (The DMA approach is most effective for identifying levels of accountability in specialist jobs, as will be shown in the next chapter.) This bottom-up process confirmed the number of work levels required and also flagged areas of sub-optimal organization, such as *compression* (more than one layer of management within one level of accountability, which is a block to motivation), for subsequent action.

Step 2

The probes must start at the frontline and progress inclusively to the top of the organization.

The issue of size

In both companies we recognized that underlying the respective obsessions with job classes and management grades was the legacy of the impact of size on the evaluation of jobs. Historically the bigger the job, the higher the job class or grade. The job evaluation schemes were quantitatively based. They did not assess the value of a job or what it added (or did not add) to the organization. The job was largely evaluated on the sales, budget, value of assets, number of subordinates, and the like. These were invariably factorized in different schemes, which led to higher points, grades or whatever. The other criteria never overrode the impact of the size criterion. These systems led to a perennial chase for more resources to manage to achieve higher recognition from the grading mechanism, and the most common response was to add a layer into the hierarchy and deliver another 'promotion'. *The DMA principle of one line job per work level eliminates such grade-creep.*

DMA therefore challenged this culture, which was not comfortable for those well versed in the art of grade-creep. It focused on quality of decisions. It was not simply driven by size, although size and number of assets managed might lead to different activities and quality of decision making, which might lead to the higher work level. For example, in PPE, the four largest countries had lead innovation centres, each developing and manufacturing a specialist category of product for the other 14 countries in Western Europe, which did not have such innovation or manufacturing facilities. This led to the allocation of a higher work level in the four lead countries. However, it was not therefore simply a matter of size that resulted in that outcome.

Although size is taken into account, it does not drive the levels of accountability, unless it changes the quality of decisions being taken. So, for example, adding one work-level 3 job to another does not create a work-level 4 role. This is a fundamental departure from traditional job evaluation schemes.

DMA exposed the worth of the previous 'administrative promotion' mentality and therefore disturbed some of the existing status relativities. Thus the fact that managers previously with different grades were now in the same work level was not easy to stomach for those who had clawed their way into the higher grades over a number of years. They felt they were losing out in the new approach. Although the loss was really only relative and psychological, it was nevertheless very real and had to be taken account of in the change process, outlined in Chapter 9. These were typically the older, more senior managers who were very influential in their respective constituencies.

Psychological factors such as these quickly emerged in the pilot studies as key sources of resistance that had to be managed.

Step 3

Key management must be trained in the use and understanding of the DMA solution set.

In Unilever, training workshops focused first on the highly influential HR function which, it was decided, would have to carry the brunt of the analysis and counselling work, which would accompany the move to the new system. This called for many workshops worldwide.

At the same time, extensive briefing and discussion sessions were organized for the top managers who would be leading the change process. Draft ideas and materials were presented and discussed at these meetings. This helped ensure the new system was seen to be workable, that it was improved by input from the most influential people in the business, who in the process became more understanding of and committed to the change. (The five-phase communication model used will also be discussed more fully in Chapter 9.) The investment in time and money on training and communication was enormous but it was an essential ingredient of the overall process to ensure successful implementation.

The training and briefing in Tesco was equally meticulous. Nine project teams were set up and trained by the central Tesco One Team Rewards project team (in place for nearly two years) and myself, to be able to identify work levels across the business. In contrast to Unilever, these project teams were led by line managers on a full-time basis working to a detailed activity plan. This plan included consistency meetings and analysis (read-across meetings), which culminated in main board approval of the individuals' levels.

Step 4

Verify decisions taken against the following descriptions of the DMA elements and identify which roles have operational, strategic or governance accountabilities as the balance of their work.

Step 5

Having established the level of accountability, verify whether the jobs are line or support roles.

OPERATIONAL ACCOUNTABILITY (WORK LEVELS 1–3)

Operational work focuses on improving the performance of existing assets, whether they are people, technology, budgets, systems, services or any potential combination of these.

Work level 1 – Demand response

In work level 1, the tasks are essentially demands: make this product, sell this product, deliver this product, install this system, repair this system, deliver this service. The output or service is prescribed: the jobholder is working towards objectives that can be completely specified beforehand, according to defined circumstances, which may present themselves. In Tesco, well-defined 'routines' often set the framework for level 1 work. The key elements of work level 1 are as follows.

1. Nature of work

The jobholder is accountable for concrete tasks, each of which has a prescribed output. They are often summarized in a manual or contained in an electronic database, which can be communicated during training. The work will often require significant skills and qualifications, although the tasks remain predictable with the outcome known in advance. Work at the bottom of level 1 (unskilled work) may leave little room for individual discretion. Work at the top of level 1 (for example, a supervisor) may well demand considerable knowledge and experience and the jobholder would be expected to work skilfully and use considerable initiative within the defined boundaries.

2. Resource complexity

Those in work level 1 are not accountable for budgets, or subordinates. This is a key consideration is establishing the difference between a support role and a line role at the work level 1/work level 2 interface. Resources are restricted to those needed to obtain the prescribed output or service. An example of work at this level would be an individual working in the distribution or transport department expected to deliver products at 4 o'clock in the afternoon, to the local supermarket. The driver cannot change the schedule otherwise he will jeopardize the supermarket's loading schedule. Nevertheless, he is expected to drive a heavy trade vehicle safely through a metropolitan area and would be required to have a licence to drive such a vehicle. This is a skilful task and although unexpected events such as an accident or a detour could be incurred, these are events that probably have been anticipated and in such exceptional circumstances, guidelines have been laid down outlining the appropriate action.

3. Problem solving

Problems have discrete solutions that are often defined by the boss, or requested by a customer or supplier. The expected output, or outcome, can be visualized in advance in concrete terms. When the appropriate response to a problem is not clear, guidelines exist for referral to the relevant authority. Such procedures for coping with the unexpected or emergency situations are typically laid out, for example, in the responsibilities of a shift supervisor, who may be the senior person on site during the nightshift.

4. Change

Jobholders are not accountable for making a change to a given schedule, but they are expected to seek improvement within that schedule. Examples include instigating changes to lessen downtime between line changes in a factory, or seeking quicker delivery routes within the supply chain. Empowerment initiatives are aimed at encouraging these continuous improvements in performance. Clear guidelines indicate appropriate change limits; for example, when to close down a line or to contact a supplier or customer.

5. Natural work team

Colleagues in the same work level often work at a single location (for example a factory line, office workstation or laboratory bench). Empowerment and team-working initiatives are extending the physical mobility of jobs and therefore the lateral interaction that can occur across, usually, a department.

6. External interaction

External contacts typically involve a fixed number of customers or suppliers, generally within a framework for regular contact and liaison. Salespeople working within a territory will typically have a regular routine, a suggested call pattern and an indicative price list to work with. Individual customers may be varied but will tend to come from a given location or community. More extensive use of IT is changing the frequency, but not the fundamental nature or purpose, of many of the external contacts at this level.

7. Time frame

Results of unskilled or even semi-skilled work can be known within seconds or minutes. As the work becomes progressively more complicated and complex, so the time for task completion can be extended through days or weeks, up to three months.

The **upper boundary** in this 'demand zone' means that a jobholder would not be expected to make significant judgements on what output to aim for, or under what circumstances to aim for it. If he or she is in doubt as to which task to pursue, it is prescribed that he or she take the matter up with his or her immediate superior.

I was recently visiting an impressive call centre, run by IBM in Europe, serving a number of different companies across 15 countries. There were a number of operators working at various workstations who were highly skilled in solving certain IT problems and many of them could speak more than one language. Interestingly, I was told by one of the employees that, by and large, it was unheard of to encounter a problem or request that hadn't been covered in the training or the manual and had not come up previously. In such an occurrence the operator would immediately work with his or her superior to ensure that there were appropriate guidelines to handle just such a problem in the future.

Typical jobs in work level 1

- **Sales representative** – meets customer demand from a price list as part of an agreed monthly plan.

- **Multi-skilled factory employee** – ensures specific line outputs in accordance with production schedule and repairs faulty equipment as specified.

- **Office employee** – ensures databases are used to provide timely, reliable information, as specified, to meet the demands of a company head office, a national head office, or the corporate centre.

- **Supervisor** – a support job that assists someone in work level 2 to manage work level 1 subordinates, by helping to train, monitor and improve performance.

Impact of trade unions on work level 1

In many countries around the world, jobs in work level 1 are variously classified in accord with local trade unions, collective agreements, national pay systems, or various forms of legal agreement. It makes little sense to attempt to maintain consistent forms of evaluation and assessment of work at level 1, around the world. However, from work level 2 and above, referred to as 'management', there is a strong effort to maintain consistency. If a large international organization has a policy of internal promotion and development, it is important to have a reliable instrument to measure responsibility of management jobs around the world. This does not mean, however, that pay rates or remuneration profiles are the same in China and Chile, for example. This latter issue will be covered in greater detail in Chapter 6 on reward.

Work level 2 – Diagnostic response

Within the second level of accountability, results have to be achieved in specific situations, but now the output required can be only partially specified beforehand. Now the jobholder is carrying out work where the precise objectives, or tasks to be achieved, have to be judged or diagnosed according to the needs of each specific, concrete situation or case that presents itself. The work is such that it is impossible to demonstrate fully beforehand just what the final outcome should look like, as this can only be established by actually completing the task concerned, which may require professional know-how.

1. Nature of work

Accountable for responding to situations that have to be judged one by one before an appropriate response can be made. The response is no longer prescribed, but depends on an assessment of other people's needs. Until the task is actually tackled, only a general indication of the optimum outcome can be given. The needs of a specific case or situation are judged and matched to the appropriate concrete solution. An idea of the difference between level 1 and level 2 can be illustrated by considering a request for training to a training manager from a line colleague. A work level 1 response would be simply to enrol the manager or the subordinate as instructed, or requested. A work level 2 response would be to further consider the request from the line manager by analysing the training needs of the individual under review, and then, perhaps, suggesting a more appropriate programme of learning based on this diagnosis. Authoritative specialist knowledge, often requiring professional accreditation, emerges as a requirement at level 2. The first layer of management, with accountability for level 1 subordinates, now emerges.

2. Resource complexity

Resources are restricted to the framework of existing products, geography, customers, suppliers, technology and systems. The design of guidelines, manuals, or routines for work level 1 workers would normally be an indication of work level 2 responsibilities. The management of budgets starts to become an important issue. The most common resource will be a team of work level 1 people. The other important resource to be managed is know-how. Thus, professional accreditation as an engineer or an accountant, for example, is often necessary to perform key tasks of a job at the second level of accountability. The frontline for such specialists is usually work level 2, although they might spend a brief training period in work level 1.

3. Problem solving

Analysis is required, but in the context of concrete situations where specific solutions can usually be visualized beforehand. The work requires fact gathering and diagnosis of a given situation, often making use of specialist knowledge and expertise. Interpretation of events and short-term concrete data (such as variances in performance), usually within the framework of accredited know-how, is expected.

4. Change

The jobholder can 'flex the schedule', ie make short-term changes to plan, based upon an analysis of the specific job context. For example, a production manager in a factory can change a daily or weekly production plan given an unexpected shortage in raw or packaging materials. The work entails accountability for improving performance and productivity, usually as set out in the annual plan.

5. Natural work team

Interaction with colleagues in the same function or process, typically across more than one site, in order to share and build on the knowledge of relevant situations. This may mean regional/international collaboration and may lead to the establishment of interdisciplinary teams.

6. External interaction

Customers are more likely to be organizations rather than individual consumers or users. The number of customers or suppliers tends now to become more variable and may well cover more than one location, or region. An example from the retail grocery trade is an accounts manager who handles the outlets of a grocery chain in a particular region.

7. Time frame

Work at this level is bounded by the annual operation plan and therefore the task horizon is up to one year.

Typical jobs in work level 2

- **Factory HR manager** – manages recruitment, payroll and development issues and advises on employee relations and local legislative matters.

- **Data centre manager** – plans and maintains an efficient hardware service (typically 7 × 24) via a bank of operating systems, supporting various software applications across a number of units.

- **Brand manager** – monitors and evaluates performance of product(s)/brand(s) against targets; ensures launched and re-launched networks are implemented in line with the annual plan; identifies variances in the product/brand performance and recommends appropriate responses.

At the **upper boundary** a work level 2 jobholder is not accountable for making decisions that would be commitments on how future possible situations are to be dealt with. This would be the responsibility of the boss at a higher level.

Level 3 – Integrated response

At the third level of accountability, it is necessary to go beyond responding to specific situations, consumers, customers or suppliers one by one, or on a case-by-case basis. It is now necessary to envisage the needs of a continuing sequence of different situations, some as yet in the future and not yet materialized, in terms of the patterns of responses that may need to be established. In this way, work from different sections needs to be integrated as part of an overall response. In the supply chain, for example, it might be a case of developing a system for handling manufacturing orders for a particular type of product or process. Work at this level is also concerned with developing systems and procedures, which may establish a framework for the way future diagnostic response-work has to be carried out.

This is the level of operational general management. The 'dwell-time' in work level 3 is typically longer than in work levels 1 and 2. Conversely, too little time spent in work level 3 can jeopardize individual growth and development, as will be demonstrated in Chapter 8.

1. Nature of work

Accountable for a flow of work that must be understood in the context of an integrated system or unit. The jobholder must move beyond coping with discrete situations and must now manage the interaction between them in order to achieve the planned outputs. Distinctive jobs required in national/international head offices typically emerge at level 3. Work at this level is still largely operational because the jobholder is in the realm of concrete and given resources and is not accountable for more strategic outputs. This is the fundamental difference between work level 3 and work level 4.

2. Resource complexity

Resources are still given but need to be managed and balanced within the context of an integrated system or unit. Financial targets start to become more important and contributions to capital expenditure plans are increasingly required. Jobholders must ensure that resources are used effectively and that continuous improvement and increased productivity are achieved. Project leadership at this level will involve the integration of a number of disciplines and teams. Authoritative specialist knowledge is often essential to perform the key tasks of level 3 jobs.

3. Problem solving

Problem solving involves identifying patterns in the actual performance of existing products, or organization units such as supermarkets, factories, or systems and services. This requires scanning a series of activities; establishing and evaluating linkages between situations; and analysing trends. The jobholder may not be physically present at every stage in the flow of work, but concrete and specific ratios are available for analysis (eg output per shift, per department, sales per customer or area, market shares per brand). The jobholder is expected to signal developments that could affect the current annual plan and/or have consequences for the following annual plan. At this level problems are challenging but remain concrete and largely operational in nature.

4. Change

The jobholder is accountable for ensuring that existing products, systems and processes continually attain new levels of performance.

Integration of different elements of work (often involving subordinates at levels 1 and 2) to ensure improvements is expected. Working to improve the performance of existing physical assets or modifying existing products or systems is called **development**. It differs fundamentally from the invention and discovery expected at work level 4 and above. At level 3, an advisory contribution to policy and strategy is expected. The focus is on today, but tomorrow's needs have to be taken into account. Significant projects emerge at work level 3.

5. Natural work team

Interaction now tends to occur with colleagues in the same organization usually across functions or units and often across more than one country, in order to improve the performance of existing processes, operational systems and products within the operating environment. Knowledge of these working networks to achieve results is expected.

6. External interaction

Interaction with the external environment tends to involve customers or suppliers in a network of different locations. This is in contrast to level 2, where external contacts are primarily local, or within a district, whereas at level 3, this environment can include national contacts, for example the key buyers in a national grocery chain. It might also involve key officials at national, government, trade union or comparable institutions.

7. Time frame

At this level the jobholder is expected to achieve the current annual plan but is also accountable for the quality of contributions to the next year's annual plan.

In Unilever, a critical planning time frame, which is used for jobs at the third level of accountability, is a rolling eight-quarter plan. Level 3 managers are responsible for managing this plan and achieving the results set out in it.

In considering the **upper boundary** a manager at work level 3 is not expected to make any decisions on the reallocation of resources to meet as yet un-manifested needs for the given kinds of services or products within, for example, a given factory, or national market. This would involve the reconfiguration of resources that would be expected at work level 4.

Typical jobs in work level 3

- **Distribution manager** – delivers the annual warehouse operations plans and ensures that productivity and service targets are achieved, based on a good understanding of the business in its local environment.

- **National accounts manager** – responsible for one or more retail customers who normally cover a total (national) geographical domain; develops and plans tailor-made responses to a network of customers.

- **Marketing manager** – contributes to design and improvement of marketing launch networks and policy; analyses the performance relationship between existing products and market needs.

- **Factory manager** – understands and manages, within given resources of staff, equipment and buildings, a system capable of responding to any likely flow of orders.

STRATEGIC ACCOUNTABILITY (WORK LEVELS 4–6)

Strategic work involves the realignment of assets, based on an assessment of resource gaps and market opportunities, to ensure future plans will be met.

According to Henry Mintzberg (1989), 'Strategy is the organization's "conception" of how to deal with its environment for a time.' At the level of strategic work, the constraints and restraints concerning resource configuration and its application are lifted. Jobholders are accountable for identifying new opportunities and resolving gaps in the know-how, the application of systems, the delivery of services and the meeting of untapped or new needs. The ability to think and move outside the box becomes essential. Strategic responsibilities are a decisive jump forward. Refuge in change limited to superficial trend analysis, fads and the changing of labels (such as calling 'Personnel' 'Human Resources') is a disguise often worn by those who cannot cross the Rubicon from operational to strategic responsibility. This is a journey which, it seems, relatively few can successfully accomplish. In large organizations about 1 per cent of the total employees either have strategic responsibilities or have the potential to reach that level.

Observation suggests that over-reaching ambition will lead many across this line with disappointing results. The discipline of DMA logic can help avoid this trap, firstly by organizing the work to make clear where genuine strategic accountability resides and secondly (as will be explained more fully in Chapter 8) by ensuring that individuals are given the appropriate combination of challenge and time to demonstrate they possess strategic competence.

Perhaps it is worth repeating that we are again talking here about accountability for the implementation of strategy. This is not to say that people in the lower work levels cannot make significant contributions to strategy or think of radically new approaches. Clearly, those who have the potential to operate at strategic levels will make these contributions and as part of their personal development should be challenged to do so. Apologists for hierarchy are not arguing that all key decisions and bright ideas can only be thought of at the top of the organization. This was perhaps the favoured thinking of theorists earlier in the 20th century, such as Alfred Sloan, but modern standards of education and technology have fundamentally changed this approach.

Work level 4 – Authoritative response

At work level 4 it is necessary to think beyond the product, system, unit or service being managed in levels 1 to 3. At work level 2, the purpose of the activity being managed is limited by the existence of certain given, or specified, systems and processes, together with the availability (or not) of key resources. At work level 3 the former constraint disappears, as **development** of systems and processes is expected, but the latter constraint remains. By contrast, at work level 4 both constraints no longer exist. In a global organization many roles have a responsibility that is part of a greater whole. Work level 4 jobs might lead activities[1] such as marketing, supply chain, customer service, finance or human resources. In these different areas, authoritative expertise is called for. In a research lab a work level 4 scientist might be a world authority in the applied research of a particular discipline.[2] What is therefore called for, or expected at this level, is an authoritative and expert response to an identified strategic need. For example, a marketing executive at work level 4 would be accountable for the quality and substance of the marketing plan which is in turn a component of a work level 5 business plan.

1. Nature of work

Accountable for work that is more strategic than operational, the jobholder must make authoritative recommendations for change based upon an analysis of the gaps in the availability and performance of resources, products portfolio and systems. This entails identifying opportunities and constraints and initiating the introduction of new products, systems or services as well as the withdrawal of old ones. In addition to preparing and achieving annual plans, jobholders are expected to contribute to longer-term and strategic plans. They often manage groups of key operational general management jobs, for example a supply chain director managing a number of factories, or a regional director with a group of superstores.

2. Resource complexity

Resources are still largely given but have to be planned and negotiated. Jobholders are expected to make knowledgeable recommendations, to add/delete resources or start/stop a project within their specific area of accountability. Performance is now increasingly measured in financial terms such as the management of a capital expenditure programme.

Many jobs can only succeed with the help and support of subordinates. The network of subordinate roles is referred to as *infrastructure.* Understanding the infrastructure is important in helping to establish the correct work level. Thus the presence of subordinate positions up to work level 3 helps confirm the genuine value-added of a level 4 role.

Scientists at this level, who might have no infrastructure of subordinates, undertake applied research, which discovers new linkages in existing knowledge, typically within a scientific discipline, and which results in new products, services or applications that better meet existing needs. In the Unilever Corporate Centre, level 4 jobs exhibit regional leadership in part of the world for a discipline or category.[3] An example of a work level 4 resource issue is the identification of a gap in an existing product range which requires modification of the marketing strategy, the identification of company-wide implications and, where agreed, then changing the product portfolio.

3. Problem solving

Accountability for solving problems of a strategic nature emerges at this level. Abstract and conceptual analysis is required to identify problems and assess potential solutions, including new formulae, products, technology, systems or policies. Tomorrow's solutions may not yet physically exist and, therefore, have to be conceptualized. This modelling process entails identifying the causes of patterns and linkages in consumer or customer behaviour that may have been identified at work level 3 in the performance and capacity of plant, people and systems.

4. Change

The jobholder is accountable for establishing new linkages among existing bodies of ideas, practices and policies. Tomorrow's requirements are as important as today's. Accountability for applied research emerges at level 4. The jobholder spots gaps and received wisdom and makes authoritative recommendations for change. An example of level 4 accountability for change is the identification of products that meet the breakthrough criteria of the consumer value/technology matrix. See Figure 5.3 on page 133.

5. Natural work team

This typically involves membership of a network, which enables jobholders to collaborate with colleagues beyond their accountable operating environments in order to deliver the work expected of them. For example, in Unilever the director of an innovation centre in a particular region might need to contact colleagues in the research laboratory who are outside the normal operating domain of the local company. This collaboration requires a wide knowledge, which often takes many years to establish, of the relevant concern resources.

6. External interaction

External contacts often with national governmental trade and industrial institutions. Increasingly, given the developments of the retail grocery trade, these contacts in consumer goods companies are becoming international. Responding to these contacts requires decision making and can, therefore, have a significant impact on the results of the organization. Strategic external interaction becomes increasingly proactive rather than mostly reactive as in the operational levels. External agencies have to be influenced to change their behaviour, plans or actions.

7. Time frame

In addition to managing the current annual plan and ensuring an authoritative contribution to the next annual plan, managers at this level are accountable for making key contributions in their particular area to the strategic plan. The task horizon therefore is now up to three years.

Typical jobs in work level 4

- **Category director** – responsible for a portfolio of products covering at least one market, which need to change to meet new customer needs.

- **Financial director/vice president**[4] – produces company plans and verifies their financial viability; monitors overall financial performance; highlights significant variances from plan and initiates appropriate action; introduces key system changes (for example, IT) to ensure financial soundness and improved company performance.

- **Category research manager** – manages the process of category innovation in a research laboratory and is accountable for delivering against agreed innovation plans.

The **upper boundary** of work level 4 is covered by the defined activity for which the individual is accountable. Decisions on the allocation of resources between parallel activities or the integration of such resources is not expected. This is the prerogative of a more general manager in work level 5 and constitutes the critical difference between these two levels of accountability.

Work level 5 – Comprehensive response

This is usually the first level of strategic general management accountable for a fully resourced operating unit, division or company (often national).

At level 5 the scope is widened still further by moving from a framework of an existing or established range of markets, products, technologies or services to one that aims to meet a more basic or general need or set of needs. Work at this level entails the management of resource boundaries, identifiable as complete entities. Depending upon their nature and extent, these boundaries could be national or international. The response has to be more comprehensive than anything called for in the lower echelons considered thus far. This could mean establishing or deleting complete ranges of products or services or entering or leaving separate markets. These changes must take into account not only what is desirable but also what is financially, technologically, politically (externally and internally) possible.

Definitions change and move further from the concrete towards the conceptual. A case in point is a category: see note 3 above. Thus, a manager with global responsibility for tea beverages no longer considers just the particular brands of tea, but seeks to define underlying needs that might form the basis of an archetypal response meeting these common consumer needs across the world. This might result in the global architecture of a new master brand positioning. **Comprehensive** can refer to separate command of a fully fledged standalone unit in a defined geographical domain such as a country, or accountability for a category, function or discipline on a global basis, which would require leading-edge know-how.

1. Nature of work

Accountable for a single, cohesive entity, the jobholder must assess proposals from specific units, set priorities and reconfigure resource boundaries by adding or deleting products, systems or services. Jobholders are accountable for the delivery of agreed annual and longer-term company plans.

A level 5 role is often that of the CEO of a fully fledged standalone national company, in eg Thailand. A 'fully fledged' company would usually possess the following features:

- a full range of functions or processes;
- complex (relative to the industry) technology;
- presence in key markets;
- the ability to have a material impact upon the performance and reputation of the regional business.

A standalone business typically has 1) a significant record of ongoing growth, and 2) self-sufficiency and strategic resources, reflected in a work level 4 infrastructure. There may also be international level 5 companies that are a collection of national markets which, when added together, provide significant international presence made possible by common technologies and products. In level 5 companies, innovation essentially entails the management of development.

But with level 5 jobs in research or the international head office, jobholders would be expected to extend the boundaries of existing know-how, disciplines and/or categories. They are perceived as international experts internally and externally. These jobs typically demonstrate company-wide influence. The jobholders are recognized as the leading practitioners and custodians of corporate disciplines or categories.

2. Resource complexity

The performance of existing resources, while important, is only a starting point for identifying future needs and appropriate responses. Jobholders must make comprehensive recommendations for allocating resources among different parts of the company or division. Competing resource recommendations must be resolved to the benefit of the overall operation. In addition, managers at this level are typically charged with delivering profit targets for their company, division or unit. An example of a work level 5 resources issue is to allocate funds among competing proposals from different parts of a company.

3. Problem solving

Longer-term strategic direction is now the focus of level 5 problem solving. The abstract and conceptual analysis required at level 4 must now be applied to a wider range of products, activities and/or geographies. Managing a single, cohesive entity (such as a national company) requires the level 5 jobholder to evaluate and prioritize proposals for change. Competition for resources and conflicts of interest must be resolved. In contrast to level 4, where a typical problem is to identify gaps in an existing product range, a level 5 problem is to assess whether the product range itself is viable.

At this level the very language being used starts to change. It moves from the concrete (products, things) to the more abstract (needs to be met); from, for example, Dove toilet soap to the daily need for personal hygiene. This is a permanent, universal need that offers continuous possibilities for new solutions. There is the pull of competition.

4. Change

The jobholder is accountable for the discovery or invention of new knowledge and/or its application. This does not mean that the individual must necessarily discover or invent personally: however, the jobholder must set priorities and manage resources in order to drive innovation and make it possible. An example of the change at this level would be a project that has an impact across the total organization. The focus now is very much on the future.

5. Natural work team

A key task is to negotiate and identify sources of ideas, products and resources to help ensure, for example, that a company delivers its plan in the agreed time frame. Work at this level typically entails membership of a corporate-wide network. These links are vital for negotiating and agreeing priorities in delivery or agreement to launch of new initiatives. It is important in Unilever, for example, for securing relevant ideas and proposals, which can then be entered early into the research laboratories' innovation programmes to ensure appropriate product or service delivery for the unit in question.

6. External interaction

In scanning the environment it is critical to assess what is socially, politically and environmentally feasible. Sometimes what the business unit wants to do is not always possible either absolutely or even relatively in terms of place, time and scale. In which case the challenge is to have the external possibilities prioritized so that they can be appropriately managed. The external contacts will often include the leaders of major national institutions and, sometimes, their regional or even international counterparts.

At this level of accountability, links with the national environment move beyond collaboration. The jobholder must manage the environment, which, at times, may work against the aims and objectives of the company. This will often require proactive contact with the leaders of these national organizations.

7. Time frame

A level 5 leader of a business unit, for example, must ensure that the annual plan is being achieved and that the next year's annual plan is being put together to meet the short-term challenges facing the business. But, in addition, a key responsibility now is the unit's plan, and contribution to the overall business plan is expected. The short-term, and long-term paths must both be navigated successfully at the same time. The time frame now is up to five years.

The **upper boundary** of work level 5 is defined, or limited, by the responsibility for which comprehensive know-how or accountability is called for. There is no expectation for any decisions to be taken in the reconfiguration of resource or organization boundaries beyond those currently allocated. Thus the CEO of a company in Thailand would have no authority to realign supply chain resources in Indonesia. The global manager for Lipton Tea would have no responsibility for changing the brand architecture of Organics Shampoo.

Work level 6 – Extensive response

The definitions of work levels 6 to 8 are based predominantly on the work undertaken in Unilever.

At present, the Tesco main board is in work level 6, which in that case includes a significant amount of the governance responsibilities outlined in work level 7.

The key consideration is the context of the accountabilities, which determines their balance – see principle 2, page 55. Thus in one organization level 6 might be at a strategic level, while in another it might be at the governance level, even the chief executive. The flexibility of the DMA approach was illustrated in Figure 4.1, page 77.

At work level 6 the challenge moves beyond responsibility for a single level 5 domain. The sixth level of accountability calls for the integration of a number of these domains, which are therefore managed as a cohesive *network*.

1. Nature of work

The manager at level 6 is accountable for integration of a network of separate companies, divisions or units, one or some of which must be at work level 5.

Work at this level is accountable for the delivery of annual and longer-term regional and international plans. Jobs at level 6 have a recognizable material impact on the performance and/or image of the whole organization. In Tesco they are part of the board governance process. Strategy shifts from a focus on national markets to the needs and opportunities of a 'seamless' network of markets. Customers are increasingly international, markets tend to be interlinked and, as a result, the supply chain in company infrastructure is more complex and interdependent.

2. Resource complexity

Resources must be allocated among a network of companies, divisions or units. Company and national priorities and resource boundaries may need to be modified in order to achieve overall business strategies. The financial assets managed at this level are significant. An example of a level 6 resource issue would be a decision to enter or leave a particular country.

3. Problem solving

Abstract and conceptual analysis must now be applied to problems of integrating a network of level 5 resources, often with concern-wide implications. Problems that are tackled at this level involve establishing leadership in regional markets and managing the relationships between concern categories. An example is international leadership of a continental business group in Unilever.

4. Change

The jobholder is expected to lead breakthrough developments in categories, disciplines and/or technology, or an industry, again by managing (and sometimes dramatically changing) resource configurations. An example would be reconfiguring a major supply chain across several national boundaries. Changes in disciplines or technology initiated at this level invariably permeate the entire organization.

5. Natural work team

Managers at this level establish what is both desirable and feasible in ensuring rapid communication and commitment to strategy across the world. They are a most critical organization-wide network. They are regular, authoritative contributors to the process of corporate governance, given their leadership roles as guardians of significant business interests. The natural network at this level will be other colleagues who are regularly expected to contribute to, and implement, corporate strategy.

6. External interaction

The political, economic, social, technological and educational trends and events assume critical importance, particularly because of the increasing pace and complexity of change. Work at this level calls for a wide understanding of these global events and trends as these impact on jobholders' network of resources which inevitably straddle the boundaries of nation states. International and, increasingly, even worldwide networks are a feature of work level 6 accountabilities. This increasingly diverse and complex environment will include key national and regional politicians, such as the European Commission, the leaders of national institutions and international bodies, such as the World Bank and the International Monetary Fund (IMF). Global competition means that national interests must increasingly be managed within a regional, and sometimes wider international context.

The **timeframe** now therefore stretches up to seven years.

The **upper boundary** of work level 6 in Unilever is global strategy. Managers at this level are accountable for implementing components of that strategy and contributing to the concern governance, which emerges at work level 7.

ACCOUNTABILITY FOR GOVERNANCE (WORK LEVELS 7 AND 8)

Beyond operational and strategic work one moves into the realm of governance, which entails legal and fiduciary responsibilities to society. This includes setting the mission, values and resource limits governing the work that can be achieved at the operational and strategic levels within the organization.

According to Bain and Band (1996), 'Good Governance is the Board's duty.' They also state that 'The central concern of Governance is to add to as many organizational stakeholders as is practicable. The underlying driver at board room level is to see how value can best be created.'

Responsibility for governance

In small family-owned operations, governance functions can be assumed at a relatively low level of accountability. It is then also likely that governance responsibilities will be relatively straightforward and will not occupy the balance of tasks being carried out: see principle 2, in Chapter 3.

But in large (with sales revenue greater than the gross domestic product (GDP) of more than half the world's countries), complex, international businesses of public liability, key governance duties cut in at work level 6. For those with very significant international reach (ie presence, not just selling, in at least 50 countries), this probably commences at work level 7.

Bob Garratt (2003) sees corporate governance being underpinned by three values: honesty, openness and accountability. 'The ideals behind these three values are rooted in the notion that people with an official position in the private, public, or not-for-profit sectors should not abuse their office.'

But as recent events at Enron, WorldCom, Merrill Lynch, Salomon and even the New York Stock Exchange confirm, the fish does indeed rot from the head (see Garratt, 1996). In the 1990s I was somewhat taken aback when attending a programme at Berkeley to be told, 'The United States is the most ethical country in the world.' When I asked the professor in question for his evidence his revealing reply was, 'Because the United States has more legislation on this issue than any other country!' The issue of governance and accountability has finally staggered, lurched and stumbled to the centre of the North American stage – and not before time.

Although the hard-hitting Garratt stresses the importance of accountability in the governance process he does not really provide an airtight definition. The DMA approach does, as will now be demonstrated.

Governance at Unilever

Unilever has sales in excess of US $50 billion and is present in about 100 countries, while its products are known and sold in over 200. Governance responsibilities at Unilever cut in at work level 7. It has a unique governance structure. Given the Anglo-Dutch cross-shareholding, there are two chairmen: the Chairman of Unilever plc (representing originally the British shareholders) and the Chairman of Unilever NV (representing the Dutch shareholders). This legal structure has led to the expensive establishment of two international head offices, one in London and one in Rotterdam. It is complex and difficult to manage, but it has been made to work.

Single point accountability

One of the driving principles to the dismantling of Unilever's ineffective matrix organization in 1996 was the principle of single point accountability. Indeed, work levels were quoted by the Chairman Elect at the time, Niall FitzGerald, as a driving force in the logic of this process: 'The reorganization and work levels share a common objective – clarity. Accountability is key. The concept of accountability goes right to the heart of what work levels are all about.' But, somehow, the principle of single point accountability evaporated at the top. To add to this complexity, the executive board of Unilever consists of full-time Unilever employees (as indeed does that of Tesco). The only outsiders are non-executive directors (often people with impressive public credentials such as Romano Prodi, now Chairman of the EEC Commission, and the American politician George Mitchell).

This preamble is simply to make clear that the governance structure of Unilever is not exemplary. Nevertheless, I will now endeavour to outline what should be the substance of work at work levels 7 and 8.

Work level 7 – Stakeholder response

1. Nature of work

Moves beyond meeting needs on a regional or limited global basis. The key responsibility is to determine how value can be established across all of the activities (functions, processes) and categories worldwide. In line with the overall mission or corporate purpose of 'satisfying everyday needs of people everywhere', it must define which permanent and universal needs should form the core of the business. This must be done in a way that satisfies a wide range of stakeholders. In short, they must help the chairmen establish the core strategy and ensure that appropriate performance is achieved in line with that strategy.

2. Resource complexity

The key givens are the values in the corporate purpose (Unilever's mission statement), key constraints being the availability of core resources such as people, finance and technology. The board must then identify which categories are to be resourced in which geographies. It must drive the achievement of synergies, which can come from scale and scope. It must ensure that common shared assets such as people, finance, brands and technology (including IT) are appropriately and continuously harnessed. It must define common processes to be shared to ensure that scale does deliver real efficiency.

3. Problem solving

Given the identified categories and the strategic agenda, the board must set the priorities to ensure the maximum positive exploitation of the key opportunities that have to be met from finite resources. This must be balanced with the sometimes conflicting interests of the stakeholders.

The outcome of this process leads to the establishment of agreed key business drivers such as sustained profitable growth, return on assets, efficiency of capital, and the level of profitability to be achieved in the long term, bearing in mind the context of social responsibility and environmental sustainability.

4. Change

The board is accountable for implementing global reconfiguration of the business.

This could entail disposal of businesses (for example, Chemicals) or the acquisition of new businesses (for example, Bestfoods) based on geographical priorities (for example, expansion into Central and Eastern Europe), category strategy (for example, the move into ice cream in Brazil), or the establishment of new businesses (for example, China) or extended investment in existing businesses (for example, Arabia). It must ensure global leadership in innovation by harvesting sources of internal and external research to deliver breakthrough solutions to meet defined, permanent and universal consumer needs.

5. Natural work team

Board directors have well-defined personal accountabilities but in law share accountability for concern governance. Critical collective responsibilities include helping management identify and resolve strategy and performance issues, and ensure that all legal and ethical priorities are maintained. In addition, they must work with their board colleagues in order to integrate personal areas of accountability with those of the concern as a whole. For example, the personnel director, whose key stakeholder responsibility is the firm's employees, should ensure that best practice is achieved based on state of the art thinking in the areas of recruitment, learning, reward and career planning within the context of the priorities of the corporate long-term strategy.

6. External interaction

Most key stakeholders such as shareholders, consumers, customers, suppliers, trade unions, media, governments and local communities are external.

Management of and proactive communication with these groups is a key board responsibility. This also includes active responses and initiatives with pressure groups and non-governmental organizations (NGOs) on an increasingly international scale. The board is responsible for driving initiatives in the areas of social and environmental responsibility and managing the issues relating to the management of existing and new technology's impact on sustainability. It must ensure that the company's activities do not have a deleterious impact on the environment. Managing all these communication channels successfully is a fundamental responsibility, but none more so than that of sharing information with shareholders (especially large ones). Going beyond the bare minimum required in law demonstrates that a company both appreciates its shareholders' need to be informed and values their involvement. The board's ultimate purpose is to add value to the entire business. The management of shareholder and investor relationships is the board's most critical external challenge.

7. Time frame

Value derives from investment. An enterprise that intends to be in business for the long haul needs to think carefully about investing in resource replenishment and discovery (research). Interestingly, Jaques (1989) noted, 'Seven to eight years is the longest forward that human beings seem to be able to plan or carry out specifically budgeted projects. Larger scale projects have to be broken down in to seven year or shorter sub-projects or phases.' This squares with observed experience in Unilever. Thus, the time horizon at work level 7 is up to 10 years.

DMA principles and governance

The principles set out in Chapter 3 also apply at work levels 7 and 8. There should therefore be only one layer in each of the governance work levels. The reason why so many CEO/COO combinations are ineffective is they often appear to be operating in the same work level. It is interesting to note in this context that Coca-Cola did away with its COO role in March 2001. This situation occurred in Unilever prior to the reorganization in 1996.

In the late 1980s Unilever had three separate directors (called coordinators) each respectively responsible for a significant part of Unilever's food business (about 50 per cent of total sales), in what was known as the Foods Executive. One director was 'placed in charge of two others' and was referred to as the Chairman of the Foods Executive. DMA analysis revealed that they were all operating in the same accountability level and that the Chairman of the Foods Executive was not the boss of the other two directors. They each carved out discrete product and geographical areas that meant the objectives of the Foods Executive's plan to achieve synergies were not really obtained.

'A vacant work level 6'

The organization at the next level down became even more diffuse. New organizational forms such as European Category Boards (ECBs) and European Brand Groups (EBGs) were set up and dismantled on a regular basis.

During this period I interviewed all the work level 5 food general managers and encountered widespread frustration and confusion in Europe and North America. In addition, those in the rest of the world were convinced their concerns and priorities in food were being neglected by a Euro-centric organization. Many of these individuals in Europe were being asked to wear more than one hat (covering product, national or functional responsibilities), were travelling extensively, frequently attending meetings, but were invariably unable to make critical decisions other than on issues that were within their own compass, for example their own company. Divisions of 'responsibility' were seemingly based more on politics than on business knowledge. For example, it was agreed that leadership of the margarine business was a critical role, but five different managers were each given the lead in one aspect of the project (for example 'health', 'diet' and so on). This was a sure formula for the dissipation and ineffective use of resource. Comments such as 'the EBG is too complex, too time consuming and too slow', 'there is considerable overlap and little coherence between strategy and operations', 'I report to a foods operations member, but the job adds no value. We can agree but then we both have to go to the director together for a decision' (a strong clue that these managers were in fact working in the same level of accountability, reinforced by meaningless titles), were encountered all too frequently.

By mid-1995, it was clear that the Foods Executive was struggling. It had endeavoured to establish a number of category boards and 'committee type' structures of equals below the board, but they were given no real commensurate accountability.

In other words, work level 6 was de facto vacant and there was no value addition to the role of these general managers below the Foods Executive.

This was in contrast to developments in the detergents and personal products coordinations, when the more open trading conditions started in Western Europe during 1992. Each coordination established pan-European companies (Lever Europe and Personal Products Europe respectively) with clear accountability at level 6. It was immediately noticeable that these companies were reconfiguring their European supply chain, IT, marketing and advertising while the Foods Executive continued their debates and discussions in various committees.

Over-layered and under-led

In the mid-1990s the Foods Executive had managed to achieve something one would have thought was impossible (although this phenomenon has been found elsewhere): it was in different parts both over-layered and under-layered, and therefore under-led, a sure formula for ineffectiveness. There were two layers of directors in one work level, which did not function as a team, with no decision-making accountability in the next level down, leaving a group of overburdened and somewhat frustrated general managers across Europe. During this period Unilever's market performance slipped in comparison to the latter half of the 1980s.

In the 1996 reorganization two foods business groups were established in Europe and one in North America (all at work level 6), and, not entirely coincidentally perhaps, their business ratios have all improved since.

Sub-optimal structures can occur at any level

In the late 1990s the business in India, consisting of a number of very successful level 5 units, was well run by the local CEO who clearly operated at work level 6. This was established following over 50 interviews in the field during 1997. But he reported to a work Level 6 'Business Group President' with his entourage in London. There are examples in the military of one four-star general reporting to another. This and the previous example demonstrate that sub-optimal organization design can occur at any level in the organization.

Work level 8 – Directive response

Work Level 8 is the CEO level in Unilever. Level 8 calls for a directive response for, as President Truman said, 'This is where the buck stops': the ultimate accountability. Ultimate accountability demands leadership, which in turn sets directions, subject to certain constraints.

Accountability for assessing those constraints resides at work level 8 in Unilever. Achieving this in a global business requires the establishment of key links with world leaders, opinion formers and drivers of change, whether economic, business, social, political, religious, educational or cultural, on any part of the world stage. What succeeds the current business and how to ensure its successful survival is a key concern and challenge.

In businesses of the global reach, complexity, diversity and size of Unilever this is the level that sets the mission, vision and strategy. It also establishes the ethical standards and outlines the norms and guidelines for doing business. In short, the defining of the corporate culture, values and performance standards.

1. Nature of work

Work at this level entails defining what business the company is to pursue and deciding which permanent and universal needs are to be met on a global basis. The chairmen must ensure that underlying linkages in science, technology (including information technology) and brands are maximized while driving for effective synergies in the deployment of finance and people across the business. They set the corporate purpose, define the values and ethical standards to be followed. They are the ultimate guardians of financial probity and long-term strategy.

An example of this was project 'Growth Opportunities' in the first half of the 1990s, which led to a new prioritization of categories and greater focus on consumer goods, a process which has greatly intensified since.

2. Resource complexity

Resources are constrained at this level by corporate purpose and strategy. This level is accountable for the continual improvement in performance reflected in results and the 'rate of return' for the main stakeholders: shareholders, employees, customers, suppliers and consumers. This involves the provision of functional excellence across the business and the reinforcing of the international linkages of key resources. Prime areas of investment focus for the long term are capital expenditure, advertising investment and management succession for the top echelons of the business.

3. Problem solving

The essential difference between levels 7 and 8 within Unilever is the move from responding to consumer needs in isolation to proactively identifying and driving the emerging linkages between them, taking into account the organization's capabilities. There is a constant need to ensure that the political economies of scale and scope are fully realized. The size paradox: namely small is beautiful, large is beautiful, has to be optimized in the face of changing technology, such as the Internet, which is rapidly reconfiguring the world as we know it. This calls for achieving a dynamic balance between categories, functions and geography.

4. Change

Maintaining economic buoyancy in a heaving sea of change is probably a CEO's most demanding challenge in today's world. The challenge of change is not new, as de Tocqueville pointed out in 1835, but as Warren Bennis noted in 1966: 'One thing is new since de Tocqueville's time, *the acceleration* of newness, the changing scale of change itself.' But not even a Bennis could have foreseen the impact on business and individuals of the Internet meteorite. Today CEOs are making investment decisions as if in the heat of a military battle where the boundaries of engagement are being constantly realigned. This is an unnerving experience for people used to making measured decisions based on careful objective analysis and assessment. The rules of this game are unfolding in real time across the world. This is not just accelerated newness – it is *unprecedented*. CEOs will not be forgiven for getting it wrong, notwithstanding that many decisions amount to a flutter on the e-roulette.

In contrast to level 7, accountability for change now entails the potential reconfiguring of all or any of the concern's management groups, geographies or principal activities. Eight years ago the organizational focus of Unilever was the national company. In 1996 that moved to a regional focus, such as Western Europe, North America, Latin America and so on. Although this was the most radical reorganization probably in the company's history at the time, within three years it was past its sell-by date in Europe, given the pace of change in technology and the developments of the retail grocery trade. The company has embarked on a move along the organizational spectrum from national focus to ultimately a seamless global organization. It has not reached that destination yet but the challenge is to decide at what pace to progress along this continuum. The decision is not 'if' but 'when', but it has immense repercussions for stakeholders, particularly employees. It was no surprise when, in February 2000, the chairmen announced that during the next five years they would jettison 75 per cent of the current 1,600 brands, close about 100 factories and remove about 25,000 jobs.

Notwithstanding the enormity of these figures in today's world, analysts actually questioned whether this decision-making process was radical enough and whether the time frame envisaged was sufficiently urgent.

5. Natural work team

Jon Katzenbach (1997) has pointed out that 'Even in the best companies a so called top team seldom functions as a real team.' Although, somewhat incongruously, Unilever does have a joint team of two (an executive office) running the business, normally lateral teamwork is not so obvious for the CEO.

In normal circumstances, a key discriminating attribute is the quality of leadership demonstrated. Intriguingly, Campbell, Goold and Alexander (1995) refer to the parenting influences at this level in organizations, and, as we all know, children are very adept at playing one parent off against another. Thus, in Unilever the joint chairmanship can achieve consensus, but the flipside can be inertia.

Nevertheless, governance is shared with the board, especially the non-executive directors, who lead the independent Governance Committees, such as Audit, Remuneration and Appointments. There are clear examples, such as BP, General Motors and IBM, where CEOs have been removed for lack of performance. Even at this level, lateral teamwork can never be taken for granted.

6. External interaction

When outlining a survey of a board's 'top 5 tasks' in 1995, Felton, Hodnut and Witt made no mention of the environment. But today, environmental concerns and the issue of social responsibility loom ever larger on the governance agenda. Incidents such as Shell's problems over the Brent Spar episode or their difficulties in South Eastern Nigeria graphically illustrate the growing importance of this challenge.

Responding to the need for greater social responsibility, Shell has developed the concept of the triple bottom line. It now reports on:

- financial performance;
- physical environment;
- corporate social responsibility performance.

Targets and standards are set for all three bottom lines.

The French retailer, Carrefour, initiated a similar enhancement of its governance reporting in 2001 with its Sustainability Report. Multinational corporations (MNCs) must play their part in sustaining the environment, and Unilever's initiative to support the World Fishing Organization's sustainable fishing programme is a good case in point. Tesco also takes its community responsibilities very seriously.

The chairpersons of global companies need to forge links with world leaders, opinion moulders and drivers of change in many different walks of life, be they economic, academic, business, political, religious or cultural.

The demands of performance management in its widest sense are at the heartland of the governance process. As Drucker noted in 1990, 'Even non-profit organizations have to be governed by performance.'

The challenge of balancing the various external forces impinging on global performance management has arguably never been more daunting.

CSR in Europe: a cautionary tale.

The EU's so-called 'Rhenish' model for corporate social responsibility is badly conceived. It consists of inflexible labour laws, an obsession with politically correct initiatives, which load the dice against wealth producers, leading to increased unemployment, while it lacks both fiscal and budgetary control and the integrity to tackle the ludicrous commitments to early retirement provisions that cannot be met. In short the EU fails the governance values of honesty, openness and accountability.

In similar vein the British government encouraged the Higgs Report to suggest that the heads of public businesses should not select their subordinates. This sadly revealed a fundamental misunderstanding of the nature of accountability.

The above merely emphasizes the enormity of the task facing the CEOs of leading organizations who need to proactively influence the environment in which they operate.

7. Time frame

Long-term strategy was considered the number one task of the board, highlighted by the Felton study referred to above. In Unilever this accountability ultimately resides with the two chairmen. For an organization that is avowedly in business for the long haul, securing management and board succession is a key role, which calls for a 15-year lens at CEO level. This is the critical time frame for most critical investment decisions relating to capital, technology, and line of business. They are responsible for managing the overall portfolio – adding and subtracting – as well as setting clear performance priorities for the direction of resource.

Step 6

If steps 1 to 5 reveal a sub-optimal organization, set out a plan of action for return to health.

CHAPTER REVIEW

This chapter has outlined the DMA solution set as applied in two large international companies. The differences between operational, strategic and governance levels of accountability were highlighted. Six major steps were outlined, showing how the DMA analysis can be used as a reliable form of health check. The next chapter describes in more detail how DMA can be applied in the supply chain and in areas of innovation such as a research laboratory. The book then goes on to demonstrate how it further links with reward management, leadership development and the management and communication of change.

NOTES

1 The definition of an activity is 'Major recognisable functions or processes, typically represented at the executive level of an operating company. E.g. the finance activity'. *Unilever Work Level Manual*, March 1997.

2 The definition of a 'discipline' in the same *Work Level Manual* is 'A specific subset of an Activity. For example, accounting is a discipline within the finance activity.'

3 'A Category is a grouping of products that share similar characteristics from the perspective of consumers, usually meeting a permanent and universal need.' *Unilever Work Level Manual*, March 1997.

4 It is important not to be misled by titles. For example, the term director often denotes a work level 4 role in a large international business in Europe, but a level 3 role in the United States.

5
How to stimulate genuine empowerment and innovation

This chapter will demonstrate how the application of DMA principles can lead to genuine empowerment and enhanced innovation. Empowerment became the buzzword of the 1990s. It was seen as the natural successor to, and indeed extension of, earlier work such as Theory Y, job enrichment and Theory Z. However, unlike these earlier developments there was no identified thought leader such as MacGregor, Herzberg or Ouchi to help prescribe the right medicine. By the end of the decade empowerment was starting to get a bad press. In this chapter I will highlight the importance of accurate thinking about viable spans of control, and describe how a US factory was reorganized and empowered as a result of applying DMA logic.

Innovation is also becoming a vague and overworked term. Marketing hype has devalued the meaning of the word 'new'. Probes undertaken in European research laboratories will provide critical insights into how the innovation process can be managed more effectively. The consequences of responsibilities straddling more than one work level will also be examined.

THE EMPOWERMENT ILLNESS

The first symptom of the illness is the lack of a clear definition of empowerment. No theory or recognized research exists that has established and refined the key concepts. It seems to have been unleashed by management journalists as a tenet of aspirational management. The first reference to empowerment I can recall came at a Tom Peters management seminar in Frankfurt in February 1988, where he was essentially promoting his book *Thriving on Chaos*. He was long on exhortation but short on explanation. Nine years later, Dave Ulrich was equally vague: 'Successful empowerment approaches to culture change are more than gripe sessions. They are built on the principle of "no blaming no complaining". Empowerment efforts are focused on translating a specific mindset into a specific employee behaviour.' In 1994, Aileen Stewart concluded: 'To sum up: empowerment allows organizations to respond rapidly, flexibly and efficiently to customer and market demands. The result is reduced waste, delays and errors and a work-force in which staff are a fully utilized resource.' Good evangelical stuff, but what is it? Which brings us to the second symptom.

Empowerment seems, broadly speaking, to describe a greater freedom of decision making. However, no method for determining the appropriate levels of responsibility and freedom for the 'empowered' decision maker has been identified. Not much thought has been given to the practical achievement of 'empowerment' through appropriate organizational structure. The simplistic notion is that talent will be released merely by removing layers in the hierarchy, the assumption being that all the talent residing at the bottom of the pyramid is needlessly compressed by the dead weight of a less competent cadre of individuals above them. Simply remove this organizational plug and employees' natural brilliance will uncoil, with spectacular results. But frustratingly for management, once again no one has outlined **how** to unerringly tread this path to motivational nirvana.

Thirdly, since no one seems to have satisfactorily defined empowerment it is difficult to say what it is not. Thus, removing a management layer in an organization that is appropriately structured will traumatize employees, not empower them. The knowledge and experience of competent individuals in the middle echelons of an organization do not migrate to their subordinates once the former have been removed. This defies the logic of accountability and common sense. Vacuums of accountability cause stress and sub-optimal performance. Re-engineering guesswork has often led to the removal of genuinely value-adding jobs which in time aggravates the pain of an unhealthy organization. In these cases pathologies then masquerade as empowerment.

Often a CEO states that his or her organization is empowered. The popular mythology is that a flat organization is an empowered organization. But if neither flatness nor empowerment can be defined or measured it is impossible to prove or disprove the case. I well remember a CEO in Italy, running a company that had an excellent record of successfully innovating new products, claiming that his factory was empowered and correctly organized. He had assumed that the presence of a highly effective development department indicated that the rest of the organization was equally well organized. Unfortunately, when I visited the factory and carried out a series of interviews of key production managers I discovered that 'there were five layers of management where only two were strictly necessary, and that the production organization was opaque as a result'. The workers at the frontline were not highly motivated or empowered.

SPAN OF CONTROL

One of the most common blockages to empowerment seems to be muddled thinking about the span of control, or span of management. This refers to the number of people who can be managed as direct reports by one person. As Fisch (1963) pointed out, 'if the number of people reporting to each manager is too small the organization will be top heavy, expensive to operate, stifling to initiative and a barrier to communication throughout the organization'. Allen Janger (1989), from the New York Conference Board, noted in a study of 105 separate units that managers' spans of control averaged between 2.3 to 83.45 with a median of 7.8 and a median number of layers of 5. Interestingly, this supported his earlier findings in 1960, when he established that the median span of control of the CEOs in 81 companies was 8. In 1974 David Van Fleet quoted earlier work by Dale in 1952: 'with a median at 9 in 100 large (5,000 or more employees) companies'. From the above study the Conference Board concluded, 'units with fewer than five layers are flat, and those with managerial spans less than 7.8 are narrow'. But note what this means in terms of the DMA model. An organization with 6 layers of management (ie with the top job at level 7) and an average span of control of 7.8 throughout would have more than 225,000 employees, and one with 7 layers in excess of 1 million employees! This would suggest that there are very few flat or truly empowered organizations, despite the empowerment hype.

One of the main reasons for this seems to be the lack of accurate distinguishing between **line** and **support** jobs (see Chapter 3). Invariably, support jobs are drawn on organization charts on the spine of accountability as if they were the bosses of those sketched below them. The span of control fallacy, which believes that six is the maximum number of people that one can manage, only compounds the error. This mistaken belief is most common in the people-intensive units of the business. For example, Figure 5.1 shows the official organization chart in an English factory in the early 1990s.

Analysis revealed that the factory manager was work level 3 and the production manager work level 2. The shift superintendents spent most of their time ensuring that the supervisors – whom they considered superfluous – were doing their job properly. There was no evidence that the superintendents had to do anything other than responsible level 1 work. They worked according to 'common sense and accumulated experience'. There was surprisingly little contact with the production manager. There were four layers where only two were required. Despite this, the frontline was not effectively managed

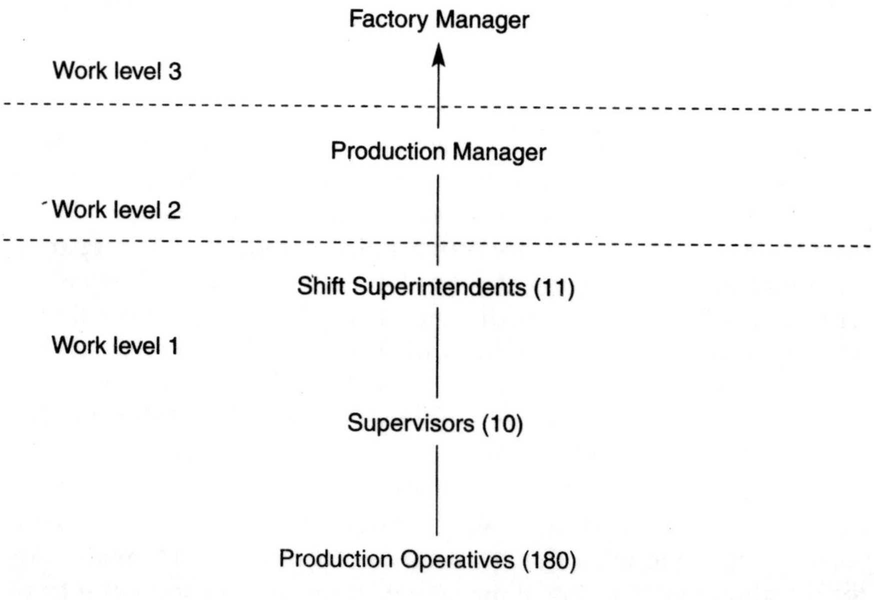

Figure 5.1 *Official factory organization chart (production)*

and as a result the workers turned to a whole variety of different people to solve their problems and grievances. Not surprisingly, the factory had a history of brittle industrial relations, yet much of the supervisory and management effort allegedly went into 'improving motivation'. The workers were adamant that the supervisors were unnecessary. The supervisors in turn saw their key task as 'motivating people'.

It is amazing how often over-managed departments are frantically busy with work and yet key tasks are consistently omitted and the frontline complain of lack of job satisfaction (or empowerment). Long hours and overtime demands are not always what they seem when the structure is sub-optimal. Often, therefore, the workforce is frustrated by management's preconceptions of how a factory should be organized.

The solution in this case, as set out in Figure 5.2, was to delete the role of supervisor and to redefine the superintendents' role as support jobs (and maybe operate with one less superintendent, depending on how the day shift was organized).

The superintendents were to assist the production manager manage the entire department of around 200 – ie the de facto span of control would be 183. He or she would know each individual personally. I have encountered de facto spans of control of this size on many

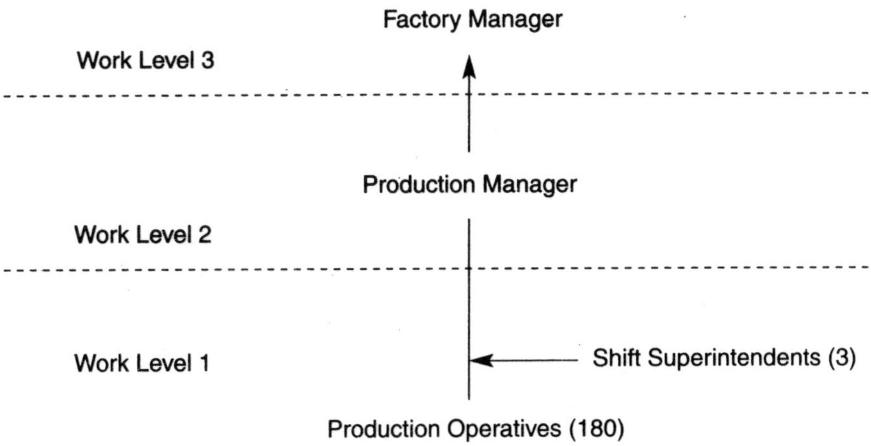

Figure 5.2 *Recommended factory organization chart for production department*

occasions, despite the official depiction on the organization chart. The production manager would be accountable for the performance of the department and every individual in it. He or she would decide who could come into the department, what work they would do, their objectives, deadlines, how they would be trained and when they would move on from the department. The production manager would be responsible for daily, weekly and monthly production schedules. The superintendents would provide shift cover and assist with induction, training, monitoring performance of staff and machinery, disciplinary and factory line administration, including shift patterns and variances against departmental targets relating to volume, quality, waste, absenteeism and productivity.

Importance of support roles

Once the concept of a support role is fully understood, traditional, limited thinking about viable spans of control gets blown out of the water. Some of the operatives may need to be designated leading hands or team leaders working on the line. These titles are akin to rank and may have higher pay rates as a result. An analogy to this production department would be a (single shift) platoon in the army. The lance corporal/corporal would be the equivalent of team leaders on the line, while the sergeant would equate to the superintendent in a support role to the officer in charge. So-called autonomous teams and leaderless work groups conform to this model. I have observed work in Volvo and Saab factories in Sweden organized along these lines. The empowered teams were variously arranged in work level 1, with accountable managers in the equivalent of work level 2 enjoying wide spans of control (in excess of 100). Another automotive company, Fiat, has average spans in excess of 80 at the frontline of one factory.

What has been established so far is that traditional thinking about spans of control or spans of management is conservative and incorrectly captured on most organization charts. The lack of distinction between line and support jobs and the inaccurate assessments as to which support jobs are essential aggravate the overall situation, contributing to over-management and lack of empowerment. Lyndall Urwick made very clear in 1956 that 'the span of control is not a rigid rule to be applied woodenly in all situations'. As we also discovered as early as 1979, 'the optimal management span of control is not simply a single uniform figure: judgement is required bearing in mind a number of different factors such as the nature of the superior's tasks, the nature of the subordinates' tasks, the location of subordinates' (Roès, 1979). Additional factors include the interdependence of subordinates, (see the work of James Thompson (1967)), which is also consistent with the 'interlocking' concept of Urwick and with Graicunas (1937). Additional factors identified by Tomasko in 1987 include 'the quality of the subordinates' and the manager's training, the manager's tenure, subordinate turn over and rotation, strength of the lateral communication channels, investment in automated information systems, the number of performance measures needed, the use made of job enrichment and the existence of a shared culture'.

One company, since it introduced levels of accountability, has given guidance to its management on how to establish realistic spans of management. It has established a grid of the key considerations to help decide how wide spans need to be. This has resulted in genuine empowerment and significant cost reduction, as superfluous jobs were identified and the individuals moved to other roles.

Earlier work on spans of control

In 1963, Fisch radically challenged conventional wisdom: 'what I have seen in business leads me to state that the maximum span of management for middle management might well be 50 and for supervisory personnel as large as 100'.

In 1977, Van Fleet and Bodeian reminded us that as early as 1955 'The General Electric Company suggested spans might go as high as 50 or more.' Implicit in this insight was firstly the realization that often the work of large numbers of subordinates did not interlock; for example, 'the 40 departmental heads reporting to a Sears Roebuck store manager' referred to by Tomasko (1987). Secondly, the key support jobs could carry out many of the relevant interlocking activities on behalf of the boss. It is the understanding of these support roles that is the key to managing large number of subordinates who can be empowered in the process. The 1989 Conference Board study referred to above concluded as follows: 'the age of the computer and advanced telecommunications has carried the participating companies, especially those in the automotive and electrical machinery companies in a number of new directions. To meet their strategic need for greater economies of scale, they created larger functionally organized production units. They have kept units flat, however, by using improved planning, scheduling, and logistic systems; by amalgamating formally separate production and engineering units; and by using more highly trained, self co-ordinated workers. They have pushed average managerial spans over 20:1 (close to 100:1 at the first supervisory level) and kept the number of layers within or below the "normal" range of large unit benchmark.'

WHAT IS THE CURE?

Misconceptions and bad practice tend to suggest that what is understood, in some cases, as empowerment is an illness and not a cure for demotivation. The problem is that many spurious initiatives masquerade as 'empowerment'. The validity of the idea is not new. It was recognized years ago by Mary Parker Follett (1949): 'The important thing about responsibility is not to whom you are responsible, but for what you are responsible.' In 1995 Nohria wrote: 'I find that Follett offers one of the clearest statements of what the current buzzword "empowerment" really means. She argues firms can be more effective if they emphasize power-with rather than power-over.' Her definition of value-added comes from her suggestion that we 'think out the form of organization whereby authority may go with 3 things: knowledge, experience, and the skill to apply that knowledge and experience'. But empowerment is a journey, it is not a destination. Changing technology sees to that, and 'the full potential of the new technology is not being realized' according to Child and Loveridge (1990). Nohria further points out the fragility of this process: 'I think organizations based on the principle of empowerment or power-with will always remain fragile and especially susceptible to reversion to a command and control system during times of change in leadership.'

DMA and empowerment

The empowerment label is simply another way of saying that effective organizations need a motivated workforce. It is further recognition that tall hierarchies suppress and frustrate the efforts of talented and educated employees. However, even where these shortcomings are recognized this does not automatically unlock the key to motivation and future success. **The DMA approach** can provide the answer by ensuring that all employees are working within the correct level. Once the necessary levels of work required have been identified, the next two steps are to design an organization that reflects that reality and then match individuals with the requisite ability to function effectively at each level. As reported in Bain and Mabey (1999), 'empowerment means having the right number of jobs with the right people in them at the right Work Levels'. This is illustrated in the following example.

Evidence of the cure

In 1991, I completed an analysis of the Chesebrough Pond's organization in the United States. It was a successful company of around US $1 billion sales but despite its earlier success it had developed a very rich organization with an average span of control of just under five and around seven layers of management in the main functions of the business. It was decided to undertake a Greenfield Organizational Review – a zero-based approach to building a new organization.

First, the business strategy was revamped. In order to achieve greater focus and simplicity it was decided to divest some elements of the business. The shape of the executive team at the top was redesigned. I then worked with that top team, preparing them for a one-week meeting in which together they designed a target organization, working bottom-up. The top team were convinced that we had to design a company in which the president's job should be at work level 5. In other words, no part of the organization justified more than four layers of value-adding management. This was quite controversial at first for a company of this size and complexity. It was particularly taxing in the people-intensive areas of the business such as the supply chain, including the factories and customer service. The Chesebrough Ponds Vice-President of Human Resources, Jim McCall, played a key role throughout, especially in the implementation stage.

The company had a number of factories, one of which was at Jefferson City. Historically the factory had more layers of supervision than envisaged in the target organization. The top job was now pitched at work level 3, which meant that the plant manager had scope for only one layer of management between himself and his frontline employees. He set out to build an empowered factory.

Empowerment means organizational change

Previously there had been three layers of management in the Jefferson City plant, but two had been in work level 2, as it transpired. One layer (departmental managers) was removed. This had been a crucial step since it not only corrected a structural anomaly but it released talent in levels 1 and 2 which had previously been circumscribed. But this could not be achieved before the old jobs at work level 1 and 2 were redesigned.

There was less emphasis on departmental boundaries. Individuals were encouraged to make contacts with people who could solve their problems. Most contacts were lateral within the work level but vertical and even external contacts, for example with suppliers, were encouraged when appropriate. This was noticeably reinforced by single status initiatives: managers did not wear ties, jackets or white coats and so blended into the background; there is one canteen and no reserved car parking spaces. New titles have been introduced to enhance people's importance and reflect the new vision. Factory Operatives, whose work was redesigned, were known as Associates. The leading hands had new roles and were designated Team Coordinators. Supervisors are variously known as Process Leaders and Coaches. These imaginative titles tend to reinforce the new work culture, which underlined the empowerment initiative.

Furthermore, Associates in level 1 saw the removal of a layer of management as clear proof that top management really meant what they had said. It has been subsequently recognized that this was when the empowerment really started to take off because trust was established as the bedrock of the entire process. Prior to that, those in work level 1 bore the brunt of cost reductions 'to improve productivity' while managers had been left undisturbed.

The empowerment of Associates has enabled them to move higher into work level 1 and assume greater accountability for their work; for example, everybody now undertakes some machine adjustments; they can physically leave the line and contact other departments or even suppliers. On occasions, they now travel to suppliers to help commission and, as a result, 'own' new machinery. These were tasks typically done by supervisors in the past, most of whom would have been work level 1.

A fundamental feature of the work of the Associates today is their mobility. In the past their job was static, fixed to the machine's site. As one Associate put it: 'We are now responsible for what our machine is doing in volume and quality. We are responsible to coordinate what it takes to get this production. If there is a problem, we can't let it go on. In the past, I would do what I was told; for example, quality assurance says the product is OK so run it. Even though I could see it was not OK I would run it. Today I would shut down the line and get help, solve the problem, stop the waste and avoid rework and perhaps unnecessary overtime. Previously only the supervisor could do that. Empowerment means we are constantly thinking. We are not brain dead as in the past.'

As one of the managers described his role: 'In Jefferson City the way people are treated is different. Associates are not treated as extensions of the machine. The purpose of management is coaching and direction and not the day-to-day management of the shop floor. My boss lets me do my job and I am learning how to let my people do their jobs.'

By the mid-1990s, there were just over half the number of managers and supervisors that there had been in 1989. Ongoing empowerment is likely to lead to even fewer process supervisors in time as the Associates continue to develop. New Process Leaders or Coaches are key support jobs at the top of work level 1 who essentially enable Associates to achieve their output objectives. A further role was introduced at Associate level, namely that of Team Coordinator. These are currently rotational roles which one Senior Line Operator occupies each day. The role, therefore, does not involve seniority or more money but each day one of the Associates is the point of contact for a line and is responsible for essential paperwork. Empowerment has led to changed roles.

Working in the correct work level

One of the challenges for managers has been to remain in their work level and let their subordinates work effectively in their own levels. The work of those in work level 1 is basically to respond to the production schedule and in turn meet that schedule, while that of those in work level 2 is to respond flexibly to customers within the schedule, ie change the short-term (one or two weeks) schedule as appropriate. The plant manager at work level 3 sets the goals and targets for the plant as a whole while encouraging levels 1 and 2 to assess how these can be acquired. He will then allocated resources to ensure the plants' internal and external customers are satisfied accordingly.

As one process owner (supervisor) summed it up: 'Cross-training our associates has led to much greater flexibility and cooperation. They know what needs to be done; they do not have to be told. Information is open to everyone, not just management. Teamwork exists from the top down. Everyone sticks together. There is no feeling of status or hierarchy. There is a real open door policy. We try to keep the big (business) picture while all the time trying to improve. The people make the decisions; you guide them. Being in an empowered factory is more difficult but it is more interesting: you can do more.'

Information sharing and training

It was noticeable, walking around the Jefferson City plant, that there was a lot of key information about annual targets, past and present performance on display. Statements of philosophy, mission and vision together with key plant objectives were posted in the foyer and entrance to the production hall. The use of and training in IT was an impressive feature of the plant. There were a number of very creative programmes; some initiated by associates themselves, to improve computer literacy. The associates clearly use IT as a tool of work and do not seem to view it as a threat to their job security. Indeed, it is known in the plant that people will not lose their employment if their jobs disappear, as a result of new changes leading to enhanced productivity. The general impression is that people thrive on this information and sense of openness and seek more not less communication. It was very clear from associates' comments that there was a strong correlation between communication and a sense of empowerment. When information sharing had waned, people felt distinctly less empowered to the point where suspicion and conjecture were starting to take root and needed to be resolved.

Training and education seemed to be critical elements in the achievement of empowerment. Initially issues such as business education and computer literacy need to be met, but as a state of empowerment develops and becomes more mature, so the training needs change, requiring more skills and process training. In short, the process of informing people that they are empowered to build in mechanisms that will identify *how* the empowerment process can be taken a stage further. A proactive, dynamic training culture is vital if momentum is not to be lost.

Chesebrough Ponds had established a total quality philosophy in the past. It was clear that that philosophy provided an important foundation on which to build empowerment. It is a moot point whether the plant could have progressed so far so quickly without the corporate total quality initiative.

The reward culture

The plant had established an impressive reward culture based on celebration and recognition of success. These recognitions are often small, but they seem to be frequent, timely and very effective. Initially, much of the celebration focused upon individuals. As teamwork developed and became more entrenched, the maturation of empowerment suggested that there is a time when focus upon the group is both more appreciated and more effective. Another very significant feature of the Jefferson City empowerment phenomenon has been the lack of fundamental change in pay systems. There are no new gain-sharing or major productivity payment mechanisms. The recognition features referred to above rarely involve cash and, when appropriate, the amounts paid are not significant. This experience is contrary to the widely held view that behavioural change will only occur when reward systems are remodelled.

Two local features may have contributed to this success and should not be underestimated. The employees seemed to feel they were well paid. It was significant that during 30 or so interviews across all levels and areas of the plant, not one person commented negatively about compensation. Secondly, the plant has a very stable workforce. The average length of service approaches 20 years and in some cases there are third-generation family members employed in the plant. As one person remarked, 'This sort of loyalty money can't buy.' Another commented, 'It is not money which gets you out of bed in the morning.' There is also an evident pride in the local culture, which has a strong belief in the value of work. The plant is non-unionized and does not have a legacy of antagonism to management. These environmental considerations might help explain why empowerment has taken root without a major additional investment in compensation changes.

The quality of leadership

The key element in the empowerment mix was undoubtedly the quality of leadership of the plant. Vision, determination to change, courage to manage uncertainty and the ability to lead are essential, as are high interpersonal skills and integrity. If the top management are not truly committed and capable of lasting the distance, it seems inevitable that empowerment initiatives will fail. There is little doubt that principles of empowerment, when well managed, lead to a competitive advantage of a type that is virtually impossible to copy and match, since it continues to advance. Improvement does not happen on its own and even an initiative as successful as that of Jefferson City would lose momentum without the right hand at the tiller. I will cover in Chapter 8 the issue of personal development. But I have noticed on more than one occasion that for change to be successful the change leader often has to have potential for higher levels of accountability. Thus, the individual who led the change at the work level 3 plant at Jefferson City had clear potential to move to level 4. But he was subsequently moved to a position which, although a grade 'promotion', was still in work level 3. It entailed coordinating the other factories reporting to a level 4 supply chain vice president. The position was a new one, effectively a span breaker, aimed at developing the superior who was given a wider than normal span of control. This was a good example of a manager being constrained by 'promotion' within the same work level. A few months later this talented manager resigned.

WHAT THEN IS EMPOWERMENT?

One person at the Jefferson City plant described empowerment as 'the work of the supervisors has come down to the workers'. A supervisor described it as 'getting people to motivate themselves', whereas a manager felt the main change in empowerment was 'what people now know as a result of training'.

Associates have moved from unskilled to semi-skilled work within work level 1. Their work is still prescribed and essentially consists of 'responding to a schedule and meeting that schedule'. Process supervisors who work at the top of work level 1 are seen as coaches who are inwardly focused and who 'guide associates to make the right decisions'. The management at work level 2 are more outwardly (to the factory) focused because of their links with marketing and development departments. They must service the customers external to the company by being able to flex the production schedule. The plant manager sees his task as constantly improving that schedule. He sets broad, demanding annual targets for the plant within the company's strategic plan and then plans and provides the resources that will facilitate their achievement.

Based on this example at Jefferson City, the key elements of an empowered unit seem to include:

- clear definition of accountabilities;
- minimalization of departmental boundaries;
- mobility and flexibility within the frontline;
- proactive training and coaching;

- open information and use of it;
- minimizing status demarcations;
- focus on recognition;
- focus on results;
- one management layer per management work level;
- good leadership;
- business orientation;
- ongoing, proactive communications right to the frontline.

In summary, empowerment means enabling people to work at the right level without being crowded from above. It entails training and development and amounts to encouraging people to take decisions and make improvements around their jobs. True empowerment guarantees correct accountability per level of work: **ie the right number of jobs with the right calibre of people in them at the right work levels**. It also ensures that individuals are accountable for outcomes which are clear and transparent in an environment which meets their learning needs, fosters participation, teamwork and a sense of personal worth.

In December 2003, CEO Ross Perot Jnr explained these ideas in this way:

> You have to take care of your team, and recruit the right people. It's a little bit like basketball. I can get onto the court and play some games. But the truth is if I am doing my job right I shouldn't have to get on the court. I have to discipline myself to be a good delegator – general manager rather than a team coach.

The Jefferson City plant is one example of where the right organization design is coupled with appropriate accountability, clear processes and real scope for personal development. The catalyst of this empowerment was the principles of DMA, which guided the reorganization of the company first, and then the factory. This shows that DMA is an integral part of the empowerment cure.

INNOVATION AND ORGANIZATIONAL SCHIZOPHRENIA

Just prior to resigning to join a competitor, one of Unilever's senior marketers said to me during a work-level interview in the mid-1990s, 'Over the past 50 years the major breakthroughs (in detergents) have been in machinery. Probably most of our research is development.' Yet just prior to that a bouncy research scientist had waxed lyrical about his worldwide 'research budget of £32 million (part of the detergent portfolio)', and described his 'research function as a business function and that 80 per cent of his time had nothing to do with the laboratory. That the line structure of the laboratory had nothing to do with the work in the lab.' This rang a few alarm bells as Unilever had just experienced a high-profile detergents marketing failure because of technical shortcomings in the product. And although we were assured the lessons had been learnt, the evidence was thin on the ground. As one scientist put it: 'Our exploratory scientists do a lot of routine stuff. I have worked on five projects in five years. We keep moving areas.' This person then requested a move out of exploratory science in order to do something more challenging and long term!

What is innovation?

I first started working in the research laboratories in 1989. At that time, there was confusion about the meaning and role of innovation. A number of important questions surfaced. What was the role of the research laboratories? Development or research? How should they interface with the business, should projects be science driven or led by marketing? How should the laboratories be structured as a result? How should the work and careers of scientists be organized? What was the right balance between science and management roles?

It had been pointed out as early as 1989 by Dive that 'an analysis of layers of management in a number of different units in one country last year indicated that the most heavily layered section were in Research and Development. Yet there is a compelling consensus outside Unilever that tall hierarchies do not facilitate innovation.' A series of assignments over a period of almost 10 years helped uncover a number of issues, which have hindered creative work in the laboratories. The application of DMA logic identified a way forward. This approach has been equally effective in other areas of work that are said to be creative, such as marketing.

Need for a clear mission

Research laboratories in industry are often caught on the horns of a dilemma. If they become too enmeshed in academic science they may generate high-quality inventions but fail to generate sufficient new products for the marketplace. Ashok Ganguly (Unilever's Research Director for much of the 1990s) described this in 1999 as large 'R' and small 'd'. This was said to be one of Philips's problems in the 1980s. If on the other hand they focus too much on the marketplace and the current product range they are apt to miss out on the breakthrough creative work. More a case of 'incremental R&D: small "r" and big "D"'. Thirdly, it is possible to fall between both stools, achieving neither a flow of breakthrough work nor a steady stream of high-quality new products. In the early 1990s, prior to Ganguly's appointment, Unilever was more prone to the third option. The big question was why? For although, compared to, say, the innovative industries of electronics and pharmaceuticals, Unilever's spend on research and development as a percentage of sales is low, it is nevertheless substantial, running into some hundreds of millions of pounds.

The first foray into one of the European laboratories revealed a number of serious organizational and people development issues. First, the mission of the laboratory was not crystal clear. There was no common view of the place of the research laboratories in the wider scheme of things within the company, from those interviewed at the time. Although labelled a 'research' entity, most of the work was not research.

Organizational schizophrenia

The laboratory betrayed symptoms of organizational ambivalence, positioned uncomfortably between what can be loosely described as 'industrial' and 'academic' models of organization. A small but significant indication of this schizophrenia was rampant confusion over titles, ie whether to favour a university or an industrial model. This uncertainty over mission led to a fundamental lack of coherent structure, compounded by a further uncertainty about the level of work at the frontline. Research work is not done in work levels 1 to 3, only the support work. (In 1999 one of the research labs had 89 per cent of its management in work level 2!) The effects of this organizational schizophrenia seemed to reverberate throughout the laboratories. Areas and levels of work overlapped, lines of accountability were blurred, there was no common pattern of jobs or career paths, issues such as management of science, customers and administration were confused and tangled, and individual capacity (especially that of PhDs) was under-utilized with a consequent loss of synergy, creativity and motivation.

A lack of organization charts and short, clear role descriptions of accountability can be most revealing in a large complex organization. It turned out to be so in this case. The scientists employed many personal metaphors to describe the workings of the laboratory, such as 'the beating heart' or the 'propeller model', but in reality these meant little to others across the unit. The 'charts' made available primarily represented functional groupings and teams without distilling key levels of responsibility or real lines of accountability. Significantly, these charts were regularly changed with impunity by upper middle managers throughout this particular project. Not surprisingly, a lot of frustration was encountered lower down in the laboratory. The clue to unravelling much of this tangled organizational skein came from applying the principles of DMA to the scientific work of innovation.

LEVELS OF SCIENTIFIC WORK

Scientific work, like other forms of endeavour, can be analysed in terms of its level of complexity and response to problems. Sometimes this analysis is hindered by over-reference to umbrella terms such as innovation, which can mask critical distinctions between development and research, whether basic or applied. Work in the laboratories indicated that scientific work could be broken down into different levels.

Work level 1

The work undertaken in the research laboratories at this level was predominantly defined output following agreed procedures and bench routines. It often involved assistance in areas such as laboratory experiments, including relatively routine analysis, which would require some tertiary qualification in chemistry or biochemistry to ensure that the correct protocols were both understood and accurately followed. The titles of the jobs, such as technical assistants, reflected the nature of this work.

Work level 2

The work typically entailed being in a position to accurately set up and run experiments and *interpret* the results. To meet the required accountability, this involved quite detailed knowledge of a body of scientific theory often referred to as part of a discipline. The titles encountered tended to move from assistant scientists to scientist. In this context one could expect capable university graduates with a good degree to begin work in level 1 jobs and move to level 2 scientific posts in about two years. A scientist with a PhD intended as preparation for a research career should start, for example, in the equivalent of work level 2 and move fairly rapidly to work level 3.

Work level 3

At this level the jobholder used existing science and technology to establish methodology and programmes to deal with concrete requests from the business that required a scientific solution or application. Although the solution was new, it did not demand discovery or invention. The science required was *development*. Job titles at this level included senior scientist or assistant principal scientist.

A note of caution at this stage about titles: as already indicated, the very titles used in the laboratories reflected a certain ambivalence as to their true role. As it emerged that these laboratories were over-managed, different titles on occasion straddled more than one work level. Titles were inconsistently applied across the different laboratories. They did not mean the same thing, or involve the same nature of work, even within the same programme. It was noticeable that some groups, dissatisfied with the existing nomenclature, had chosen their own variations. As one individual put it: 'This place is a maze: and one which changes almost daily.' It seemed there was a clear recognition of a problem without accurate diagnosis of the cause. Thus, the titles aligned to the different work levels in this chapter can be taken at best as only indicative.

Development

What has emerged thus far is that for the first three operational work levels, scientific innovation culminates in development. It has already been established in Chapter 4 that working to improve the performance of existing physical assets or modifying existing systems or products amounts to development. This is the level of scientific work that often underlines 'the new and improved formula'. The operative word here is 'improved'. New science is not involved. There is no technological breakthrough at this stage. Clever refinement, adaptation, modification (possibly requiring patents to legally protect the innovation) is involved but within given technological, scientific and marketing constraints specified at the outset of a project and bounded by relatively short-term milestones (up to two years) and budgets. The importance of development work is not to be underestimated. It is the lifeblood of innovative marketing programmes aimed at better understanding and meeting consumer needs. Without it, consumer goods companies and others would founder, and their constant challenge is to speed up the innovation chain from product idea to the marketplace. Development time frames are under constant pressure, as the application of software becomes more widespread. As Quinn, Baruch and Zien (1996) have pointed out, 'at the development level, virtually all design of physical systems, sub-systems, components and parts now occurs in software'.

Discipline and innovation

It is a paradox that innovation occurs most regularly within the confines of an orderly and disciplined approach. The principled rigour of the research bench needs to be mirrored in a similarly ordered framework of organization and accountability. While mechanistic rules and structures can stultify scientific endeavour, as Burns and Stalker (1961) and French and Bell (1973) have pointed out, their organic and dynamic organization models do not espouse disorder and chaos. Unclear missions, objectives, priorities and accountabilities for operational and/or strategic innovation spawn confusion and frustration, which is reflected in a waste of talent and indifferent output and results.

The work of Professors Wheelwright and Clark of the Harvard Business School has had a very pronounced effect on the thinking and action of Unilever in the area of innovation during the 1990s. Their approach was written up in 1995. It led to a major revamping of the innovation process at Unilever, with the introduction of an innovation funnel (of which more below) to ensure an optimal flow of ideas into products and on to the marketplace. Part of this innovation overhaul was the establishment of what became known as the consumer/technology matrix, already referred to in Chapter 4: see Figure 5.3.

Referring to Figure 5.3, the operational levels of science (up to work-level 3) would relate to Brand support, Derivative products, and Platform products. As can be seen from Figure 5.3, the degree of enabling technology or science is fundamentally incremental, or

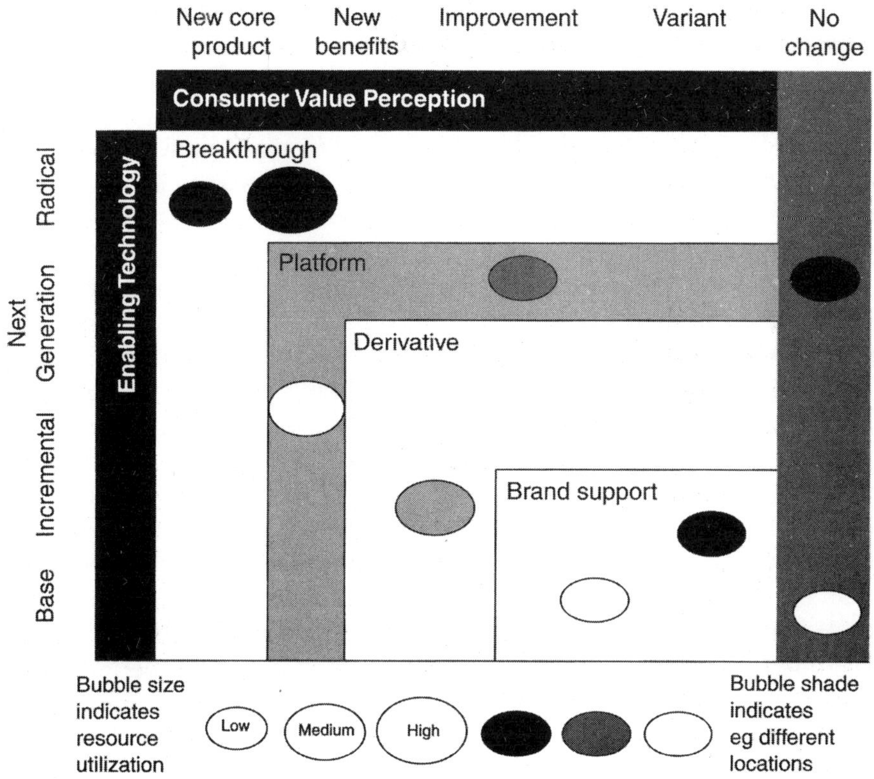

Figure 5.3 *Consumer/technology (C/T) matrix*

developmental at this stage. The fundamental change takes place in the Breakthrough quadrant (of Figure 5.3), which involves the migration from development to research, from operational to strategic innovation, from level 3 to level 4. As already indicated, this is a critical divide. There is no guarantee that the holder of a PhD will make a good research scientist at the strategic level, but he or she might become a good manager of operational scientists or, to put that another way, the presence of scientists at level 4 does not necessarily mean that a laboratory is doing either applied or pure research.

Work level 4

This is the level at which *research* begins. The scientist is accountable for spotting and closing gaps in existing bodies of scientific theory. This involves genuinely abstract work and mental modelling.

Fundamental experimental design based upon radical hypotheses is called for, as is the modelling of complex phenomena and the interpretation of the experimental results that lead to the discovery of new linkages in scientific theory. At work level 4 this would typically amount to *applied research*. The work is still firmly linked to practical data about markets, science and technology. This linkage is the source of a defined and identified need, which will be the catalyst of any major innovation.

At this level (eg principal scientist in Unilever), the individual's work would normally be externally recognized by other leading academics (some such scientists are university professors) and usually the incumbent will have built up a list of internationally recognized referees, have established a scientific track record, together with published papers and invitations to speak at and participate in international symposiums, as a result of his or her work and reputation.

The *Breakthrough Stage* in product marketing terms would be manifested by being first to market with a core product meeting a permanent and universal need, which exploits a radically new technological or scientific application while also offering unique consumer or customer value. The commercial advantage stems from the fact that the new product meets a previously unmet need offering a new form or function, which stimulates new consumer usage.

Work levels 5 and above

At levels 5 and above, the expected impact of the work is the building of new scientific theory that has an increasingly broad impact on society and even civilization. This is the realm of *pure* or *basic research* – the blue skies of inventors and Nobel Prize winners. The link with existing data, markets and scientific applications is increasingly tenuous as the exploratory process moves into unknown and serendipitous territory. The consumer/technology matrix links back to DMA as follows: Derivative and Platform innovations equate to the operational levels, ie up to and including level 3. This would be development. A simple example would be another perfume variant in an existing range of deodorants applying existing technology without a significant shift in consumer perception or behaviour.

Breakthrough innovations would equate to strategic levels, ie 4–6. This would be research. An example might be the discovery of appropriate laser technology to clean clothes. This would reshape the technology of cleaning equipment (probably decimating the white goods industry) and would radically change consumer perception and behaviour.

Harnessing creativity

One misconception about the DMA model of accountability is that it implies that creative ideas can only occur at the top of the organization when 'we all know that anyone anywhere in the organization can be the source of a brilliant new idea'. Accountability for creativity should not be confused with the practice of creativity. In fact, as will be shown later in this chapter (see 'Multi-hatted responsibility'), combining tasks of strategic innovation with those of operational management is not a recipe for success. However, a manager at the top of a unit is responsible for stimulating and harnessing a flow of suggestions and ideas that might progress through a project stage to emerge as successfully launched policies, systems or products. This crystallized in Unilever during the 1990s as the 'innovation funnel'. The inspiration for this came from Kim Clark, Professor of Business Administration at Harvard Business School, adapted from research he had undertaken into the work of engineers in the automotive industry.

The basic purpose is to stimulate ideas, which are then scrutinized against common standards and criteria to determine which should attract project resource and progress through predetermined screens to implementation. The key stages are idea generation, tests of feasibility and capability, which if met, result in launch. While ideas are encouraged from all sources, those in operational levels can be responsible for progressing projects through the funnel while those in strategic levels would be accountable in the main for managing the screens and deciding which projects should progress further and which should not. Indeed, for strategic projects with, for example, global reach, the screens would be part of the governance process.

Ashok Ganguly and Antony Burgmans, the Chairman of Unilever NV, adapted Clark's funnel to drive innovation in Unilever: see Figure 5.4.

In this model, the Charter gate could be managed up to work level 3. In a large, complex organization the Contract gate accountability would reside at a strategic level, for a global product probably not less than work level 6.

In the absence of such an overall framework, it is amazing how disruptive and demotivating creative departments can become as they slide into a downward spiral of less successful output and more frenetic activity. I have seen this with young marketing directors who

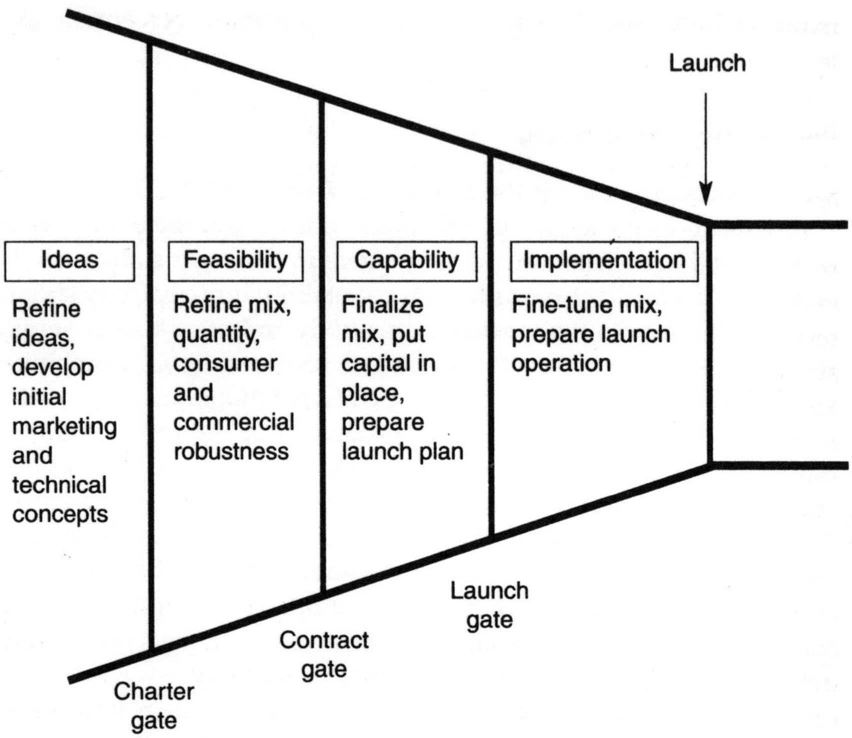

Figure 5.4 *The innovation funnel*

want to stimulate creativity 'with everyone in everything together', in the name of teamwork with 'multi-attendees at muddled and time-consuming meetings with seemingly unending agendas' in pursuit of the 'big idea'. It is a basic confusion of style and accountability.

Multi-hatted responsibilities

There are different pressures in organizations that encourage the wearing of more than one hat of responsibility.

For the accountants, it is cheaper. For the organization development specialists it is the outcome of the matrix organization. Some might feel that people cannot serve two masters, such as God and mammon, and yet we are encouraged to 'render under Caesar what is Caesar's and to God, what is God's.' Can the logic of DMA throw any light on this subject?

Experience suggests that in small departments *within the operational levels* (1–3) managers can successfully wear two hats. For example, the manager of a small buying department with subordinates at work levels 1 and 2 might also be able to operate as a specialist or chief buyer as well as running the department. It works most effectively if the manager has level 3 buying responsibilities in a specialist area. But combining job responsibilities (even in small departments) *across the operational/strategic divide* is not recommended.

I have seen strange combinations where, for example, global responsibilities have been combined with the somewhat menial task of administering the board's payroll. In this situation the short-term operational requirements tend to override the more important strategic issues. 'Bad work drives out good' according to the well-known dictum. This was confirmed from interviews with various members of this department. One noted somewhat whimsically, 'On implementation, I do not report to anybody'. Another commented: 'According to the chart I report to X, but I hardly ever see him, in fact I do not know whom I report to'. (The evaluation notes referring to this interview concluded: 'yet again we have confirmation that there is no real line of accountability in this department'.) Yet another individual confirmed, 'I see my boss about once a month.' This is abdication, not delegation, and seems to be symptomatic of mixing strategic and operational responsibilities. Those who had to deal with this department bemoaned its obsession with detail, together with its inability to make timely decisions.

The combining of strategic and operational work in large departments or divisions is also not recommended. Experience in Latin America and Europe reveals that it can cause great stress.

Given the general theme of this chapter, let us look at an example from the research side of the business. First, perhaps, let us be clear what the double-hatted role is not. It is not a person in work level 4 managing 100 scientists in levels 3 and 2 who are engaged in operational levels of science. That is a clear case of a level 4 role with managerial responsibilities, albeit in the area of innovation. What is being referred to here is someone who is expected to do *both* strategic innovation *and* manage 100 subordinates. Experience indicates that this is an impossible combination of tasks and usually the one that suffers is the level 4 innovation role. This is the old dilemma of the career path for specialists versus generalists, who become responsible for administrative and managerial work. If strategic innovation is the expectation of the work, it is incompatible with extensive management and departmental responsibilities. Invention and the management of others are not easy bedfellows.

A typical example of this confusion of roles comes from the interview notes of a person designated Principal Scientist, Technology Platform Leader and Unit Manager. Even the elaborate title hints that the job is straddling the strategic/operational divide. When the incumbent was asked: 'What is your most important job?' the reply was quite revealing. 'As far as I am concerned it is the role of Principal Scientist. However, the company thinks that the Platform Manager role is the most important and the laboratory thinks that the Science Unit Leader role is the most important!'

Finally, even major roles *combining different levels of strategic work* (for example, work levels 4 and 5) seem to be unworkable. Again an example from research (although others could be provided) illustrates the point. At one stage, Unilever attempted to combine its research laboratories around the world into a single Borderless Division. The aim was to have 'project teams operate freely across the current borders of geography, hierarchy and functional specialism' according to a Unilever Research and Engineering paper in 1992. A critical feature of this organization was the combining of the roles Head of Laboratory and Head of Research for different product areas of the business. The former would warrant work level 4 in its own right and the latter work level 5 as a rule. Doubt quickly emerged, among those asked to carry out the combined role, about its viability, because:

- there were different kinds (and levels) of work each of which required full time commitment;
- the combined burden of work was too great;
- different models of the combined roles emerged in the different laboratories to handle the workload, which was seen as proof that the model could not work as envisaged;
- new roles, such as deputy and assistant, emerged in the laboratories to cope with the workload;
- interviews revealed that none of those working in the role, or close observers of its operation, believed it was either working or would work.

This doubled-hatted role was subsequently dismantled. Although this particular organizational solution did not work, it does not invalidate the idea of a 'borderless laboratory'.

CONCLUSION

This chapter has demonstrated that the logic of the DMA solution set can guarantee that workforces are truly empowered and creative talent is fully utilized. Identifying line and support roles helps dispel myths about the number of direct subordinates one can manage. The disciplines of consumer value matrices and innovation funnels can be most effective when coupled with the identified levels of accountability. The dangers of multi-hatted roles were outlined, especially when straddling the borderline of operation and accountability.

Analysis of the different levels of accountability highlighted how some of the problems of organizing 'creative' work can be resolved. Over-managed hierarchies, blurred accountabilities, excessive operational work, diffuse teamwork together with disorganized and poorly defined project work (which is covered more fully in Chapter 10), are unfailingly exposed by the X-ray of the DMA probes.

To test whether your organization is really empowered, or whether your creative units are optimally organized, apply the six steps outlined in the previous chapter. But in step 5, examine spans of control more rigorously, taking into account the contribution of support roles.

6

Broadbanding: fool's gold

Broadbanding of money is the pay phenomenon (fad?) of the 1990s. It was not even mentioned in Ed Lawler's authoritative book *Strategic Pay* published in 1990. Yet by 1993 enthusiasts such as Hofrichter described it as 'The most effective pay tool to emerge in recent years'. Experience suggests this is a highly questionable claim.

Chris Ashton (1999) noted, 'As the concept of the flatter, more flexible and more responsive organization has emerged in the 1990s, internal structures and processes changed accordingly. In this type of organization convention-bound hierarchies and grade structures have been consigned to the Corporate Archives and replaced by Broadbanding systems.'

Others, such as Brown and Armstrong (1999), were more circumspect about the effectiveness of broadbanding.

WHY BROADBAND?

During the 1980s most leading international companies recognized that their hierarchies had grown out of control. Delayering and re-engineering were in vogue. The link with strategy was invariably nebulous.

By the 1990s many businesses had come to the conclusion that, given their flatter organizations, they were left with a surfeit of management grades. There was a growing realization that their grading system(s) had helped spawn the growth of their sprawling structures. Given the simpler, leaner organization structures then emerging, there was a corresponding need for simpler pay structures.

There have been six main claims made for broadbanding pay scales.

1. Less administration

The first reason given for espousing broadbanding was administrative simplicity. As Arabella McIntyre Brown (1997) argued, 'Now that the pyramid has been squashed, companies have had to develop new pay systems to cope. One solution is broadbanding, a system developed in the U.S. to simplify highly fragmented and hide-bound public sector organizations.' This initiative quickly migrated, with the help of consultants, to the private sector. Some companies, such as General Electric, took extreme steps and collapsed 27 position grades into 7 or 8 bands.

Others were less radical, such as Pepisco, who folded 10 executive levels into 5 pay bands. Broadbanding reduces burdensome administration, it is argued, because fewer grades mean less work on job evaluation, administrative changes to salaries and benefits. Market alignment is also easier and less complex. Fewer pay reviews and committees are required to manage the system on an ongoing basis.

2. Greater flexibility

The second reason cited for adapting broadbanding is that it affords greater flexibility. Alison Smith put the typical argument forward in 1996: 'Broadbanding is being used to reflect the flatter organization structure and allow more pay for flexibility, while at the same time reducing employee pre-occupation with grade status.' She goes on to say that around a third of all companies have already either introduced this approach or are planning to do so. By 1997 a Towers Perrin European study with a sample of 303 companies reported: 'Over half the surveyed participants (55%) have made changes to their pay and grading structures over the past 2 years, primarily through reducing the number of pay grades and increasing the width of pay ranges. 70% planned to make changes in the next two years.' It is a little worrying that the responses from highly numerate remuneration managers exceed 100 per cent. It seems to suggest that almost half the recent changes had failed within two years! The Towers Perrin report also made the point: 'The prime objective in making such changes has been greater flexibility.'

3. More emphasis on career development

The third reason frequently given for broadbanding is that it enables more emphasis on career development. According to McIntyre Brown, 'Broadbanding encourages team working and lateral career development as pay rises are not dependent on promotions to a higher band.' Lew Nerish of Nabisco was already referring to lateral promotions in 1995. Watson and Wyatt maintained in 1999, 'This more flexible type of framework has been able to integrate reward with individual development focusing employees on "the how" and not just on "the what".' General Electric, for example, labelled its broadbands 'Career Bands'. The company had been concerned that undue focus on its 27 position levels was hindering moves across its 12 businesses. This worked against Jack Welch's desire to emphasize the 'boundarylessness' of the organization. The decision to move to bands was to improve organizational effectiveness, by increasing the speed with which moves could happen; improving resource allocation; providing better career development; and reinforcing the company's values (such as 'boundarylessness', 'stealing with pride', ie 'sharing best practice').

Arabella McIntyre Brown, Alison Smith, Duncan Brown and Michael Armstrong together with the Towers Perrin study, all referred to above, state that broadbanding fosters (lateral) career development.

4. Facilitates culture change

Fourthly, it is believed that broadbanding is an essential feature in the driving of a corporate culture change: for example, enabling greater pay differentiation based on performance, since pay rises are not dependant on promotion to a higher band. GE was also aiming to achieve this with its career bands. As Brown and Armstrong remind us, broadbanding 'reduces unhealthy emphasis on hierarchy, status, job titles and job descriptions. It reinforces culture/mind set change.' The idea is that broadbanding supports a broadly skilled workforce by encouraging employees to evaluate skill acquisition in terms of professional development, not simply grade promotion.

5. More focus on the customer

Fifthly, it is argued that as more companies are preoccupied with focus on the customer broadbanding helps support an external focus. The traditional highly structured system of grades is a reflection of an organization concerned with what is happening internally, which can insulate managers from the outside world. The prevailing culture then is more concerned with plaudits from the boss rather than brickbats from the customer. This internal focus explains why some companies find their grade-creep has outstripped the real growth in the business.

6. Closer link with competencies

Finally, according to Abosch (1995), 'Broadbanding promises to add value by supporting employee efforts to improve their competencies and skills.' Competency-related pay is the other major topic in reward management to emerge during the 1990s and it is not surprising to see the two linked together.

A number of these reasons and future plans are summarized in a table from the Towers Perrin 1997 study already referred to – see Figure 6.1.

It has been quite noticeable in recent years that the number of respondents to questionnaires 'thinking of implementing broadbanding' consistently outstrips the number who have actually done something about it. Is this significant?

BROADBANDING OF WHAT?

Broadbanding in the literature that I have reviewed thus far is synonymous with *broadbanding of money*. It is assumed that fewer grades must be accompanied by broader pay ranges. But there seems to be no agreement as to what constitutes a broadband. The Towers Perrin study already referred to reported, 'The median of pay ranges for management was 30–60% but only 15–30% for non-management' (there was no definition of management). Only 10 per cent were operating with pay ranges of 80 per cent or more, which Wilson (1994) argues is needed for 'genuine broadbanding'.

But is the broader pay range the necessary consequence of fewer grades? Charles Handy's exposition on portfolio careers in 1990 suggests not. He has observed that people are increasingly living

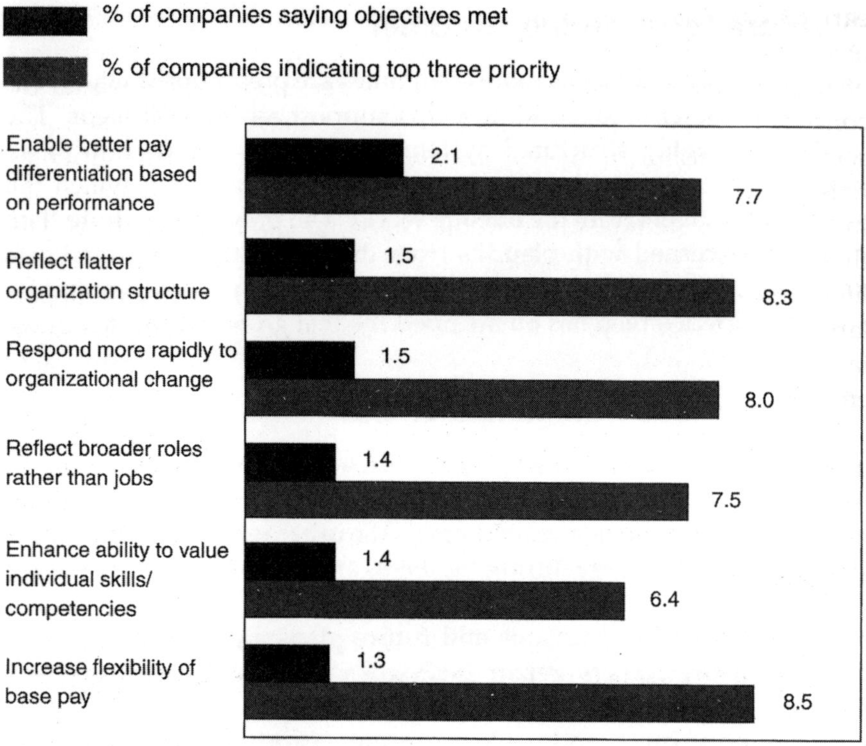

Source: Towers Perrin UK (1977)

Figure 6.1 *Pay restructuring objectives – last three years (percentage of companies reporting pay restrictions)*

portfolio lives, part of which entails a lifetime package of different jobs, projects and contracts and consequently a series of different employers, sometimes in parallel. The net result of this is that people on contract employment are paid a 'rate for the job'. The concept of pay according to a 'range for the job' has become increasingly illogical. Furthermore, the increase in meritocracy, even in Europe, means that young employees are not prepared to accept base pay significantly less than a colleague just because the latter is older and by implication 'wiser'. The grey brigade do not run the world of e-commerce.

These days, base pay is only a component of a more complex total reward strategy in which most leading companies are paying more attention to variable pay, profit sharing, stock options and long-term incentives. Given today's low inflation rates and less punitive tax regimes in many countries, compared to the devastating inflation and high tax rates favoured by the socialist governments of the 1970s and early 1980s, principally in the developed world, people are less obsessed with base salary rates. Concern for survival, then, in a period of unrelenting rises in the cost of living has now been replaced by concern for wealth creation. It is hard to believe that 25 years ago socialist governments in Europe wanted to restrict income differentials to a ratio of 1:5 from the bottom to the top of large organizations. In 1976 it was demonstrated to the Diamond Commission in the UK that, given the then prevailing tax rates and these assumptions, the lifetime net earnings of a university-educated manager running a large factory would be 1:1 to that of an unskilled worker in the same factory. Fortunately today, even governments are a little more enlightened.

The key point, though, is that the emergence of the broadbanding of money is not the solution to today's flatter organization structures. It is not a reward strategy in tune with the real world or the aspirations of young executives. Societal trends are moving in precisely the opposite direction.

SHORTCOMINGS OF BROADBANDING MONEY

If the last statement is correct, what about all the advantages of broadbanding listed above? The fact that a CEO lists a series of objectives as the rationale for restructuring a business, or an HR director claims as the advantages of broadbanding, does not guarantee they are achieved in practice.

For example, Unilever's management reward policy since the late 1960s has stated that the company pays for responsibility, performance and potential. A close examination of the facts in 1993 revealed that practice was not in line with stated policy. The company operated with overlapping pay scales (which is still commonplace in the market, especially in those companies that have broadbanded). It was possible therefore, and not unusual, for an older subordinate, high in his or her pay range, to be paid more than a younger boss. Or to put it more starkly, the person with less responsibility was paid more. An examination of discrimination on the basis of performance was even more disturbing. The average difference between the best and the worst performers was less than 2 per cent. When this was first revealed to key managers around the world, the common reaction was 'that is a typical European problem'. But the virus was surprisingly resistant and widespread. No major continent exceeded the 2 per cent average figure. The North American top management had the most entrenched 'entitlement mentality' despite their much-vaunted 'performance culture' (this is also reflected in the region's attitude to variable pay and huge stock packages which are notably devoid of performance criteria). As Crystal has pointed out in a study of 459 US companies in 1991, 'performance does not account for more than 5% of the variation in CEO pay'. Finally, when the compa-ratios (pay position as a percentage of the range maximum) of designated high potential managers were compared with their corresponding non-high-flying colleagues they emerged on average 10 per cent worse off. The company's best managers were therefore generally the cheapest for head-hunters to attract! Intriguingly, but not altogether surprisingly, the one thing that did correlate positively with pay was, in fact, age. On average, the older you were the better you were paid (and try selling to older managers in the upper echelons of an organization the need to pay more only to their younger subordinates!). This outcome was not what stated policy would have led one to expect. Thus it does not follow that the well-articulated reasons purporting to favour broadbanding are put into practice.

Let us therefore examine the reasons for broadbanding in that light.

CRITIQUE OF REASONS FOR BROADBANDING

Administrative simplicity

In essence the argument here is itself utterly simplistic. If the presence of too many grades is ineffective, fewer must be better. In principle this is right but experience shows that finding the right answer is actually far more complex. Grading structures and job evaluation systems do have their logic, albeit often increasingly of limited value these days. To replace a creaking system of outmoded logic with one of no convincing logic is not a recipe for success. It is very difficult to uncover evidence that proves that broadbanding is easier and simpler to manage. It is certainly not reflected in cost savings. A Watson and Wyatt survey of 69 companies in 1999 found that for 85 per cent of these organizations the impact of broadbanding on their payroll was neutral. As one US compensation and benefits expert explained to me, 'The first result of broadbanding is more work. The line manager no longer has a merit increase guideline based on elements such as performance, position in the range and time since the last increase. There is no longer a tight framework, which minimizes the scope for error. There is a wide band, which increases the chance of paying off market. As there is the budget guideline on increases the immediate need to is call for market data, which actually tends to create more tension between line and HR management.' Obviously the success of this approach depends on the quality of external market data. Brown and Armstrong remind us that the redesign of pay structures into fewer bands is the relatively easy part. The management of pay within the chosen bands, generally on the basis of performance and contribution, is by far the more difficult. They then indicate that two of the seven organizations they researched had experienced industrial action as they introduced their new structures because of concerns about the fairness and adequacy of the appraisal system being advocated. Broader bands from the union perspective gave greater scope for the 'blue-eyed-boy syndrome' to have an effect on pay. As one bank found, a move into broadbands was a recipe for trouble. Thus, despite the claims to the contrary, the pragmatic evidence points to no reduction in cost or workload given the introduction of broadbanding. If there is an optimal way to organize (which is the basic thesis of this book) then why let pay degenerate into a lottery?

When visiting companies that had already broadbanded I was surprised to find they had no rationale for the answer they had arrived at. If they previously had a system of 20 grades it might now be reduced to, say, 5. When asked why 5 and not 4 or 6 there was invariably no convincing explanation. The thinking seemed to be, if 20 is too many, then anything less than 20 must be better, and in fact the fewer the better. *The fundamental flaw in the argument for broadbanding of money is the complete absence of a conceptual model to identify both the appropriate number of bands and the width of those bands.* Given the lack of an underlying paradigm for broadbanding, the call for simplicity is really little more than a beguiling siren.

In practice, the fewer the bands, the wider the ranges. Invariably these overlap. Yet, as already indicated, wide overlapping ranges seem to be counter-cyclical to individual and societal needs. Wide ranges seem to mask muddled thinking about market position. Wide ranges can lead to cost inflation, as everyone is entitled to drift to the higher maximum. This has already led some companies (for example, Johnson & Johnson) to abandon broadbanding.

Charles Peck, the compensation expert at the Conference Board in New York, has pointed out that seeking market data on each job in a broadband turns every job into a grade. This is an administrative nightmare worse than that of any grading system.

Affords greater flexibility

This claim stems from the belief that the dismantling of an overly structured and bureaucratic approach of too many grades results in greater flexibility automatically. Although the broadbanding of money has not yet stood the test of time, and I am suggesting it will not, this so-called flexibility is a short-term form of longer-term chaos. The scourge of merit pay systems is subjectivism. The broadbanding systems I have so far encountered have no objective basis or robust paradigm as a bulwark against lack of management competence or old-fashioned favouritism.

Just as successful innovation and experimentation requires some outline of form and discipline, so individuals want the basis of their pay to be objectively and fairly determined. We are all aware that many prejudices lurk beneath the surface of our diverse world. The individual mix of interpersonal relationships and the scope for mistrust are significant. It is nearly 50 years since Jaques' finding that one of two key sources of stress at work was inequitable pay. The current fashion for broadbanding of pay ranges appears to be creating a plausible veneer of equity.

Two of the disadvantages of broadbanding that worry Brown and Armstrong are 'the reliance it places on Line Management and the pressure it places on individual pay and performance management'. GE's corporate compensation consultant, Dan Gilbert, already warned me in July 1995: 'The risk of inequities is higher with broadbanding and there is no conventional way of cleaning them up as there is no structural framework within which to do it.' Which is another way of saying that costs can spin out of control. Which is not the flexibility that most people have in mind when they advocate broadbanding.

More focus on career development

The management development claims of broadbanding are among its flimsiest. In his review of research findings from a 1995 American Compensation Association/Hewitt Survey of 116 organizations, Ashton (1999) noted, 'By far the two most significant areas which were less effective after Broadbanding were compensation system complexity and employee focus on promotional opportunities.'

The most common problem encountered is the concern of managers who feel less sense of advancement and earning of 'stripes' once the edifice of job classes or grades is dismantled. The psychological glow afforded by years of administrative promotions is not easy to extinguish. Administrative promotions are a negative legacy of excessive hierarchies and their concomitant bureaucracy combined with a lack of open discussion about real promotion prospects in many cases. Broadbanding is a step in the right direction but the lack of a robust and unequivocal framework suggests that the new state might be merely an alleviation of the former, not a solution. The fundamental problem of administrative promotions remains, which, with broadbanding, are perceived to be more limited than previously.

Broadbanding supports culture change initiatives

This is such a nebulous claim that it is hard to prove or disprove. But so far there has been little substantive data to make the case. Furthermore, no one seems to define exactly what this culture is, how it has been modified and where it has improved. The nearest we have come to this seems to be the assertion that broadbanding complements a flatter organization structure. But the reality seems to be a tendency towards more subjective analysis and assessment. There is also evidence from discussions in the United States in particular that the technique of broadbanding is being seen as another faddish fashion, which is already close to running its course. It is arguably of no benefit to employees who see it as just another device to save money. Thoughtful managers are critical of the abstruse and woolly thinking behind it. I have not yet come across any convincing evidence that demonstrates that broad pay bands have had a noticeable and measurable positive impact upon culture, however defined. The claim that broadbanding drives culture change is spurious.

Broadbanding is said to facilitate external as opposed to internal focus

Here again there is scant evidence to support this glib claim. At best it seems to be neutral, neither helping nor hindering focus on external constituencies. Many existing job evaluation schemes have a factor or criterion aimed at assessing external challenge. Simply burning and slashing 24 grades to 8 or whatever does not basically alter the situation. The fact that grade-creep obsession is diminished does not guarantee that more energy is thereby expended on consumers, customers and suppliers. In fact experience to date indicates that poorly designed broadbanding schemes generate plenty of internal angst as familiar and comfortable landmarks are removed and replaced by others that are more puzzling and difficult to understand. In 2003 I have also seen evidence that grade-creep re-emerges after a few years.

The better link with competencies

The sixth stated reason for broadbanding is that it facilitates competency-linked pay.

The competencies bandwagon of the 1990s seems to be approaching quicksand and competency-related pay appears to be going in the same direction. The subject of competencies is fraught with problems of definition. Competency high priest Richard Boyatzis acknowledged this at the third Italian Competencies Conference in Rome during 1998. Sparrow (1998) is even more trenchant: 'No self respecting text book on Occupational Psychology would include a chapter on Management Competencies.' He went on to say, 'Along with the language of competencies have come methodologies of variable quality, some muddled thinking and unease among psychologists about what is really being tested and assessed. The unease is heightened by the prospect that these may soon form the basis of many people's pay. There is an adage among reward consultants. "If you can't measure it, you can't pay for it".'

The problem is that competencies are variously defined. In some companies they are defined as skills, and where accurately identified help establish pay for performance. In others, such as Unilever, competencies are designed to help uncover potential, with pay aligned accordingly. There are other cases where the understanding of competencies seems to be a mishmash of the two. In fact even Boyatzis's (1982) own definition does not offer much light in this murk: 'A motive, trait, skill, aspect of one's image or social role or body of knowledge which he or she uses'.

If the foundation of competencies-linked pay is built on definitional sand it is hard to see how an effective broadbanding pay system can be constructed as a consequence. Pay for the person, not the job, always looks attractive, but in practice both are needed. Much of today's competency-related pay seems to be a return to the imperfect leadership trait theories of the 1950s. As Morgan McCall (1998) has noted, 'Even though it has been known for decades that no single set of traits defines all successful executives in all situations, the belief that it does has been resurrected in one-size-fits-all competencies.' (Ironically, leadership theories began with 'Great Man' theories but were debunked by contingency theorists, only to re-emerge as 'competencies'.)

If competencies amount to little more than personal characteristics such as self-image, attitudes, values, traits and motives then assessment is apt to be subjective. This is not a sound basis for any pay system irrespective of width of pay band.

McCall has also warned, 'Competencies also have their dark side':

For		
Team player	read	Not a risk taker
Biased towards action	read	Reckless
Analytic thinker	read	Afraid to act
Innovative	read	Impractical
Customer-focused	read	Can't control costs
Good with people	read	Soft, too easy on people
Has global vision	read	Unfocused

The claim that broadbanding forges a closer and by implication a more effective link with competencies is both unproven and of very dubious value.

Although the six reasons initially given for advocating a move to broadbanding look plausible, experience to date suggests they are illusory.

THE INADEQUACIES OF THE BROADBANDING OF MONEY

Unilever, led by Herwig Kressler, the then Head of Remuneration, looked very closely at introducing broadbands as a potential pay solution for 20,000 managers around the world. It was rejected because there was concern that a defensible basis for a universal model or set of reliable principles could not be found. 'Favourable results' seemed to be vague and suspect. It seemed at best to be only a band-aid, a temporary solution with no guarantee that it would solve our underlying problems relating to pay for responsibility, performance and potential.

Loss of cost control

The experience of other companies revealed more problems than success. Loss of cost control had already derailed some initiatives.

There was a widespread preoccupation among practitioners about how to establish a glass ceiling within the bands, particularly if they were 100 per cent or more. But efforts to get a better grip on costs led to a concomitant series of other problems.

Introduction of sub-ranges within the broadbands

There was a tendency to build sub-ranges (grades in another guise) within the bands. This in turn led to the undermining of the career development benefit if new bureaucratic hurdles to financial progress through the band started to appear.

The net result seemed to be demotivation and cynicism about the introduction of broadbanding. It had also emerged that broadbands were difficult to sell and even more burdensome to administer.

In summary, it emerged that broadbanding of money was not a viable solution and the evidence of those who had embarked on the broadbanding journey was inconclusive at best.

Others seem to have come to the same conclusion. In December 1999, Michael Armstrong said, 'Many firms are struggling to apply Broadbanding. The Lloyds Register think the solution for them is Broadbanding but they are not sure how to get there... There is enormous diversity of models but budgetary control is the main mechanism for control. Never underestimate the amount of support and guidance Line Managers need. Ownership by Line Management is often rhetoric.'

At the beginning of 2000, when reviewing the Chartered Institute of Personnel and Development's research into broadbanding, he concluded, 'The research has squashed once and for all any idea that there is such a thing as "best practice" when applied to pay systems. It is best fit that matters, and a contingency approach is the one usually adopted.'

An unprofessional solution

No self-respecting profession allows 'Anything goes'. As Hilmer and Donaldson (1996) have pointed out, 'Membership in a profession requires mastery of an evolutionary body of knowledge that typically takes years to learn and apply skilfully.' In admitting there are no objective standards to explain how broadbanding of money works, the HR profession is in danger of shooting itself in the foot. This is not the case with the broadbanding of accountability.

BROADBANDING OF ACCOUNTABILITY

Given the inadequacies of the broadbanding of money, an approach based on the *broadbanding of accountability* was proposed. This was based on the DMA principles, namely the mapping of decision-making accountability throughout the organization. Levels of accountability, subsequently implemented as work levels, were the foundation. They represented the unshakeable conceptual model and set of universal principles on which pay ranges could also be built. However, as we shall see, the pay solutions adopted in CRA, Unilever and Tesco, all differed in design.

Linking pay and DMA

The Unilever board, when reviewing the inadequate delivery against policy principles of competitive pay for responsibility, performance and potential, had to decide whether the policy itself needed modifying. After careful deliberation it reaffirmed the core policy principles as still relevant to the strategy of the business in the 21st century. But it also recognized that key changes were required in the design of job evaluation, reward management and appraisal along with marked improvements in their delivery by management. It reconfirmed that any policy must be designed to:

- 'support flat and flexible organization structure, while recognizing and rewarding higher levels of added value;
- differentiate significantly between the "good" and the "best" performance;
- reward results;
- facilitate international and cross functional management development and mobility;
- compete with a select sample of leading companies;
- respond to varying market conditions around the world with a cohesive compensation framework.'

Reward strategy

The next key step was to clarify the appropriate reward strategy, of which pay would be a critical part, given the business strategy that had unfolded during the competitive scramble for new markets following the collapse of communism at the beginning of the 1990s.

Business strategy

Unilever's corporate purpose aims to 'Satisfy the everyday needs of people everywhere'. To achieve this it saw itself as a 'multilocal-multinational' with a diverse network of management who, because of their international experience (90 per cent of those in work level 5 and above had worked outside their home country at least once), should be able to move ideas, systems, products and best practice around the world more quickly than their competitors. This is a core competence. In the final analysis competitors can copy or replicate anything the company does except the way that the organization works together.

It is important that the reward strategy, in practice, enhances the business objective. An international business conglomerate of independent fiefdoms would not need to invest in reward and management development systems, which facilitate a culture of international sharing.

Market position

The next key step is to agree the overall market position an organization wishes to adopt as a result of its strategy and policy. Given the shaky conceptual foundations of broadbanding of money, identifying a clear market position becomes increasingly difficult. The result is the emergence of simplistic mythology about the market, job families and pay benchmarks. After all, if you have not got a reliable methodology for identifying responsibilities, how can you match corresponding roles and responsibilities in other organizations, which is at the heart of market measurement? There is always a wide constellation of pay points for any commonly labelled job in any market. It is impossible to capture all of these in one broadband as a rule, although some companies seem to do so in an attempt to 'reflect the market'. The trick is to identify a relevant and sustainable position within this pay universe. The fact that so many companies blithely state that their objective is to be 'in the upper quartile of the market' illustrates the amateur depths to which much reward management has sunk as they all pursue the holy grail of the upper quartile.

Profile of reward package

Part of the answer to the market position includes a decision about the profile of the reward package. What are to be the key components? Will they include base pay, variable pay, profit sharing, stock options, long-term incentives and benefits? What mix is appropriate?

What needs to be common, at what level, if cohesiveness of an international management network is considered important? How will the package in Shanghai vary from that in São Paulo? The answer to these questions will narrow the pay band options.

Pay options within a broadband of accountability

Multiple ranges per broadband

One option is to construct more than one pay range per band or work level. This is the option favoured by Jaques and the Brunel school. See Table 6.1.

Progression rates

Jaques (1989) also believes that 'Individuals feel comfortable with pay brackets about 30% from bottom to top.'

The problem with Jaques' 30 per cent spread is that my experience of markets in about 100 countries indicates that progression rates vary considerably. The idea of a standard 30 per cent spread is becoming increasingly meaningless. In smaller countries with more meritocratic traditions, such as those in Scandinavia and Australasia, progression rates are relatively flat. In the more hierarchical cultures experienced in parts of Europe, Asia, Latin and even North America, the progression rates steepen towards the top of the organization. The trend towards steeper progression rates is increasingly being seen as one of the immoral features of unbridled capitalism, which seems to be an expression of ego and greed needs at the top of organizations. As Charles Handy reasoned in 1997, 'When senior executives of companies earn 50, sometimes even 100 times the pay of their own workers, it is hard not to feel that it is an affront to those workers.' He also notes that 'A society that does not recognize the morality of "enough" will see excesses arise which verge on the obscene as those who have first

Table 6.1 *Relating pay ranges to work levels*

Work levels	**Pay grade**
Etc	**Etc**
	3C
3	3B
	3A
	2C
2	2B
	2A
	1C
1	1B
	1A

choice of society's riches, appropriate them for themselves. Democracy will not long tolerate such an abuse of the market.' Witness Enron, WorldCom and the demise of Andersen Consulting in 2002, not to mention the NYSE's Grasso in 2003.

In reality there is no magic progression rate for percentage spread within a band if one decides to construct pay bands within a work level. The major advantage of this approach is cost control and the major disadvantage is the accidental enshrining of another system of administrative promotions, with the danger that the pay bands themselves become more important in the perception of the individuals affected by them.

This of course then undermines the whole point of broadbanding of accountability in the first place. Resolving this quandary can lead to throwing out the baby with the bath water. For example, I know of one global company headquartered in North America which threw out the idea of work levels because of the early ideas of 30 per cent pay ranges and three pay ranges per work level: 'We would merely be replacing all our old grades with 21 new ones.' The tragedy in this case was the lack of realization that work levels do not have to support a galaxy of pay grades.

The Unilever pay solution was a variation on the theme of different pay ranges per broadband, or work level. It ensured cost control but led to a dilution of the concept of genuine promotions, one of the major benefits of the broadbanding of responsibility. Indications are that in time this solution will be modified.

Single pay range per broadband

Another option is simply to operate a pay range per work level. This was the approach adopted by the Australasian mining company CRA (now part of RTZ).

In 1995 I met Terry Palmer, then Managing Director of CRA, who explained how their approach worked. Their 'strata' (accountability levels) were represented by one pay band, which was aligned to the local market.

Progress through the range was managed by a mid-point. It was only possible to progress beyond the mid-point with the agreement of a group of managers once removed from the individual in question who reviewed these cases on a regular basis.

At the time I discussed this with Terry he indicated that this system had served them well over a period of eight years. It was a pragmatic, non-bureaucratic system. It emphasized the strata of accountability and in doing so helped to change the management development debate away from grade obsession and at the same time provide a proven means of cost control by an equitable management of the mid-point within the range.

'Anchor rates' per broadband

Another way of establishing pay within a work level is by families of jobs or benchmark jobs.

The key task here is to establish relevant criteria relating to size or breadth of job to ensure that the families or benchmarks are reliably assessed within the market.

This is an approach being favoured by Tesco. They could adjust pay for different, but similar, roles within a work level. For example, factors establishing progression. Market benchmarks could be set that would relate to the pay appropriate to, say, three benchmarks in the same work level. The pay for individuals could then be linked to these key reference points.

The advantage of 'anchor rates' or 'pay reference points' is both cost control and flexibility for individual treatment without re-creating administrative promotion steps within the level of accountability.

Pay for the person

The fourth possibility is to design pay within the level based on personal qualities or attributes. At present, that tends to be referred to as competency-related pay. However, the main problem with this approach, as has already been pointed out above, is the difficulty in establishing an accurate definition of the competency or skill. There is great confusion about whether a competency is a skill and therefore influences the performance of an individual or whether in fact it is able to identify ability to take on more responsibility and is then seen as an indicator of potential. The other problem linked with the definitional shortcoming is the problem of measurement. As long as there is confusion about definition, measurement remains unreliable.

It is possible to develop skill-based pay systems. Historically though, these have usually been applicable to employees in level 1, not managers in level 2 and above. In 1999 I helped Gordon Holtshausen design a skill-based pay system for IT staff for the new Global Infrastructure Organization (GIO) of Unilever set up to run the concern's computer operations from just three locations around the world.

The advantage of this approach is that it appeals to individuals because pay is based on the person rather than the job. However, it seems that there is invariably disillusionment with this approach because it so easily becomes subjective and unsatisfactory as a form of assessment in a meritocracy. But as we managed to show, that need not be the case.

This approach probably works best at the top of the organization since the number of positions in any sample is very small and they can be market priced relatively easily and the contribution of the individual appropriately taken into account.

SUMMARY

It has been shown that broadbanding of money has not delivered its promise. In stark contrast, the broadbanding of accountability at CRA, Unilever and Tesco has been more successful.

Step 7

The seventh step in designing a healthy organization is to set the reward strategy, establish the market policy and then decide which of the four pay-per-work-level options outlined in this chapter is the most appropriate.

The purity of any approach will inevitably be compromised to some extent by pragmatism at the point of implementation. When embarking on a massive change across many countries at one point in time, the balance has to be between the ability of people to digest the amount of change required together with sufficient understanding to protect the integrity of the new process. The main message in the context of broadbanding is not to confuse the broadening of accountability levels with the broadbanding of money, since the latter is fool's gold.

7

The salmon fallacy

It is now well established that large successful companies that have stood the test of time develop their own talent. Collins and Porras (1994) have undertaken convincing research on this topic. Current popular mythology would have us believe that not so long ago everyone had a job for life and now no one has a job for life. However, the so-called war for talent is also recognized as a critical factor in achieving sustainable, profitable growth: 'For companies that are already great growers, their talent pool gives them an advantage. It takes skilled and energetic people to create growth, but growth itself is the best magnet for talent' (Baghai, Coley and White, 1999). Companies need talent and they need to retain it. Increasingly the best are doing something about it.

THE SALMON FALLACY

This chapter introduces the Salmon Fallacy, the belief that if 100 salmon are swimming slowly upstream and 10 are culled, the other 90 will then swim faster.

It highlights how leadership development cannot succeed if the focus is only on the individual to the neglect of the organizational and environmental constraints that the individual has to cope with. The importance of context will be highlighted. Lack of context is the reason most leadership development programmes fail. The chapter outlines the contribution of the DMA approach to leadership development by showing how leadership competencies can be built upon the seven Elements of DMA.

SUB-OPTIMAL TALENT DEVELOPMENT

Most companies are poor at developing their own talent. A McKinsey Survey in 2000 revealed, 'Only 3% of 6,000 executives occupying the top 200 positions at 50 large US corporations strongly agree that their organizations develop talent quickly and effectively.' It might be argued this is an American phenomenon, but anecdotal evidence suggests it is widespread throughout the world. The fuel for this thinking seems to come from the current belief that the career is dead and therefore individual development programmes are an unnecessary waste of time and money. The underlying problem is that talent development, like any scenario planning, is not an exact science. There is therefore enormous scope for enthusiastic amateurs to move into this area. In 2000, the Head of Management Development in a large multinational, with little to no previous professional experience, argued that to reach the company's growth plan, he felt it was necessary to 'Refresh the executive cadre' by getting rid of 10–20 per cent of those who were not world class. The 'world class' assessment was based on a consultant's model, which measured only three variables from a sample of only about 100 executives!

There are three problems with this approach, which seems to have been first espoused by General Electric under the aegis of Jack Welch. Firstly the framework for assessment was suspect, secondly the approach is unproven, and thirdly the focus was only on the individuals. No account was being taken of the roles, or the organizational context. Did the managers in question have real jobs with clear accountabilities? This is the most common failing of management development executives who focus exclusively on the individual. They tend to ignore the fact that *their salmon are being forced upstream and it is naïve to cull 10–20 per cent in the forlorn belief that the other 80–90 per cent will then swim faster*. It would obviously be better if the 100 per cent could swim downstream. Putting talented individuals in non-jobs, which form part of a cluttered, directionless hierarchy, does not facilitate their personal development.

In 2002/03 I saw this approach applied across Europe in a company that believed in leadership development. The company carefully recruited trainees who it believed had potential. As part of the accelerated development programme these managers were in due course promoted into small executive teams running operations in each of the different countries. Then the diktat came from the corporate office that at least one member of each executive team had to be culled in line with the '10 per cent refreshment guideline'. This totally undermined the whole approach to leadership development. It inherently admitted the recruitment process was so bad that the entire management cadre had to be replaced about every 8 to 10 years. It shattered teamwork and created a culture of distrust and disenchantment. Performance management was distorted. The 'survival of the fittest' approach to talent development is wasteful and ineffective. It also assumes leaders are born, not made.

Leaders born or made?

I do not intend to enter the old debate about 'nature versus nurture' in relation to leadership development. Clearly, some have extraordinary natural abilities, which enable them to rise above the difficulties of their situation, to do what they are meant to do. Beethoven received from his father a series of beatings that probably accelerated the deterioration of his hearing (Thayer, 2001). But just as evidently, much of the development of most of us is due to what we have received from our environment, in one way or another. Alexander the Great conquered the world, but had the exceptional Philip of Macedon as his father, and Aristotle as his tutor. (Bose, 2003).

Many executives seem to incline to one side of this debate, however. Morgan McCall (1998) has neatly summed up the most common assumptions:

> Executives, who profess otherwise, usually make two fallacious assumptions about leadership that get in the way of actually developing leadership talent. The first is that leadership ability is, in essence, something that one either has or does not. The second is that the fires of organizational life will test the mettle of the contenders and that the fittest will not only survive but will also, more often than not, end up at the top (this particular assumption is most firmly held by those currently at the top).

The last wry comment says a great deal. Most of us are inclined to view things in a way flattering to ourselves; and the view that talent prevails, despite the odds, perhaps because of them, flatters those who have happened to prevail. It also suggests that 'the odds' presented by the current environment are in some obscure way beneficial; and this alleviates some of the burden of deciding how that environment could be improved. But are all difficulties constructive? Do all the problems presented by an organizational environment call forth and develop those abilities needed by leaders? For my money, McCall and Hollenbeck (2002) have the answer: 'Managers are both born and made.' That is the assumption underpinning the contribution DMA can make to developing leaders.

LEADERSHIP DEVELOPMENT

Leadership development is complex. There has been little agreement about how to deliver it in the last 50 years, although according to Bungay and McKinney (2003), the military seem to be better at it than most organizations.

Leadership is an amalgam of factors, which are innate and learnt. A supportive context will derive the best blend and ensure both sets of components are fully developed. But most leadership studies have been mono-centric. They have been built around one idea, or set of ideas. For example talent is innate (Galton, Jaques) or simply the product of experience (Locke) and environment (Howe). In the 1950s leadership was viewed as a set of traits – except no agreement on which traits were the most significant emerged. For some, such as Eysenck, and more latterly Sternberg, the key was assessment of intelligence (IQ). For others, such as Goleman, it was to be the assessment of emotional intelligence (EQ), or in the case of Cattell, the assessment of personality. During the last couple decades of the 20th century, values, skills and competencies entered the HR lexicon. The main problem was, and is, a lack of agreed definitions. This in turn was compounded by the fact that many approaches were a mishmash of values, skills and competencies. Sometimes 'competencies' were used interchangeably with skills (Jackson) and sometimes they were referred to as behaviours (McClelland).

Some approaches were trying to assess performance, some potential, and some both at the same time. It is also true to say that some approaches did not really know what they were trying to assess. Is it any wonder that leadership development and approaches to potential assessment waxed and waned in a sea of confusion, fads, fashions and uncertainty?

A case of confusion

A couple of years ago a major company decided to enhance its supply chain performance. It invested over US $1 billion in new warehouse facilities. As part of this investment it ran an assessment centre to 'objectively chose the right incumbents for the new jobs in the new distribution centre'. So far, so good.

The assessment centre was to select people for the frontline, supervision and management roles. These jobs, especially at the frontline, called for a variety of skills. But the centre was assessing behaviours, not skills. Thus appointments were made on the basis of behaviour observed over a one- to two-day assessment centre. This was tantamount to choosing a heart surgeon on the basis of bedside manner alone.

The new organization structure was not healthy. There were too many layers and confusion about line and support roles. Predictably the new supply chain investment was not producing the planned results. So top management decided to insert another (non-value-adding) layer of management 'to sort things out'. A major investment was undermined by an incompetent approach to the handling of the people issues, which totalled a mere fraction of the total capital cost. Incorrect assessment tools were used to select people. This resulted in people being placed in jobs they could not carry out as they had inappropriate skills. The management structure was too rich, which slowed down the already ineffective decision-making processes. Too many people were at too many meetings addressing the wrong issues. And top management's 'solution' was to add another layer of management at the top of the supply chain structure. This simply aggravated an already bad situation.

Had the company been able to apply the DMA solution set to both its organization design and the assessment, appointment and development of its people it would not have made so many critical mistakes. And yet it was puzzled by the under-performance of its new warehouse set up 'because the company was using the latest HR ideas such as the application competencies and assessment centres'.

Let us now examine the DMA leadership model and the principles underpinning it. Then we can examine how this company might have implemented its US $1 billion investment more effectively.

THE DMA LEADERSHIP MODEL

Figure 7.1 sets out the basis of the DMA leadership model. It rests upon key inbuilt personal qualities, such as IQ, EQ and personality. These are mostly that part of the human iceberg that is below the water. As shown above, there is no real consensus about how these factors develop, are developed and therefore can be measured. But their outcomes can be measured and observed. These are in the main the 'stuff' of values, skills and competencies.

Values and belonging

Values are personal beliefs and attitudes held by individuals, often derived from their understanding of the purpose of life. Values are abstract, such as moral standards and ethics, which govern people's behaviour. Value-based behaviours are 'must-have' qualities. They are the cultural badge of belonging. Everyone in the 'family' must share and practise these beliefs and behavioural norms. Otherwise they should not be in the family. Values are potential derailers if not practised.

Although they show whether an individual fits into the culture of the organizational community, values cannot be used to indicate who has leadership potential. When well designed and practised, values are very powerful determinants of an organization's performance. This is what is often referred to as 'walking the talk', or 'The way we do things around here'. They determine culture.

Recent events in companies such as Enron, WorldCom and Andersen Consulting have shown what happens when values are not clearly spelt out or practised by top management. Lack of values can destroy large organizations. Conversely companies like Tesco and Wal-Mart have shown how an organization can prosper when a value such as 'Customer First' is truly practised and believed in from top to bottom of the company.

Skills and performance

Given the confused state of competency definitions already outlined it is important to note the differences between skills and competencies in the DMA model. **Skills** are the transferable abilities (professional, technical, managerial) that define how a job is to be done. These stem from the demands of the job, which might call for finance or selling

Components of outstanding leadership		
Values	**Skills**	**Competencies**
Personal beliefs/attitudes (derailers/constraints)	Transferable abilities (job requirements)	Level-based behaviours (context-dependent practices)
Value-based behaviours • Integrity • Commitment • Respect for others • Customer focus	**Technical, professional and management skills** • Manufacturing • Marketing • Selling • Buying • Logistics • IT • HR • Accounting • Engineering • Law • Project management • Time management • Change management	**Differentiating competencies** • Setting direction • Harnessing resources • Analysing and deciding • Managing change • Influencing colleagues • Managing the external environment
'Must-haves' Membership	*'Can do's'* Performance	*'Could haves'* Potential

IQ **EQ**	**Energy** Innate qualities **Talent**	**Personality**

Figure 7.1 *The DMA leadership model*

skills or the like. Skills relate to *performance within a level of accountability*, which can be measured by demonstrated capability. As shown in Figure 7.1 these are 'can-do' aspects, which can often be learnt depending upon the innate capacity shown at the foot of Figure 7.1.

It is possible to draw up skill profiles for jobs or roles and for individuals. The degrees of skill required or acquired can also be defined and identified. Unilever, for example, uses four degrees of skill: 'basic appreciation, working knowledge, fully operational and leading edge'. Tesco has three: 'bronze, silver, gold'.

The **gaps** that are apparent from comparing the overlay of role skill requirements and the skills possessed by individuals, represented in the individual profiles, are the **training needs**. These indicate which skills need development and where performance needs to be improved. An example of this overlay of profiles is given in Figure 7.2.

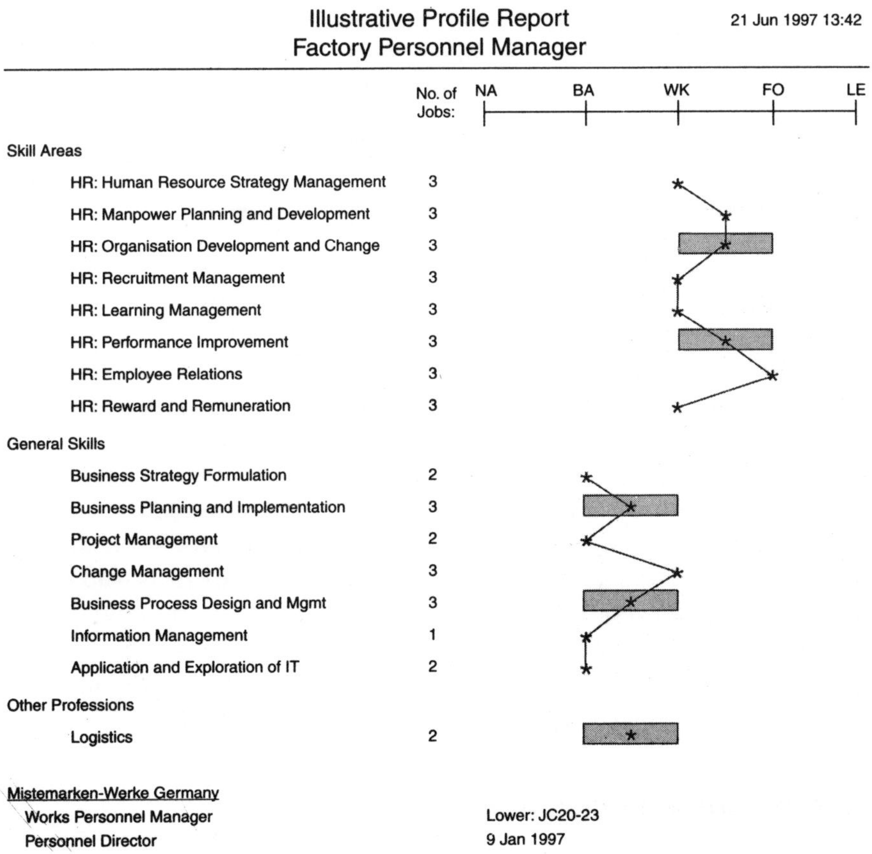

Figure 7.2 *Illustrative profile report*

As demonstrated in Figure 7.1, skills can be **technical, professional** and **managerial** or general. Technical skills might include activities such as marketing, selling, the supply chain, buying, HR and IT. Professional skills could include accounting, engineering and law, for example, whereas managerial skills refer to those skills needed to manage people. Hence the reference to 'project management', and 'change management skills', which are the more general skills that are required whatever the professional or technical skill demands. As one progresses up the levels of accountability the management skills become increasingly important and in most cases the technical skills less so.

The great problem with assessment of performance and skills is they cannot reliably gauge potential to master work at a higher level of accountability. This is because the demands to perform change qualitatively in the highest levels. As will be shown in this chapter, this is critically important when crossing the operational/strategic divide of levels 3 and 4. Yet many organizations use performance in a lower level (or grade) as the sole predictor of future performance at a higher level.

Differentiating competencies and potential

Competencies, on the other hand, define what behaviours are required to get the job done. They are what a person brings to the job, not simply what the job requires. The job or level of accountability establishes the context in which they can be assessed. They are assessed by observing how an individual acts in a given job. Competencies are the behaviours that are required in a level of accountability. Once this is established it is possible to assess a person's capacity or potential to operate successfully at the next higher level of accountability.

Differentiating competencies relate to *potential for progress to the next level of accountability within a defined time period*. The focus is leadership development. Assessment of competencies involves making judgements of a different order of complexity to those required in mapping performance. Robust sources of evidence are required. *Skills are about present leadership and competencies are about future leadership.*

What competencies measure

In 1998 George Klemp, of Canbria Consulting, Boston, USA, analysed the leadership models of 62 of the world's leading companies. He divided competencies into Practices (behaviours) – what people do on the job to get results – and Attributes (skills) – knowledge, skills and other characteristics that enable them to carry out tasks. Eight per cent of the leadership models were pure attribute models, 27 per cent were pure practice models and 65 per cent were a mixture of the two, although Klemp did concede 'there has not been a clear distinction between practices and attributes to provide rigour and conceptual clarity'.

Klemp noted that as many as 77 per cent of the Practices and Attributes recurred. As a result he identified nine 'Mega competencies'. Five were attributes and included IQ, EQ, Ego (akin to personality), technical acumen and personal development (the desire to learn by doing). The four practices were Giving direction, Influencing others, Making things happen (change) and Building relationships. These mega competencies are covered in the DMA leadership model, with the added dimension of Context, the level of accountability.

Context, context, context

Most competency models fail because they are unable to define the context in which they should be practised. *They therefore do not differentiate who has potential to progress to the next level of accountability.* It has already been shown that traditional job evaluation schemes are unable to provide differences between qualitative levels of accountability. Competency definitions out of context are useless. For example a frequent statement in many schemes is, 'is able to see the big picture'. But the different 'big pictures' that have to be viewed by a factory supervisor, the plant director, the global supply chain vice president and the CEO respectively are fundamentally different, and require different abilities and behaviours. The phrase 'is able to see the big picture' is no help if not set in context.

I would be a wealthy man if I had a dollar each time a brand manager told me s/he was 'responsible for strategy'. Brand managers are invariably at level 2, and are not accountable for strategy, although many competency models would allow for such a claim. The advantage of the DMA approach is that it sets the context in which the competencies can be observed and assessed. The competencies are derived from the Elements in the different levels of accountability. Since the Elements identify what decisions are required at each level, they provide a platform which helps align the behaviours needed to perform successfully.

DMA AND LEADERSHIP DEVELOPMENT

Part of the performance/potential conundrum stems from the fact the in assessing Potential one is assessing the ability to perform at the next higher level. But unfortunately good performance in the lower level is not a guarantor of success at the higher level. In order to assess an individual's potential for leadership development it is necessary to match levels of ability with levels of accountability. As Jaques and Cason explained in 1994:

> Any satisfactory measure of potential capability in work requires two things: first, a measure of levels of work: and, second, a method of measuring an individual's potential ability to work at a given level of work: so long as the person values doing that work, has had the opportunity to acquire the necessary skilled knowledge to do so and is not temperamentally handicapped.

One of the problems with this approach was finding companies that measured work in strata or 'levels'. Although Jaques and his colleagues, such as Stamp, have assessed individuals and plotted their 'maturation modes' (see Table 8.1) they were unable to plot these reliably against actual work being done. It was of little value to an individual to be told that s/he had capacity for level 4 if his or her job was calibrated in grades of Hay points. What level does 670 Hay points, or grade M2, or job class 27, represent? The subjective interviewing approach of Jaques and Cason was not readily transferable to hundreds of executives charged with assessing their subordinates' potential. It smacked a little of 'playing god'. Furthermore the Jaques, Cason and Stamp approach was rooted into the limited assessment of strata according only to time span of discretion.

As a final check, a number of my staff and I were subjected to this interviewing methodology. We found it unconvincing.

LINKING DMA AND COMPETENCIES

Unilever adopted a competency model to help identify which managers have leadership potential to progress in to the upper reaches of the organization. The model was developed with Hay McBer, whose work is apparently based on Doug McClelland's theory of unconscious motivation based on his assessments of fantasy behaviour (McClelland et al, 1953). By the time the competency model had been developed the total number of accountable levels of work in the company had also been established. It become clear that competencies needed to be aligned to these levels in order to help predict how individuals might progress through the organization in the future, since competencies were to be predictors of potential.

The individuals on designated potential lists were referred to as 'Listers'. These lists had planning horizons up to five years. These time horizons fitted well with work levels. It was clear that if there were six levels below the board, and most people reached the top of their career after about 25–30 years in the business, then the average time per accountability level for the very best would be about five years. As it happened research conducted into the careers of 26 directors (current and retired), levelling their career history records backwards (this research will be covered in more detail in the next chapter) revealed they did indeed spend five years on average in each work level.

Given the work of Jaques and his colleagues, and the Unilever competency model, not withstanding the imperfections of both, this already provided sufficient evidence to suggest potential assessment can be attuned to the DMA levels of accountability. In fact it suggests this could be done more effectively utilizing these levels than any other known approach to either measurement of responsibility or assessment of leadership capability. The key is to make the connection between the role-based behaviours underpinning the decisions required for each of the DMA elements across the different levels of accountability. This provides a set of general competencies accurately aligned to the work context. This alignment is set out in Figure 7.3.

As can be seen, there are six DMA competencies, since two decision-making elements, Nature of Work and Time frame, relate to the competency of Setting direction. Each of the competencies covers a continuum of increasingly complex behaviours, since the accountability levels progress from operational to strategic.

DMA elements and differentiating competencies

These competencies will help to identify an individual's capacity to handle the scope of accountable tasks at different levels of accountability. *Values, skills and most competency models do not differentiate between levels of accountability.* They are blunt instruments in the field of potential assessment. Since differentiating competencies are general in nature and indicative of leadership capability, they give no

DMA element	DMA competency	Definition *The capacity to:*
Nature of work and time frame	Setting direction	set direction for resources over time
Resource complexity	Harnessing resources	get the best from money, technology and know-how
Problem solving	Analysing and deciding	think analytically and take the right decisions
Change	Managing change	initiate, orchestrate and drive change
Natural work team	Influencing colleagues	win cooperation and commitment from others without the use of formal authority
External interaction	Managing the external environment	influence stakeholders outside the organization to ensure key objectives and mission are met

Figure 7.3 *The DMA differentiating competency model*

indication about an individual's ability to handle the technical or professional content of a given role. These content aspects, or skills, will be most marked in the operational work levels but will generally be less critical in the higher strategic echelons.

These competencies will provide the bedrock for the various career paths or tracks (fully explained in Chapter 8) which individuals may pursue as the growth in their own capabilities matches the needs of the organization, expressed as recognizable career opportunities. The primary focus of these competencies is potential, not performance, although it is acknowledged that the manner of achievement of performance can provide a window into personal qualities which may indicate scope for further growth.

At the end of the day, an assessment of how somebody will perform in a different role in the future is a guesstimate. The contribution of competencies in this context is to help lessen the inherent element of risk. Hence they can also be used as part of an external recruitment exercise as well as an internal assessment of potential. As will be explained below, they can also be used for coaching.

Setting direction

This competency complements the elements of **nature of work** and **time frame**. In order to achieve the core work or objective expected of any role or work level, it is essential that a person is clear about the purpose of the role, understands the totality of the relevant context and sees what needs to be done and how to achieve it. This is an ability to scan political, social, organizational and environmental factors, which will have a bearing on the delivery of results or achievement of the expected objective. This is the capacity that leads to what van Lennep described some 30 years ago as 'taking a helicopter view'.

This has to be done within a specified time. As target cycles lengthen in the higher echelons, more detailed planning and orchestration of events and priorities is called for. These deadlines and milestones are invariably captured in the planning and budget cycles within the organization. Hence the continuum here is from the short-term tactical to the long-term strategic. By way of illustration the full description of this competency across the levels is set out in Figure 7.4.

This format is repeated for each of the other five competencies, and for some clients corresponding negative descriptors are also provided.

Harnessing resources

This competency complements the element of **resource complexity**. (See Figure 7.5.)

This is the ability to marshal resources such as people, budget, technology, systems and the knowledge to deliver the results designated of a specific role in a defined time period. It presupposes good judgement of people, including who to assign to which activities. This competency includes the energy to take initiatives including calculated risks to achieve, and depending on upon work level, improve results. It demonstrates personal task tenacity and follow-through while generating group cooperation and commitment from subordinates where appropriate. This competency is typically shown by a self-confident person, who feels the need to achieve, thrives on feedback and is capable of motivating a team or teams to sustain consistent levels of performance.

An increasingly important resource these days is knowledge. It is possible for some jobs to have strategic accountabilities because of the know-how required, as does a research scientist with relatively small

1. SETTING DIRECTION

DEFINITION *The capacity to set direction and deliver plans over time aligned to the needs of a defined context of accountabilities.*

RELATED DMA ELEMENTS:

NATURE OF WORK
Stems from the purpose of the role and defines where it differs in accountability from those above and below.

TIME FRAME
Focuses on the time over which the impact of the majority of the decisions of the jobholder will be felt.

RANGE

Short-term operational	Long-term strategic
Low level	High level

POSITIVE DIFFERENTIATING BEHAVIOURS

WORK LEVEL 2

- Sets, communicates and holds self and others accountable for delivery of stretching, short-term (up to 12 months) operational objectives.
- Continuously reviews and acts to remove obstacles to achieving progress.

WORK LEVEL 3

- Balances potentially conflicting sub-goals or objectives to achieve an integrated plan and results for an operating unit.
- Identifies trends, patterns and priorities for performance improvement and contributes to plans for the year ahead.

WORK LEVEL 4

- Has a comprehensive view of a function, profession or scientific discipline, and is able to anticipate future needs and opportunities and set new milestones up to three years ahead.
- Able to establish specific objectives and direction from strategic intentions, and establish complete plans from identified but incompletely defined opportunities.

WORK LEVEL 5

- Sets strategy and objectives for a cohesive business entity, which may call for changes in direction, scope or pace of activities to ensure both new and existing plans are met.
- Delivers annual results while balancing this with the need to contribute to and continously achieve longer-term strategic priorites.

WORK LEVEL 6
- Focuses on setting, managing and integrating the delivery of current budgets and an overall strategy for a network of cohesive, often stand-alone, activities within the context of Group-wide plans stretching beyond five years.
- Contributes to the creation of the Group vision, mission, strategy, priorities and values, helping to determine the policy and resource requirements for the organization as a whole.

NEGATIVE DIFFERENTIATING BEHAVIOURS

WORK LEVEL 2
- Spurs itself and others to action without a clear sense of direction and well-conceived objectives.
- Ignores or fails to identify and remove obstacles to progress.

WORK LEVEL 3
- Tolerates and/or does not resolve conflicting objectives within teams at the expense of overall unit or departmental performance.
- Is overwhelmed by detail and fails to identify negative patterns and to act on the causes of poor unit or departmental performance.

WORK LEVEL 4
- Concentrates on short-term issues and immediate results, disregarding drift from longer-term plans, and fails to initiate corrective action.
- Unable to work up a concrete plan of action from an idea or a solution to a problem not previously encountered.

WORK LEVEL 5
- Maintains the current business performance but does not significantly challenge or change existing strategy to deliver better results.
- Has difficulty in simultaneously delivering the annual results for a cohesive business and the long-term plan.

WORK LEVEL 6
- Does not manage the network of activities as a whole. Performance of subordinate businesses tends to be patchy and the overall results are adversely affected as a result.
- Focuses on shorter-term problems and issues within the network which leaves little scope for quality contributions to corporate vision, mission, strategy and values.

Figure 7.4 *The 'Setting direction' competency*

2. HARNESSING RESOURCES

DEFINITION *The capacity to lead people, technology and processes in the direction of change.*

RELATED DMA ELEMENT: **RESOURCE COMPLEXITY**
Defines accountability for resources: people, technology, budgets and know-how.

RANGE

RANGE Maintenance
Reconfiguration

Low level — High level

Figure 7.5 *The 'Harnessing resources' competency*

financial and/or people resources. Consequently the continuum to be managed stretches from maintenance to reconfiguration.

Analysing and deciding

This is the competency that complements **problem solving**. (See Figure 7.6.) It is the ability to reason, think analytically and, when appropriate, conceptually, prior to taking decisive action. It assumes a capacity to develop accurate, objective, bias-free assessments of what needs to be done and in what order. It is the capability of unscrambling data into an orderly format of priorities, which helps clarify relevant actions. In difficult situations this competency presupposes integrity, courage, determination and wisdom. In this case the problem solving required stretches from the concrete to the abstract at strategic levels of accountability. At the latter level the ability to think from first principles is increasingly required.

Managing change

This is the competence that complements the element of **change**. (See Figure 7.7.)

3. ANALYSING AND DECIDING

DEFINITION *The capacity to think analytically in order to solve problems and take appropriate decisions.*

RELATED DMA ELEMENT: **PROBLEM SOLVING**
Describes the nature of problems to be solved and the path to their solution.

RANGE

Concrete	Abstract
Low level	High level

Figure 7.6 *The 'Analysing and deciding' competency*

In a world of ever increasing change, change management and innovation skills are essential. This competency assumes ability to adapt one's own behaviour, continually mastering and learning new approaches and applications in order to develop and ultimately create new solutions. It is the chameleon-like ability to reinvent oneself as the environment continually mutates, and to be capable of new business insights which result in new initiatives, processes, systems, products, services or policies, depending upon the relevant level of accountability.

While there is a certain innate quality to creativity, nevertheless the genuine innovator does learn from experience and experimentation.

4. MANAGING CHANGE

DEFINITION *The capacity to conceive, introduce and drive change.*

RELATED DMA ELEMENT: **CHANGE**
Defines accountability for driving change or innovation.

RANGE

Implement/ modify	Drive 'breakthrough'
Low level	High level

Figure 7.7 *The 'Managing change' competency*

Prototyping and conceptual modelling (which correlate with the previous competency) are a feature of a highly creative person, one who can be single-minded in driving for new levels of performance.

Organizations are innately conservative and non-adaptive, which is why genuinely innovative people steer shy of bureaucracies and why few large organizations have impressive records of timely change or innovation. Those who genuinely recognize the need for change or who, better still, can identify the change solution, are often felt to be mavericks. And as Ricardo Semler demonstrated in 1994, it is much easier to be a successful maverick if you run your own business. The need for genuine change agents within organizations has never been greater. The spectrum of behaviour required moves from the ability to modify and develop existing products or services to be able to deliver breakthrough knowledge and results.

Influencing colleagues

This competency dovetails with **natural work team**. It is the corollary of harnessing resources in the sense that leadership in an organization is power stemming from authority of position, whereas the influencing competency is the power that emanates from the authority and credibility of the person. It is persuasive rather than coercive, cooperative rather than directive, based on an individual's reputation, power-with rather than power-over, which generates rapport and support rather than compliance and obedience. (See Figure 7.8.)

5. INFLUENCING COLLEAGUES

DEFINITION *The capacity to influence others within and across the organization to achieve objectives.*

RELATED DMA ELEMENT: **NATURAL WORK TEAM**
Refers to the lateral collaboration with peers (not subordinates), which is needed to deliver accountabilities.

RANGE

Close — Remote

Low level — High level

Figure 7.8 *The 'Influencing colleagues' competency*

The fundamental ability is that which is required to build effective working relationships horizontally across the organization without the sanction of vertical or hierarchical power. It is the difference required in obtaining results with people rather than from people. Influencing power is at the heart of today's successful flatter organizations. Large institutions with global reach cannot expand quickly and operate successfully without teamwork. Much of modern management is increasingly about project management, and the skill of a project manager is in cajoling results from a temporary team of people who do not report to him/her on a permanent basis since they report to others elsewhere in the organization.

Lateral or network management is one of the critical requirements increasingly called for in the knowledge-rich companies of the 21st century. New technology has made possible virtual teams, virtual organizations, hot-desking and interconnected decentralization. When some writers refer to 'The collapse of hierarchy' maybe these are some of the developments they have in mind. It is a world in which people increasingly depend on one another to get things done, a world in which ability to influence others and win their cooperation is essential for success.

Intriguingly some departments or units protect their status quo by insidiously accusing innovators, who threaten their inertia, of a lack of influencing ability. The conspiracy shield of the mediocre will break the jousting lance of any change agent given weak top management. The continuum of accountabilities here runs from the proximate or close to the distant or remote. In truly global organizations the ability to network constructively is the hallmark of a successful top manager. Conversely, I have found that the most frequent reason for failure at level 5 and above is an inability to influence colleagues across the world and establish credibility and 'credits in the bank'.

Managing the environment with enterprise

This is the competency that correlates with **external interaction**. (See Figure 7.9.)

This is the ability to understand the changing and multiple needs of consumers, customers, suppliers and ultimately all external stakeholders who interact with and depend on the organization's services and products. Mastery of this competency is at the heartland of the organization, since it bears in upon the mission and very reason for existence. Large bureaucracies have, it seems, an inherent tendency to

6. MANAGING THE ENVIRONMENT

DEFINITION	***The capacity to influence others outside of the organization to achieve the organization's objectives.***
RELATED DMA ELEMENT:	**EXTERNAL INTERACTION** Refers to the interactions with consumers, customers, suppliers and significant external organizations (social, political and financial) to ensure the delivery of business objectives at all levels.
RANGE	Reactive — Proactive Low level — High level

Figure 7.9 *The 'Managing the environment with enterprise' competency*

turn in upon themselves and to neglect or even forget their original purpose. This is most markedly the case in large, over-layered hierarchies where those buried in the serried ranks of junior and middle management are filtered from the realities of the outside world. I suspect this is one of the reasons for the success of re-engineering in the late 1980s. The external focus of processes on 'the customer' struck a chord with those who had become understandably disenchanted with inefficient, self-serving bureaucracies. However, in dismantling the disparaged vertical silos of functions they ironically tended to build equally disruptive horizontal process silos. These worked against developing the competencies needed to **harness resources, analyse, make decisions and manage change** outlined above: in short the ability to lead.

One of the increasingly important qualities of truly enterprising managers is a sense of social and moral responsibility. They accept their organization has responsibilities to individuals and society including the environment, present and future. They are concerned to uphold a just and fair code of business conduct, while nevertheless being equally determined to influence the world of consumers, customers and suppliers to the firm's definite long-term advantage. These are managers who are enterprising businesspeople with a sense of social responsibility and cultural sensitivity. Their goal is to create increasing value for all stakeholders in the mix. Their ongoing challenge is how to balance these potentially conflicting objectives and different interest groups while also being creative, decisive leaders. Here the spectrum of behaviour moves from merely reacting to the externalities of the organization to becoming proactive at the strategic levels, working to change the external environment which would otherwise impact negatively on the organization.

Link with values

The DMA competencies differentiate behaviours needed at different levels of accountability. This helps identify individuals with potential for the next level. *Values do not differentiate*. Integrity, for example, is just as important at the frontline as at the top of the organization. In fact after the recent governance scandals such as that of Grasson and the NYSE, there seems to be more need at the top than elsewhere.

Competencies are differentiators, values are derailers (if not practised). As long as this distinction is kept in mind some organizations like to have their leadership development models made up of values and competencies. Where this occurs it seems wise to limit the number of categories to 10 or fewer, bearing in mind Gaugler and Thornton's (1989) findings 'that the accuracy with which assessors classify and rate people declines as the number of dimensions increases'. They felt up to six was optimal.

No executive is perfect, despite the somewhat god-like effect lists of competencies are apt to engender. Nevertheless it is difficult to envisage an effective manager who does not possess something of each of the above competencies. Given the tight alignment with the DMA elements, any major deficiency would probably mean that the incumbent was incapable of delivering the full accountabilities of the job at its current level, and certainly not at the next higher level, given that these competencies are designed to be predictors of potential capacity. Any deficiency or competency gaps are necessarily more serious the more senior the level of accountability and the more complex the mix of competencies required. However, as Figure 7.1 illustrates, some of the gaps can be closed with coaching and development.

Step 8

Distinguish between performance within a level of accountability (skills) and potential to move to the next level (competencies) and build systems to identify both.

DEVELOPMENT RUBICONS AND COACHING

The degree of difficulty required to move across levels of accountability varies. There seem to be critical Rubicons, such as the divide between operational and strategic levels, and between strategic and governance levels. Even the move from level 4 to level 5 seems to be very significant. Yet what is startling is how little preparation is available to help individuals move successfully through these critical transitions.

The legacy of administrative promotions based on a move through grades, points or job classes encourages the view that promotion is simply a linear progression in which the moves from grade to grade are qualitatively much the same. The logic of DMA levels and an analysis of the elements and their competencies demonstrate that there are very significant qualitative differences in moving from level 2 to level 3 compared with moving from level 3 to level 4. Even the ratios suggest this: for example in Tesco and Unilever less than 1 per cent of the employees make it to level 4.

From level 3 to level 4

The key difference between these two work levels is the requirement of strategic management. The majority of the population cannot operate, make decisions, innovate and lead at this level. For a start the degree of mental abstraction is more remote and less defined. Strategic management requires an ability to grasp the big picture, which may be complex, to identify gaps, and conceptualize this into alternatives, decide upon paths of action, given available resources, and ensure that key objectives are achieved. This may require new insights about consumers, future markets, customers, technology or society itself, which require a new way of doing business.

This involves looking beyond concrete problems, working with a time frame that extends beyond what has previously been experienced in order to gauge what may be required next to ensure business success. Managers need to be able to think from first principles, to be given a blank sheet of paper with a known problem but no known solution and think their way through to a solution. These are qualitatively different responsibilities from those encountered in levels 1 to 3. Someone successfully operating in level 3 does not necessarily have the ability to master level 4 accountabilities.

The learning and development implications are equally profound. It is relatively easy to equip individuals to move through levels 1 to 3. The work is essentially of the same mode. The world is concrete, resources are given, boundaries are defined, outcomes are expected and known, with targets and plans that are clearly specified. To progress up through the operational levels more knowledge (and experience) is required, which with the passage of time facilitates mastery of the accountable tasks. Progress is enhanced by evidence of decision making, leadership, team skills, initiatives and the ability to manage conflicting objectives (concrete) and priorities and the obtaining of results through others. But this changes from level 4. The world becomes increasingly less tangible, resources have to be identified, negotiated, boundaries are becoming more fluid, outcomes increasingly elastic and difficult to foresee, with targets more movable and influenced by increasing numbers of events and external influences. A world of challenge and reasonable certainty is increasingly becoming uncertain, less predictable, and changing at an increasing rate.

At present the quality of training given to those in level 3 is little different from that received by those moving to level 4. The next chapter will highlight how Unilever's international training programmes seem to be undiscriminating and of debatable preparatory value for this move across the operational/strategic Rubicon. In fairness, prior to 1998 and the introduction of work levels this was not such an obvious shortcoming.

From level 4 to level 5

The move from the fourth to the fifth level of accountability is also sufficiently different and significant to require specific preparation. At level 4, many jobs are directors (Europe, Africa and Asia)/vice presidents (the Americas) heading a key value chain activity as part of a fully fledged operating business unit. Jobs at level 2 and 4 invariably have 'a part of the whole', whereas at level 3 and 5 they have the 'whole cake', albeit one is operational and the other is strategic. This seems to be why 'dwell time' in levels 3 and 5 seems to have a critical impact on personal development, as will be demonstrated in more detail in Chapter 8.

The move to work level 5 therefore is typically a move into general management with full profit/loss accountability for a complete value chain. This represents a significant step 'into the stratosphere' beyond the ongoing activities of the business.

Preparation of general managers

General managers are rarely adequately prepared for this further elevation into strategic abstraction. They have now to ride two horses: they are accountable for both operations and strategy, and while others carry out the operations no one else's neck is on the line for general strategy. During 2003 Tesco has been paying particular attention to the selection and development of these general managers. They have identified what to look for and which **boundary moves** (see Chapter 8) are significant.

In most organizations it would seem there is not really sufficient preparation for those moving into level 5 general management roles. For example, there is no common guidance about what items should be regularly monitored by a business unit CEO, no suggested timings or agenda for key executive meetings. As a result all kinds of combinations prevail, and often board meetings or executive meetings in these units are overly frequent, inordinately time consuming in some cases, very detailed and operational in nature. There seems to be an almost inviolable tendency for the content of meetings to be inversely proportional to the grandeur of their title. Some 'board meetings' are weekly, lasting all day, others fortnightly lasting two hours and so on. No two agendas are perfectly alike. Finally it seems more individuals, or sometimes even layers of management, attend these meetings than is strictly necessary. It seems this is usually because the purpose of the meeting is not entirely clear.

The Royal Navy has done some very effective work in this area led by Commander Lee Dawson. The most common danger of these situations is that the level 5 general manager works in the wrong level, neglecting strategic work for which s/he is accountable and compressing subordinates in work level 4 who are apt to cascade this compression further down in to the business. The net result is the creation of unnecessary work, duplication, lack of empowerment, and neglect of key tasks.

'Level 5 leadership'

During 2001 Jim Collins produced his book *From Good to Great* in which he writes about five leadership styles, culminating in 'level 5 leadership'. His level 5 leadership is not in any way connected with the concepts of DMA leadership, which have just been outlined in this chapter.

Coaching and transitioning levels

Once the levels and competencies are established they provide the bedrock for coaching. The coaching can be trying to improve performance in the current level or preparing someone for a move to the next level. Finally they can be used to assist the newly promoted manager to master new accountabilities.

In order to help those moving across the threshold from work level 4 to 5, I have experimented by having these managers work through a series of questions. (See Figure 7.10.)

1. What must I relinquish as I take up my new role?
2. What new roles do I need to get involved in?
3. How will I add value to my new role?
4. How will my boss judge whether I am successful?
5. How will my subordinates judge whether I am successful?
6. What will be my key responsibilities – my 'nature of work'?
7. What are the key resources I should manage?
8. How can I provide for my direct reports?
9. What is the nature of the problems requiring resolution: is it strategic or operational?
10. What are the major critical changes that I must lead?
11. Who are my key colleagues and how can I make the most of their knowledge and expertise?
12. Which external stakeholders must be managed by this role?
13. What is the critical planning process that must be managed by this role?
14. What are the key deadlines by which I will be judged?
15. What are the inherent vulnerabilities of this role?
16. Have I got the right organization in place to achieve the above?
17. Am I prepared for this role, and if not, what do I need to do about it?
18. Do I feel stretched as a result of promotion, and if not, what am I doing wrong?
19. What different things do I have to do?
20. What do I have to do differently?

Figure 7.10 *Key questions to ask when promoted*

THE LEADERSHIP LOG

This list focuses on a number of questions that an individual should ask when he or she is about to be or has recently been promoted from one work level to another. Promotion to another level must see a significant shift in mindset and activity, and one should ask, 'What do I need to do differently?' (The approach in Figure 7.4 helps answer this question.) The coach's role is to make the managers aware of the tasks they need to let go of as they move upwards. To examine the specifics of delegation and empowerment, they are encouraged to write down how they think or expect they will manage in the new job. They are then encouraged to keep a brief record (personal assistants can help with this process) of how things actually turn out in the new job. In short they are asked to maintain a **leadership log**. They plot in some detail for the first month how they are actually spending their time.

The coach then reviews whether reality has matched expectations. If it has not, the key question is why not? Was the initial plan too optimistic? Was the first month untypical? Really? Why? Once the first month has been reviewed the next step is to draw up behavioural expectations for the next two months, then log events with a further review, by which time the incumbent has been in the new role for three months. By now distinct patterns will probably be discernible. The plan-log-review process is repeated at 6 months and 12 months, by which time the individual should have come to grips with the job and the way it is to be managed.

Working in the right level

The leadership log can be very revealing. Reality testing is the ultimate feedback. It helps ensure executives really do 'stay in their work level'. If they find they do not, it is important to quickly establish why they feel they have slipped into their subordinates' work levels. The quick and easy rationalization is to question the subordinates' ability and experience. Does the ex-marketing-VP-become-CEO really still have to have to final say on advertising copy and commercials? If the answer is 'Yes' then that is the time to really critique whether the marketing VP is working effectively in work level 4, and so on. If there are genuine weaknesses and/or inadequacies among subordinates it is important to establish what can be done, over what time frame with what expected results. These are typical performance management issues that emerge at level 5. Otherwise the CEO will become overburdened, trying to do other peoples' work, and is likely to neglect the true level 5 responsibilities, which may in turn jeopardize further promotion and the performance of the business unit. A leader must manage both superior and subordinate constituencies as well as maintain effective lateral interfaces across the organization.

The coaching review

The plan–log–review process can help identify where greater personal involvement or attention is required as part of the unit CEO's own learning and development. The log helps ensure learning objectives are set and evaluated, and that this particular stage in development is transitory. It also enables the new level 5 incumbent to check the effectiveness of inherited patterns of meetings and authorization protocols. How much time is spent at meetings in those early months? What is their purpose? How many layers of management must attend? Is their frequency realistic? and so on. If there are three or four layers of management in the unit, why do authorization procedures require six or seven signatures? Excessive and poorly run meetings and over-elaborate authorization procedures are, in my experience, the two greatest sources of wasteful bureaucracy which suck top managers down in to inappropriate work levels, invariably frustrating both them and their subordinates.

Sometimes a source of great frustration can be the unit CEO's boss. It is not unknown for the boss to also be working in the wrong level. This might be because s/he is incompetent, and/or the compression is coming from above. Having had that experience I know just how frustrating and stultifying this can be. This is the most difficult problem to solve. At least the log can be a source of objective data, which a skilful coach or mentor can usefully exploit, in the best sense. This also demonstrates why mentors should ideally be at least in an organizational 'grandparent' or 'manager-once-removed' relationship with the individual in question.

The coach can be internal or external. CEOs in particular are increasingly, and probably wisely, tending to use external sources for coaching. At level 5 and above there are not many shrinking violets, and the insecure ego that must take the credit for success, but distance itself from anything short of success, is unfortunately not an infrequent political problem in large organizations. This often emerges if meritocracy is superficial in practice when, for example, it is known that parent firm nationality is the key criterion driving promotions. There are not many ABBs in this world that have leaders such as Percy Barnevik (1997) who practised what he believed:

> Another challenge for global companies is to create a truly multicultural environment. You are into another league of globalization and multiculturalism when you have several nationalities on the Supervisory Board and Executive Committee. Deliberately striving for mixed teams on all levels you can go a long way towards overcoming cultural values.

Rapid growth and corporate culture can also lead to problems. Sometimes organizations grow into another level of accountability but not everyone can make the necessary adjustment. Top management have been conditioned to working in what has become the wrong level. If this situation is allowed to continue it will become a serious drag on the company's strategic development ambitions and performance. This is one of the main reasons that organic growth on a large scale is hard to deliver. As a rule of thumb, every time a business with a turnover of about US $20 billion doubles in size and complexity it probably ratchets up another level of accountability. It is a moot point whether all the top executives can master the transition to the next level.

THE GLUE

By now it should be clear that the DMA platform of accountability levels with the aligned differentiating competencies form a conceptually integrated approach to leadership development. As illustrated in Figure 7.11, one company characterized this integration as the glue that held together all its key HR processes.

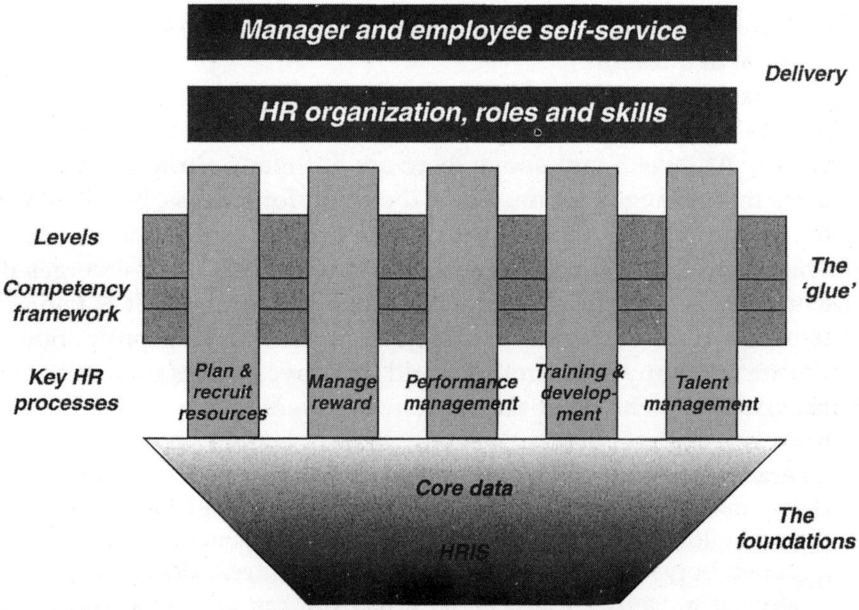

Figure 7.11 *Key components of HR strategy*

Step 9

Develop the DMA leadership model with clear distinctions between values, skills and differentiating competencies. Use the plan-log-review approach to help managers successfully make the transition from one level of accountability to the next, particularly from 3 to 4 and from 4 to 5.

SUMMARY

This chapter set out to provide an integrated solution to the problem of leadership development. It was pointed out that culling individuals from the organization allegedly for lack of (world-class) performance, without due consideration of the context within which they are working, is a flawed approach to people development.

The accountability context is not reliably indicated by a job grade or military rank. The complexity of the factors involved in identifying and developing leaders was outlined. A multi-focused approach was advocated, with clear differences between values, skills and differentiating competencies. The role of skill profiles as the basis for learning needs analysis was described. Six new DMA competencies linked to accountability levels were suggested as effective predictors of potential.

New ideas for improved coaching were described. These included a list of key questions, the leadership log and the plan-log-review process. It was shown how these approaches could help managers transition critical development Rubicons.

Finally the importance of levels of accountability and competencies as a form of organizational 'glue' was illustrated as an ideal way to integrate all the major people processes in an organization.

The case of a major company not getting the planned benefit of a major supply chain investment was highlighted. It can now be seen how DMA logic could have helped design a healthy structure, how the incumbents could have been selected on the basis of their values and skills needed for their jobs, how current and future leaders could be selected and developed, and how relevant coaching could be organized. In short, this would have delivered a successful return on the initial investment and *ensured all the salmon were swimming downstream!*

8

Tracking the salmon

The previous chapter outlined the salmon fallacy. This one focuses on how to monitor the development of the salmon. The theme continues to be leadership development, growing individuals within the organization. Significant original research will be described which gives important insight into progress through the DMA levels of accountability. A new way of *tracking talent* will be outlined as a result.

IDENTIFYING TALENT

Identifying managers who can successfully lead others in the future will never be a foolproof process. But it need not be a lottery, which it continues to be in too many companies. As McCall, Lombardo and Morrison noted in 1988: 'Management development is viewed all too often as a bag full of devices. It is instead an organization's conscious effort to provide its managers (and potential managers) with opportunities to learn, grow and change in hopes of producing over the long-term a cadre of managers with the skills necessary to function effectively in that organization.' As indicated in the previous chapter, to do this effectively one needs to be able to identify the work level or defined responsibilities and assess an individual's potential ability to operate at that level. Jaques and Cason (1994) established that it is feasible but their work was limited in extent and the methodology was essentially subjective. Jaques felt this proved his earlier finding (as set out in Figure 8.1) that people have identifiable 'maturation modes'.

After 3,000 man-hours of work-level interviewing one's ability to recognize potential certainly improves. But this is a long learning process, probably too expensive and impractical for any company to adopt as a means of training its executives to recognize potential. It was necessary to find a methodology that might be effective, transparent and objective. No method can perfectly predict the future and assessment of potential is a form of recruitment, which is always a guesstimate. But the challenge is to lesson the chance for error by basing the decision on as many sound indicators of leadership potential as possible, preferably based on reliable and objective data that already exists in the organization. *Tracking* was the answer.

TRACKING

Management development in many companies is sequenced in three- to five-year time capsules. These frames have the advantage of providing quite reliable concrete data for short-term career decisions. But given the idea of the 'maturation modes' of Jaques, Cason and Stamp, they do not easily identify the progression path of future development. Questions such as does this five-year slice of time represent the onset of an increasing momentum in a person's development curve, a slowing down or perhaps the zenith of personal development, are not really addressed. There was loose talk in the past of 'starred listers' in Unilever, which identified people who might cross the next development level within five years, but there was no rigour to these assessments, which therefore remained only shadowy prefigurings of what might happen. There was also no thought about how quickly a star should progress through the former job class system. At what pace would progression enhance or possibly endanger development and contribute, for example, to early burnout?

The idea of tracking is to plot a career path over a 15-year period and suggest the likely end point of an individual's development. In other words, the path or track a person could follow over 15 years to reach a specific destination or job in the organization. As an extension of the three- to five-year human resource planning approach it would be a series of

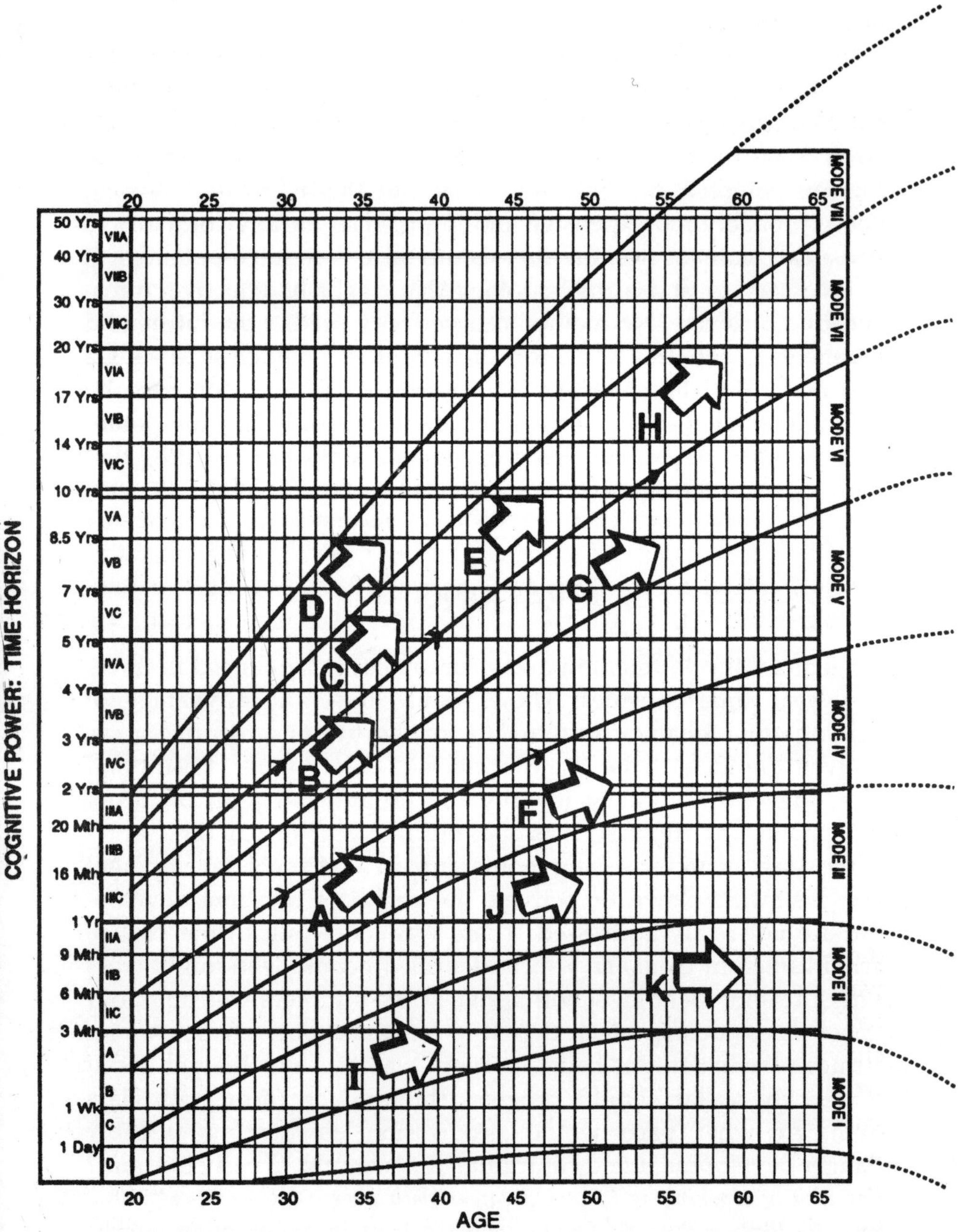

Figure 8.1 *Time-horizon progression array (Jacques, 1989)*

rolling reviews, which would be most valuable until a person reached about the age of 40.

Not every organization feels the need for career development planning up to, let alone beyond, five years. This is evident from some of the dot.com pressures outlined in Chapter 10. But, as will also be pointed out in that chapter, the new concept of personal growth, 'Time in work level', is still relevant for people moving from company to company. The principles outlined in this chapter can help them plot their own learning needs and tracks.

Tracking could be applied as follows. If someone in level 2 is considered to be demonstrating level 3 competencies he or she is placed on the work level 3 potential list. That individual is seen as a valuable potential leader and earmarked as 'List 3'. Tracking would take this a stage further. If, based on the pattern of achievement of previous executives, this level 2 person had reached a work level at an age that suggested level 5 potential within 15 years, he or she would be designated 'List 3, Track 5'. At present, when managers are placed on leadership development lists there is little idea about how far they might progress beyond the current years under review or indeed whether they are approaching a development plateau. Many will reach their limit when they are promoted to the next level. The really important challenge is trying to find those with the talent to go further.

Previous systems of administrative promotions, which expressed progress in terms of job evaluation grades, were too blunt an instrument to provide reliable and valid answers. For example, in Unilever a most important group for development, prior to the implementation of work levels, was the so-called B List, ie 'those who could achieve Job Class 30 within 5 years' but unfortunately Job Class 30 emerged at the top of work level 4. Thus this previously critical development list was identifying how many people, largely already in work level 4, could move to the top of level 4. As demonstrated in the previous chapter, the move to level 5 is a critical move within the strategic work levels. Ability to move to the top of level 4 does not necessarily guarantee that someone can move into level 5. Yet the former B List was believed to identify general management ability, effectively the equivalent of work level 5 in today's terms. Thus the company's management development system was more a game of chance – although, as will be demonstrated below, some of the marbles in the gamblers' rotating churn were heavier than others – than was realized at the time.

Deciding on 15-year lists of trackers would identify earlier the critical 5 per cent of executives who could reach the strategic work levels. It would lengthen career-planning horizons and focus on real development assignments rather than simply establish so-called succession lists of managers who are likely to deliver instant results in their next job. The theory is clear enough, and is often required in a large organization. But for the critical 5 per cent the key question remains: where is the evidence that uncovers the 15-year career tracks?

EVIDENCE FOR CAREER TRACKS

In Unilver's case the evidence for successful career tracks already existed within the organization. The key seemed to lie in working backwards into previous career paths prior to looking forward. For over 30 years the company had maintained detailed computer records mapping every job (and the job class progression) that individual managers had filled throughout their careers.

Since there was a broad correlation between the previous job classes and the proposed work levels it was possible to recalibrate a career in work levels. The correlation between the old currency of job classes and the new work-level currency correlated at over 90 per cent for jobs in work level 5 and above. This was because the evaluation of these jobs had always been carefully managed at the centre, which ensured their consistency. (As I had at one time been responsible for global job evaluation I had a good feel for most of the jobs in the sample.) The first sample of 26 jobs was limited to those who had reached the International Board, including some who had retired. Over 20 were 'lifers' who had worked in Unilever for the whole of their careers. The analysis revealed valuable information about average time spent in each work level, the age by which critical levels were achieved on average in order to proceed at a realistic pace along these career tracks. The results are summarized in Table 8.1.

Table 8.1 indicates that the ages of directors at the different work levels reveals a reasonably consistent trend in terms of the number of years spent in each level, apart from time spent in level 1, which is on average one to two years. About 90 per cent of this sample were university graduates who had also often been on compulsory military training (National Service, which ended in 1963); hence the relatively high average entry age (25) into level 1.

The analysis further indicated that these individuals seem to spend an average of five years in each level. Mathematically this is not

Table 8.1 *Average age of directors at work levels*

IN WORK LEVELS	AGE RANGE	AVERAGE
1	20–30	25
2	21–31	26
3	26–37	31
4	32–42	37
5	33–46	40
6	39–55	47
7	41–59	50
8	49–59	54

surprising but a closer examination is more revealing. Those who have been most successful historically in Unilever have spent a good 10 years on average in operational roles, with a little more of that time in level 3 than in level 2.

Interestingly, those of highest potential moved quite swiftly through level 4 (on average three years) but spent a considerable dwell time in level 5 (seven years on average). This not illogically signifies the importance of a solid apprenticeship in general management as part of the preparatory track to the board of a global company.

Jobs in work levels 3 and 5 often involve operational and strategic general management, respectively. It is logical that their average 'dwell time' is longer than for other levels. This finding was reinforced when general managers in another large organization were interviewed during 2003. Conversely, high-flyers who zoomed through work level 3 had a tendency to burn out in their late thirties. It would seem that their operational experience was too brittle a platform on which to build a successful career at the higher levels. Similarly, a good spell of general management in work level 5 seems to be a critical prerequisite for those moving into the governance levels of accountability.

It was also clear that these individuals usually spent time in a number of different jobs in each work level irrespective of their age. This presumably added value to their mix of technical and general skills experience while proving their ability to achieve results and add value to the organization. It is therefore not only important to have a realistic time to master the demands of each level but also to experience a critical mix of challenges and contrasting experiences (see 'boundary moves', page 218).

Fulcrum ages

Finally, three important fulcrum ages fall out of this analysis. These individuals have on average reached level 3 at age 31, level 5 at 40 and level 7 at 50. This suggests three ages when it would be critical to undertake a fundamental assessment of leadership potential:

- At age 30, 'Will this individual make level 5?'
- At age 35, 'Will this individual make level 6?'
- At age 40, 'Will this individual reach level 7?'

Based on the existing career maps combined with competency assessment, the answers to these questions could also give tracking indicators as follows:

- Age 30, level 3, List 4, Track 5.
- Age 35, level 4, List 5, Track 6.
- Age 40, level 5, List 6, Track 7.

Recognizing that we have not yet addressed the questions about how one progresses and what facilitates that progress, nevertheless certain useful conclusions about future career tracks can be gleaned from this analysis. This can be sharpened by focusing on the personal history record (PHR) of a CEO; see Table 8.2.

Firstly, not surprisingly, it shows that this individual actually spent an average of four years per work level to reach the top of the business. He (there are no women in this sample) also spent only three years in each of levels 2 and 3. At this stage it looks as if someone zooming through work levels 2 and 3 in five to six years has potential

Table 8.2 *Example of a work level 8 career*

WORK LEVEL	AGE	AVERAGE AGE OF DIRECTORS
1	22	25
2	24	27
3	27	32
4	32	37
5	37	40
6	39	45
7	41	48
8	49	54

for Track 8 or, and this is important, is building a brittle career base which will probably lead to burnout in the mid to late thirties. This is already a critical finding.

In the mid-1980s Unilever's Brazilian business was growing quickly and needed to develop young Brazilians to take key leadership positions.

The President of the business at the time crashed youngsters through the promotion stakes, which resulted in fearful loss rates by the mid-1990s and virtually no sustained success stories from that period. The company currently has praiseworthy ambitions for its young management in other countries. But without recourse to tracking guidelines the likelihood is that the experience of Brazil will be replicated with the current generation burning out in their mid to late thirties as they will not have been adequately prepared, notwithstanding the best of intentions.

Tesco also has very aggressive growth plans in Central Europe and Asia. These plans place enormous pressure on the need to grow indigenous management, often in countries where the management of hypermarkets is a totally new phenomenon.

Even the brightest and the best need sufficient grounding in the operational levels if they are finally to attain levels of governance accountability in the business. Evidence suggests that sufficient time in level 3 is critical in this development process. This is because work at level 3 often entails management of a large unit including many sub-units with potentially conflicting objectives and parochial priorities, which have to be integrated and balanced for the good of the whole. Examples are a large factory, a hypermarket and a significant corporate department. This is the first level that calls for a type and quality of leadership, albeit at an operational level, that will be replicated in many respects at higher levels of strategic and governance accountability. It is worth noting that certain ranks in the military, such as Captain in the Royal Navy, tend to require six to nine years' experience prior to the next promotion.

If early development experience is skimpy or in some way truncated, it would seem that one's potential growth is inevitably stunted. In the blazing sun of 'accelerated development' a healthy young plant may perish in a desert of underachievement.

A hypothetical example

Consider for a moment a hypothetical example. A talented young woman is promoted to level 4 at age 31. Analysis of the sample of directors reveals that four Unilever chairmen in the sample reached level 4 between the ages of 32 and 34 (against the average of 37 in the sample of directors). Thus if someone has reached level 4 at 31, there are a number of possible explanations:

- She might have been promoted for non-meritocratic reasons.
- She is genuinely promoted but already over-promoted.
- She is capable of being a chairperson of a complex multinational global organization.

Assuming the last, the concept of tracking changes the nature of the management development debate. This individual is an extremely capable and valuable person. Past experience suggests that she is already on a rare track to the top of the business. The challenge is to plan learning and development opportunities, postings and experience that will keep her on this track. There are 'boundary moves' – see page 218. There is already evidence from predecessors that indicate the realistic pace of this career path, to test its validity and avoid the trap of the self-fulfilling prophecy. There would be critical new challenges in this process to stay on track should this individual opt for career breaks to have children. What then needs to be done to ensure that momentum is maintained and she remains 'on track', assuming her own ambition and career aspirations are consistent with her potential?

Lions and lionesses

The concept of tracking enables companies to identify high-flyers earlier than has been customary. As Table 8.2 illustrates, it is possible to identify top talent at 26 or 27. A few years ago the Director of the Africa Middle East Group, Roy Brown, challenged us to identify a person from that region who could make the parent board within 15 years. Based on the then current development lists, there was no one over 30 identified with that leadership potential. Consequently the country CEOs were forced to dig deep into the pool of those in their twenties, which was a fundamental change in mindset. We finally developed a list of 'lions and lionesses' and mapped out detailed career moves across the next 10 years. It was quite an eye opener for without the DMA framework it was largely impressionistic guess-work. Tracking would have tightened the discipline. It would have also provided a framework against which to ask leading questions, such as 'If you think this person is so good, why is he or she only in level 2 at age 29?' In other words, there could be cases for genuine accelerated development involving a blend of cross-product, cross-function and/or cross-country posting.

Tracking managers in their twenties is becoming more critical given today's intense competition for talent. It is critical to assess the 25–30 age cohort rigorously and identify indicative 15-year tracks. Having done this, the next vital step is to carefully map out meaningful development steps and 'boundary moves' in discussion with the individual concerned. Too often at this point, it seems, especially with young women, that the career moves are really career lurches as companies react to pressures for more women in senior posts.

Quotas and affirmative action

Affirmative action is one of the key reasons why quotas rarely provide true leadership development. Officially placing someone on the equivalent of a steep track simply because they are from a minority group can do a disservice to the individual, the company and in some situations, such as in South Africa, perhaps even the country. Treating someone capable of Track 3 potential as if they have Track 5 potential is not a solution for the prejudiced and the moral transgressions of the recent past. There is evidence (based on work done in South Africa by Retief and Stamp (1996) from a database of about 8,000 interviews conducted on a population of mixed races over a period of nine years) that notwithstanding restricted opportunities for development, there are no appreciable differences between any of the racially different groups in early capability growth curves. This suggests that affirmative action should ensure that minorities are monitored carefully and propelled into level 2 positions as early as possible. Thereafter tracking could help dictate the appropriate selection of career development and learning opportunity. Retief's research would seem to indicate that tracks based on limited racial groups or men only could nevertheless still serve as a guide for leadership development for those of different ethnicity and sex. The same can be said of this sample of male, largely Anglo-Dutch-Unilever directors.

OTHER CRITICAL DETERMINANTS OF TRACKING

So far we have focused on the career tracks of those who reached the top of Unilever over the past 20 years. This still does not reveal what intrinsic or extrinsic factors lubricated these tracks. What other sources and/or propellants of tracking exist in Unilever? I next decided to examine a larger sample, involving virtually all those in levels 5 or 6 in 1997. This was compared to a cohort of managers who had been listed in the previous 10 years but had not reached level 5. Kate Phillips, then at LSE, was a key contributor to this study.

Who reaches work level 5?

The first step was to identify the group of managers to be studied. We analysed 286 PHRs of work level 4 and above personnel, whose career histories were reconstructed into work levels. This was done based on my knowledge of the jobs in question and then critiqued against the job class correlation referred to earlier. About 100 of the sample had at one stage been formally identified as having potential to progress further within five years but had not in fact reached level 5. We set out to identify what intrinsic or extrinsic factors had been significant, in a Unilever context, in propelling their career forward and whether there were any obvious gaps which helped to explain objectively why some plateaued, albeit on a lofty ledge, in the company's management pyramid.

Intrinsic factors

We grouped together skills and competencies under this heading. These, along with values and attitudes, cover the know-how required and the behaviour displayed in meeting the challenges presented by a particular job. Intrinsic attributes, although evaluated and assessed, can form the basis of further development, which in turn can be directly influenced by the individual. The key question is therefore, is success in reaching level 5 in Unilever based solely on an individual's personal (intrinsic) competencies and skills, or do other (extrinsic) factors exert equal or greater influence in this process?

Extrinsic factors

These are more objective, environmental factors, which cannot be easily changed by the individual once they have started working. Thus at the point of entry into the concern, people are a particular gender, nationality, age and may possess certain educational qualifications which may be required of a specific job into which they are recruited. Additional factors may come into play during a person's career, in which, while the individual can have a large say in the final decision, the ultimate call is made by the company. Examples would include participation in key development courses, foreign assignments, postings to the corporate centre and the type of assignment, function, category or geographical location of the job an individual occupies.

While it can be assumed that these intrinsic and extrinsic factors will influence performance, potential and therefore leadership development, there is one area that often remains unspoken and unexplored. This is the area that might be called *political factors*. Typical of these might be knowing the right people, being part of the right network, having an informal but powerful mentor. These political factors can skew organizational career planning and undermine the trust, credibility and transparency of the official process. Generally it seems that the weaker and more ineffective the management development process, the more rampant the politicization. Successful career planning will be able to bring these issues into the open, and in the case of mentoring, for example, incorporate them in the official practice so that their impact can be assessed along with other extrinsic factors.

The objective was to examine the impact of the extrinsic factors on career tracks. The following 10 extrinsic factors were isolated for further study:

- Age on reaching work levels 2, 3 and 4.
- Time spent in work levels 2 and 3.
- Foreign assignments.
- Corporate centre assignments.
- Function worked in work levels 2 and 3.
- Home country.
- Level of entry.
- Manner of entry.
- Possession of a professional qualification.
- International training.

The data was then analysed to track career histories in order to detect whether the extrinsic variables had any significant bearing on the achievement of success. Success in this context was defined as the reaching of level 5.

Results and conclusion

The broad conclusion is that only some of the extrinsic factors play a part in reaching level 5 and above. A very distinct profile emerges, which facilitates progress to work level 5. Whether this profile of favoured sons (women are largely non-existent in this sample) is the right profile for the 21st century would be a key question to resolve prior to endorsing the favoured career paths, or tracks, for the future.

Turning now to each of the so-called extrinsic factors. When interpreting the results, those who were listed but failed to reach level 5 will be referred to as 'potentials', while those in level 5 and above will be referred to as 'leaders'. This is admittedly a relative distinction, but one that distinguishes these sample results.

Age

The difference between leaders and potential leaders (potentials) in reaching level 2 is marginal:

- 92 per cent of leaders reach work level 2 by age 30 compared to 80 per cent of potentials. The gap widens at level 3, where the ratio is 2:1 (see Figure 8.2).
- 79 per cent of leaders reach level 3 by age 35 compared to only 36 per cent of the potentials.
- The gap is significant by level 4. The ratio is now 3:1 (see Figure 8.3): 67 per cent of leaders attained level 4 by 40 compared to only 22 per cent of potentials.

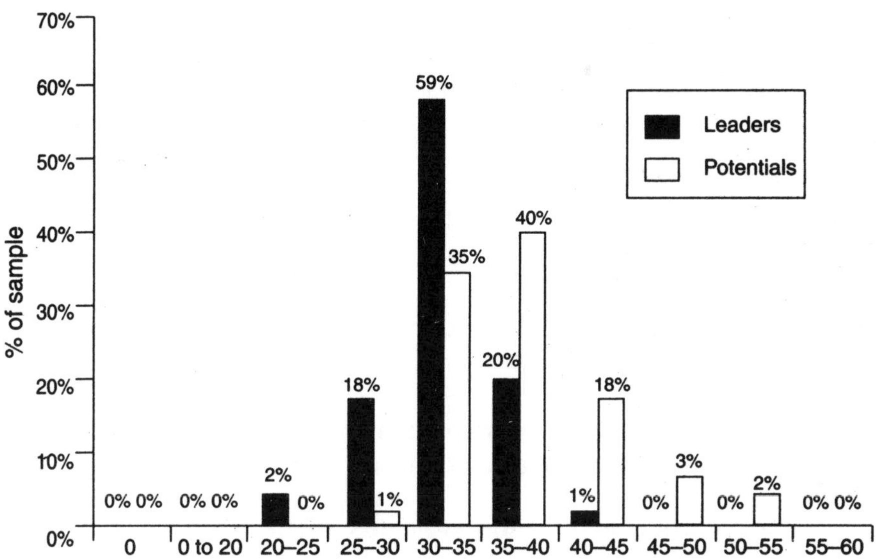

Figure 8.2 *Leaders vs potentials comparison: age at which level 3 reached*

Conclusion

There are critical ages in an individual's career, which represent fulcrum points or benchmark stages, indicating which track an individual is potentially on. Age 30 seems to be an important time to assess individuals' potential for Track 5.

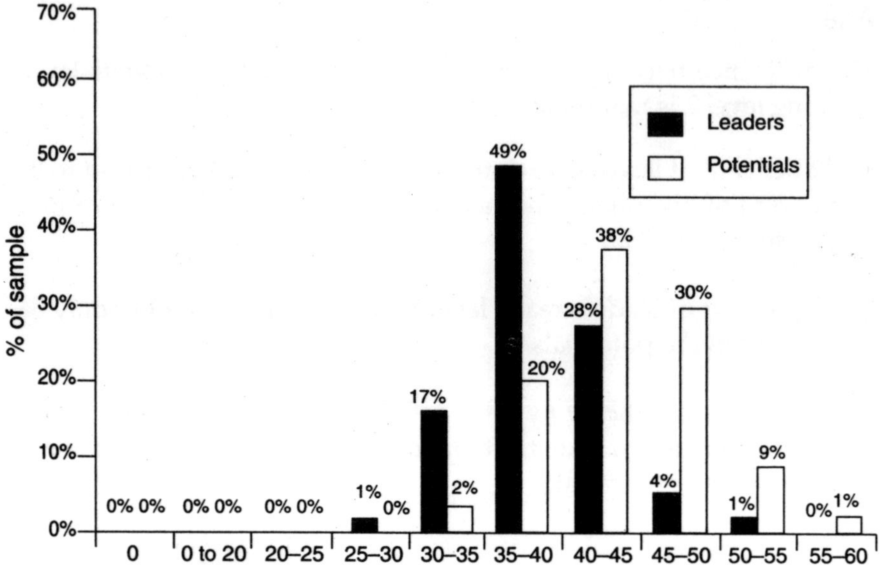

Figure 8.3 *Leaders vs potentials comparison: age at which level 4 reached*

Time spent in work level

On average leaders pass though work level 2 faster than potentials. (See Figure 8.4):

- 69 per cent of leaders spent two to seven years in level 2 compared to 30 per cent of potentials.
- Only 7 per cent of leaders spent more than 10 years in level 2 compared to 39 per cent of potentials.

The same pattern holds true for level 3 (see Figure 8.5):

- 63 per cent of leaders spent two to six years in level 3 compared with 44 per cent of potentials.
- Only 8 per cent of leaders spent more than 10 years in level 3 compared to 26 per cent of potentials.

Conclusion

There appears to be an optimum time of between three and seven years in both work levels 2 and 3 to become a leader. If more time than

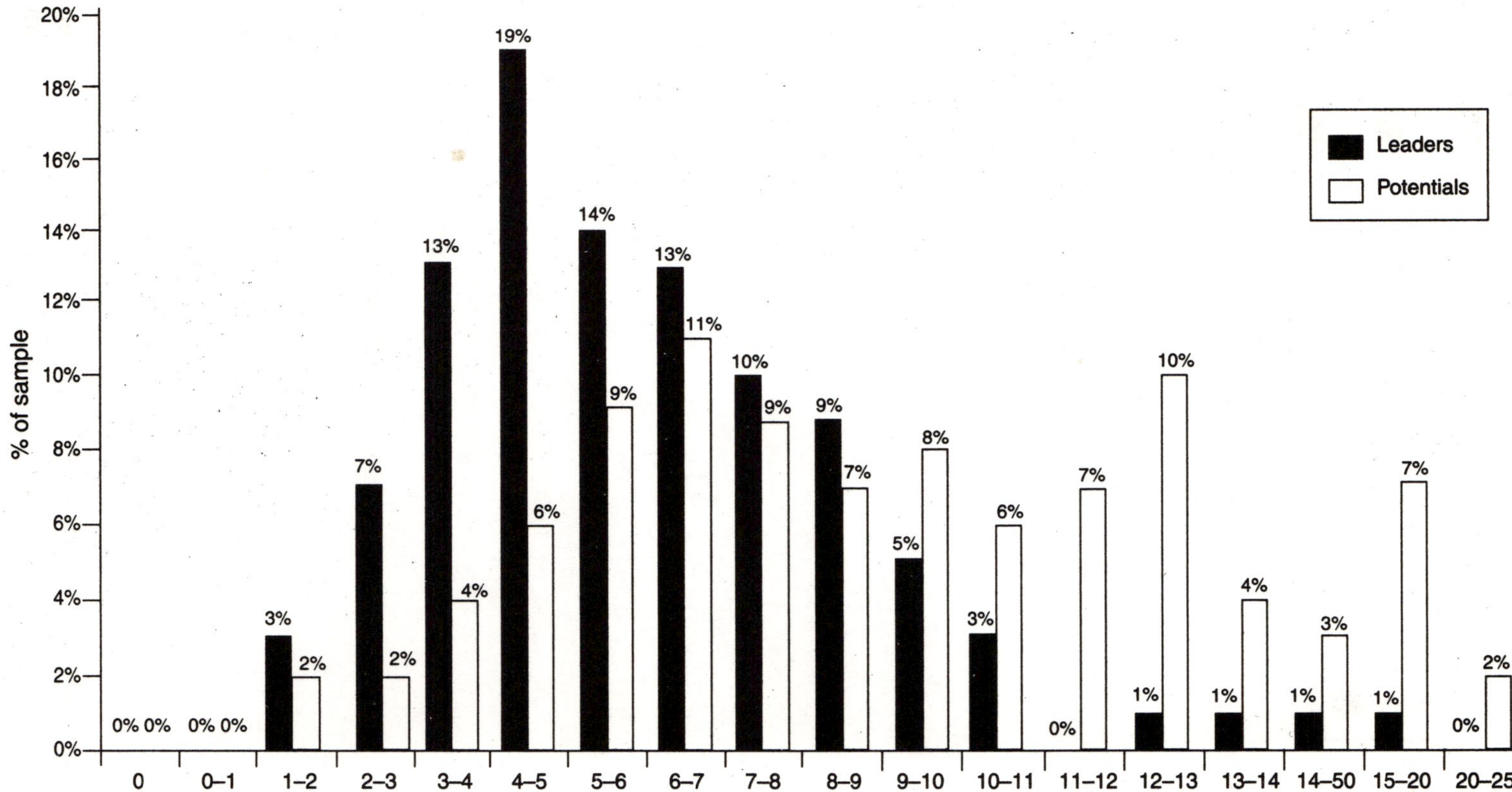

Figure 8.4 *Leaders vs potentials comparison: time in level 2 (years)*

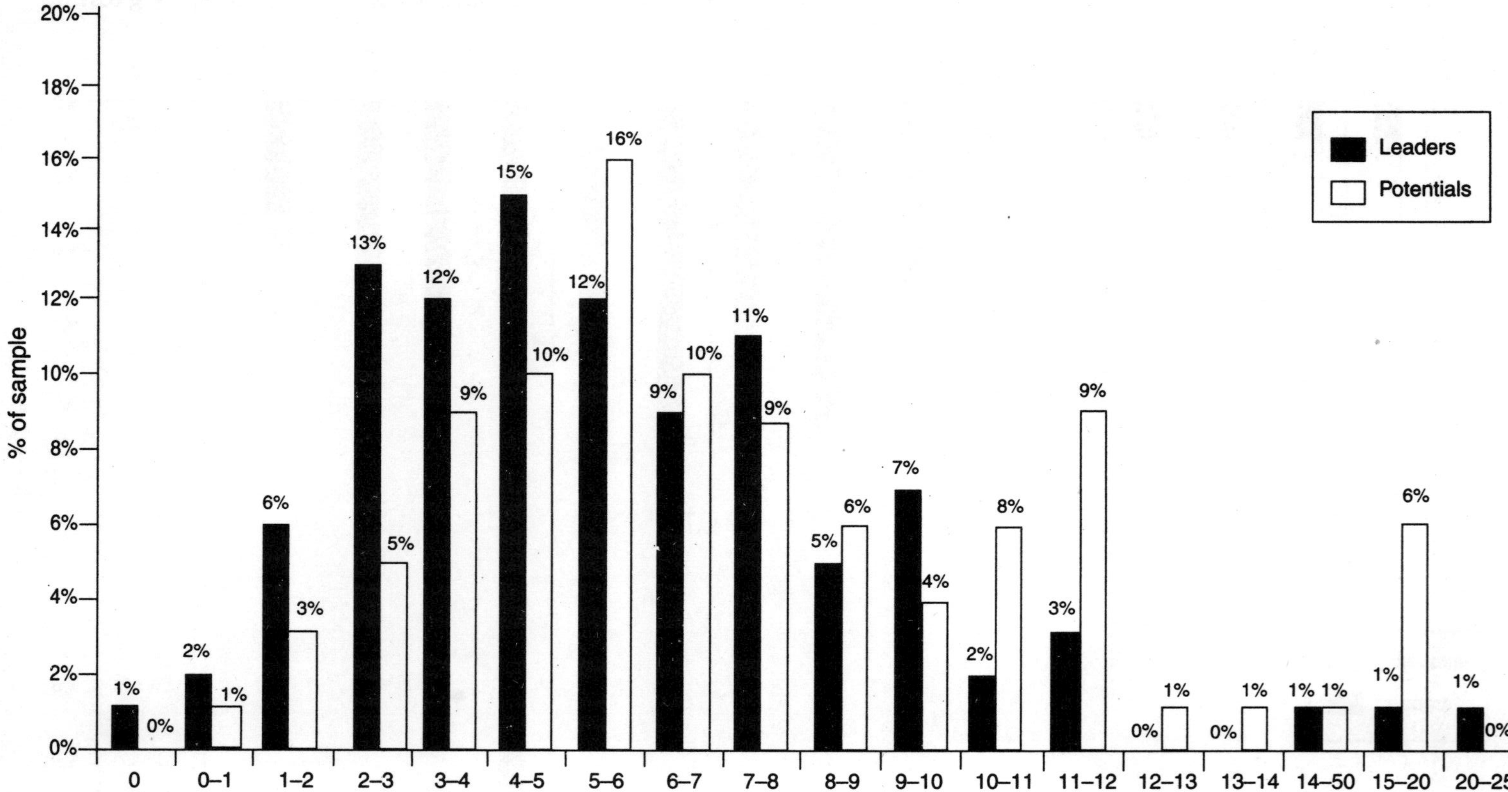

Figure 8.5 *Leaders vs potentials comparison: time in level 3 (years)*

this is spent in these levels, the possibility of becoming a leader in at least level 5 clearly diminishes.

This compares consistently with an average of five years for level 2 and 3 for directors, but about three years for potential chairpersons. It reinforces the importance of identifying potential leaders in their late twenties. This is not going to guarantee that all those identified will in fact reach level 5 and above, but it will ensure that more people who might have the potential to do so are given the opportunity.

Foreign assignments

Leaders experience more foreign assignments than potentials:

- 84 per cent of leaders had one or more foreign postings before reaching level 5 compared to 69 per cent of potentials at the same stage in their career.

Conclusion

This illustrates the importance of foreign assignments in the company's culture. At least 90 per cent of those in level 5 have been abroad at least once during their career. Given the finding above about time in work level, the key consideration would seem to be at which level the first foreign assignment occurs.

Corporate centre assignments

There is a strong informal belief that assignments in the corporate centre are an important contributor to progress in one's career. What did the facts reveal?

- 61 per cent of leaders had at least one corporate centre job compared with 26 per cent of potentials (see Figure 8.6).

Conclusion

A corporate centre assignment is an important catalyst of career development. Given the significance of Unilever's international network, it is important to be known and time in the corporate centre provides that opportunity.

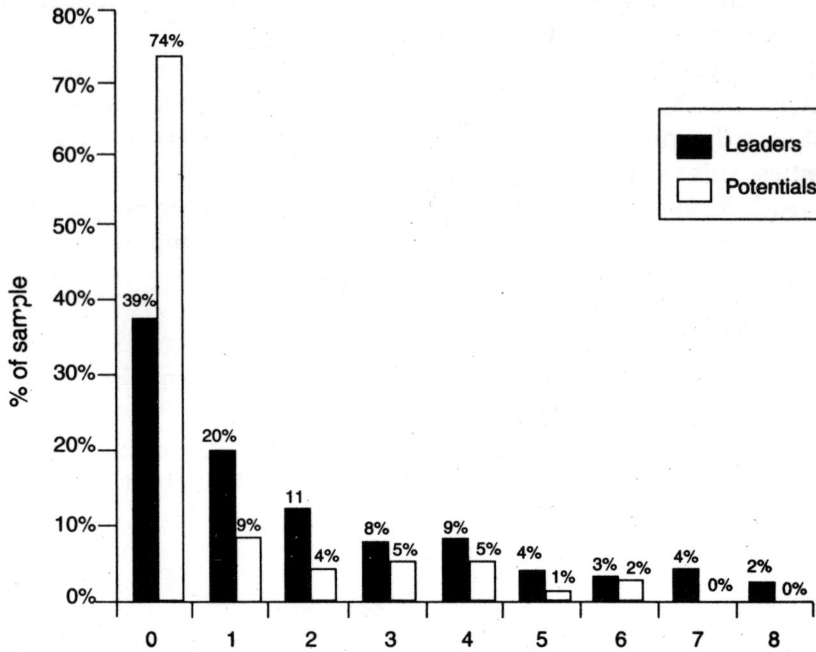

Figure 8.6 *Leaders vs potentials comparison: number of head office postings*

Function worked in work levels 2 and 3

When examining which function produced the most leaders the results were quite clear-cut. Those who had worked in marketing at both work levels 2 and 3 were most likely to become leaders:

- Work level 2 (see Figure 8.7):
  - 38 per cent of leaders came from marketing;
  - 20 per cent of leaders came from finance;
  - 82 per cent of marketers became leaders;
  - 70 per cent of finance managers became leaders.

- Work level 3 (see Figure 8.8):
  - 38 per cent of leaders came from marketing;
  - 18 per cent of leaders came from finance;
  - 76 per cent of marketers became leaders;
  - 69 per cent of finance managers became leaders.

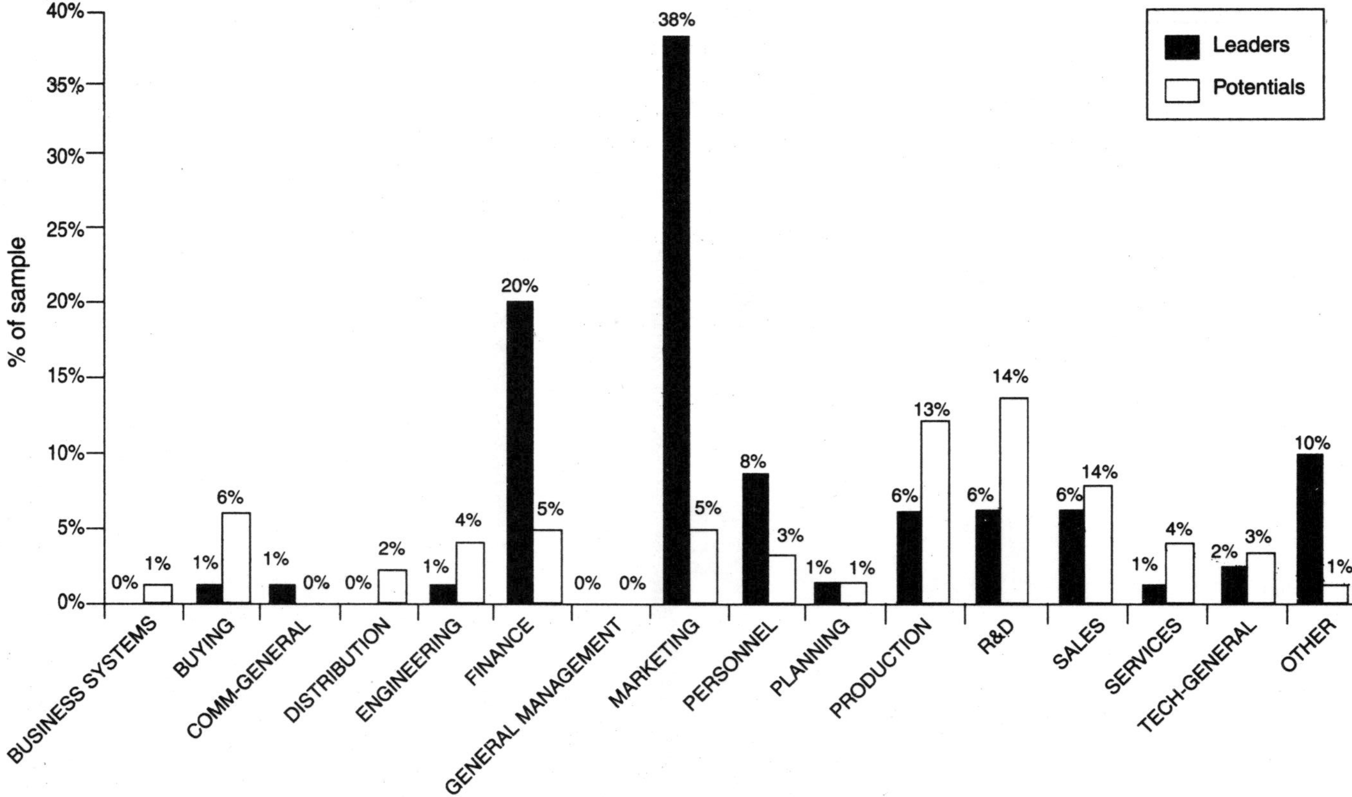

Figure 8.7 *Leaders vs potentials comparison: primary function worked – level 2*

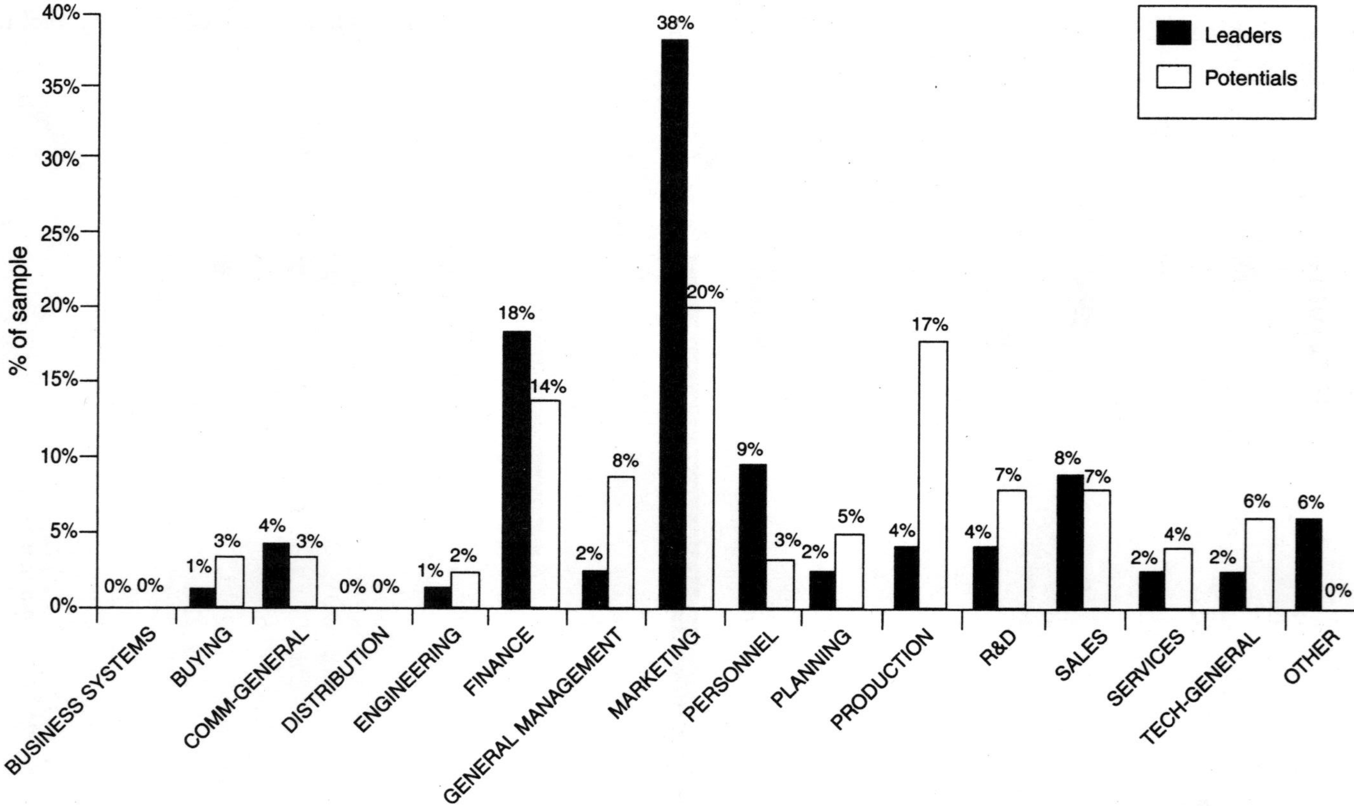

Figure 8.8 *Leaders vs potentials comparison: primary function worked – level 3*

Conclusion

Unilever considers itself a marketing company, thus it is not altogether surprising that the marketing function provides such a clear route to the top. The emergence of finance as the overwhelming second source of leaders at first looks surprising, until one realizes that finance in Unilever includes IT and, until recently, most of the supply chain functions other than manufacturing.

Nationality

Here the aim was to identify which countries produce the most leaders, which countries have the greatest success rate of potentials becoming leaders and what percentage of leaders came from non-triad countries:

- 50 per cent of leaders came from the UK (36 per cent) and the Netherlands (14 per cent), followed by Germany (8 per cent) and the United States (7 per cent).
- Non-triad countries produced only 13 per cent of leaders. Just over one-third of these came from India.
- The highest conversion rates of potentials to leaders were:
  - the Netherlands 90 per cent;
  - UK 70 per cent;
  - Germany 65 per cent;
  - United States 35 per cent.

Conclusion

The Anglo-Dutch (male) culture of Unilever is reflected in its percentage of leaders. It is not yet as diverse as it would like to be. The threefold success rate of Dutch achieving top promotions in contrast to Americans is a statistic that would puzzle most observers. It probably reflects the influence of the home country, which tends to be the norm in multinationals.

Level of entry

- 70 per cent of leaders entered Unilever in work level 1 compared with 71 per cent of potentials.

Conclusion

Entering the company as a management trainee in work level 1 was not a positive factor in leaders attaining level 5 ahead of potentials.

Manner of entry

The percentages indicated that leaders did not enter the concern in a different manner to potentials.

Professional qualifications

'Professional qualification' was defined as a university degree or professional body qualification in accounting, economics, marketing or an MBA or its equivalent. More leaders (67 per cent) than potentials (49 per cent) possessed a professional qualification. Although it might be argued that this is a significant difference, the complexity of defining a professional qualification means that these findings must be treated with caution. They naturally correlate with the findings in the section on 'Function' above, and arguably don't add significantly to that finding.

Training

Unilever has for many years run two important international leadership development programmes at its International Training Centre just outside London. One, the International Management Seminar (IMS), is for those who in today's terms are List 3, and the General Management Course (GMC) is for those who on a similar basis are List 4:

- 40 per cent of both the leaders and potentials attended an IMS but a greater percentage of potentials than leaders took the GMC course. (see Figures 8.9 and 8.10.)

Conclusion

Contrary to popular belief in the concern, IMS training does not seem to help or hinder those on development Track 5. In fact more reach level 5 who have not attended an IMS. The GMC is also not a reliable guide as to which leaders attain level 5. This raises fundamental questions about the role of those international training courses. The inadequate formal preparation for those currently crossing the work-level

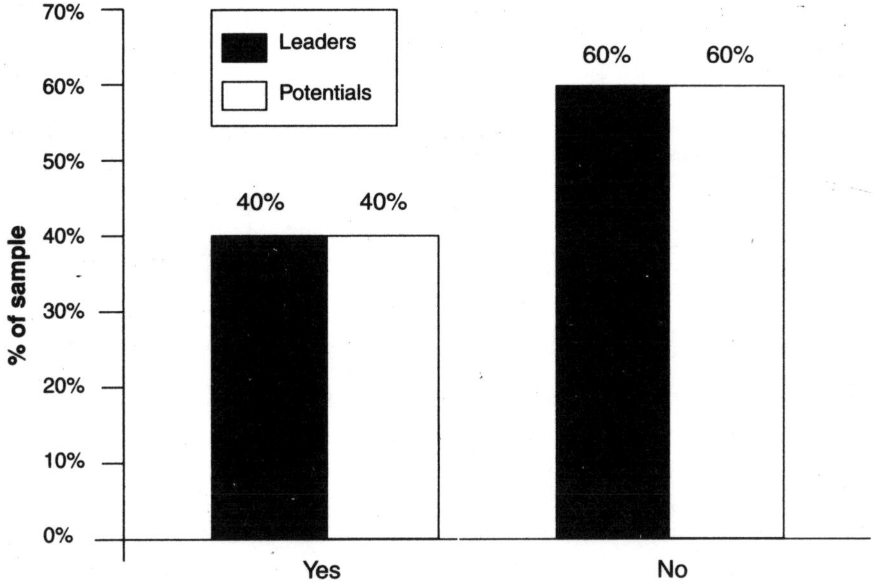

Figure 8.9 *Leaders vs listers comparison: IMS*

4/5 Rubicon has already been referred to in Chapter 7. These two programmes are currently under review at the time of writing.

Summary

Five of the ten variables are significant in identifying career tracks within Unilever, namely:

- Age per work level.
- Time in work level.
- Corporate centre assignments.
- Function.
- Nationality.

The most unexpected finding is that 1 of the 10, Training, does not seem to have a significant impact. This is worrying given the investment in that area of the business and the general belief that such training is a critical influence in the development of leaders.

DMA AND THE LEVEL PLAYING FIELD

The analysis below demonstrates the power of the logic of decision-making accountability in establishing an effective platform for leadership development.

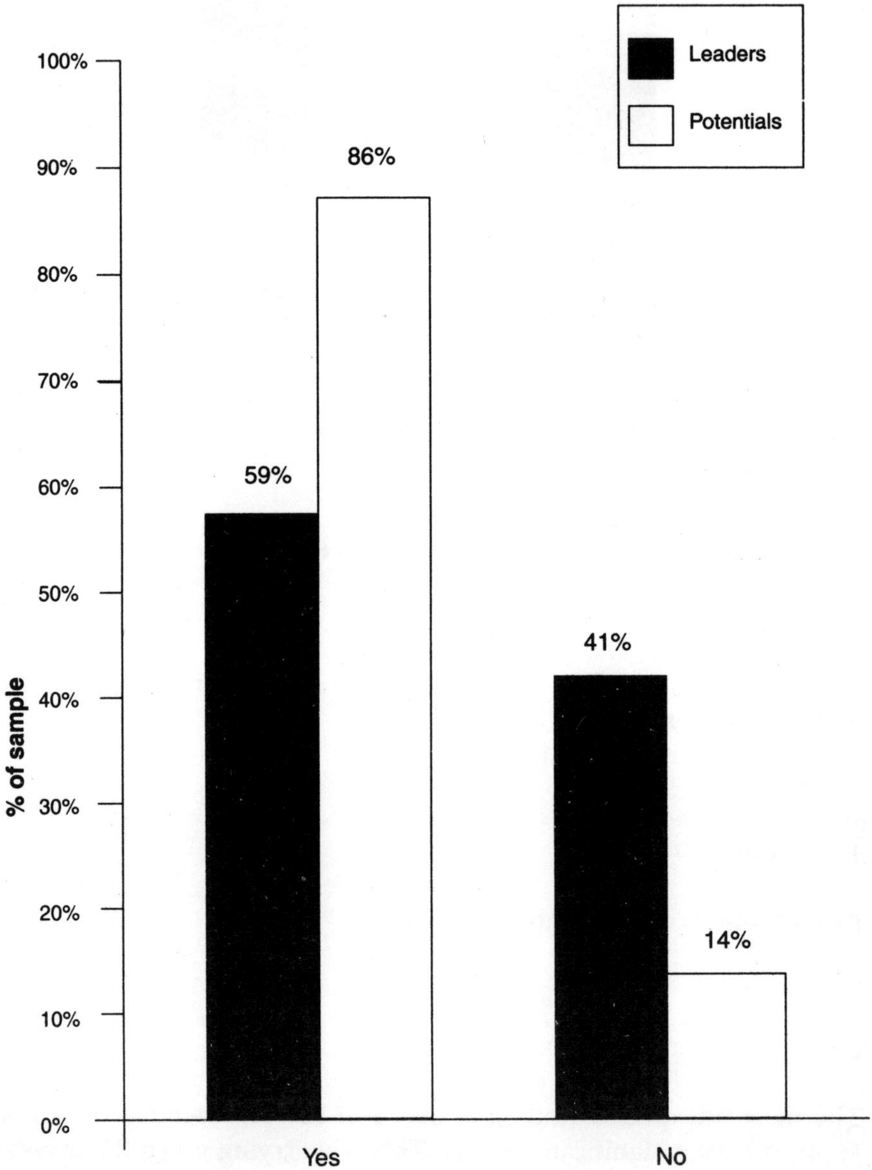

Figure 8.10 *Leaders vs potentials comparison: GMC*

The aligned competencies (described in Chapter 7) can help identify who has potential to progress into higher levels, while the patterns of (previously) successful managers can help identify career paths, or tracks, which can lay the basis for career planning at least 15 years ahead. Finally, they can help ensure that the playing field really is level, devoid of undue corporate cultural biases such as nationality, race or gender.

DEVELOPMENTAL EXPERIENCES

So far in this chapter we have talked about who makes good leaders and what paths they can follow, but more needs to be revealed about how to orchestrate meaningful development experiences. In 1988 McCall, Lombardo and Morrison noted:

> Companies that effectively identify and track their high potential managers do the following:
>
> - They dig deeply, to ensure young talent is evaluated.
> - They look widely.
> - They apply common criteria.
> - They reassess frequently.
> - They bring a corporate wide perspective to bear.
> - Exposure to job content is not so much the issue, as what one has to do while being exposed.

In 1998 McCall developed the last item, highlighting 16 developmental experiences that high-flyers can learn from. In 2002, he and George Hollenbeck applied the earlier learnings to the development of global executives. They studied a large number of executives of different nationalities at a number of large multinationals such as ABB, Ericsson, Ford, Johnson and Johnson, Shell, Unilever and others. The developmental experiences identified can be mapped in DMA terms.

Early work experiences

Executive development starts before a person reaches executive levels. One of the key constructive experiences is being moved out of one's comfort zone early. Many companies insist that their trainees start at the frontline for a short period, in the store, on the road or on the night shift. In these pre-supervisory (ie work level 1) jobs people often get their first taste of the difficulties of working with other people. They meet difficult customers or suppliers, and make early contact with some of the company's external constituencies. All of which is valuable learning provided the assignment is not too long that the trainee moves 'out of flow (see Csikszentmihalyi, pages 219–20). Industrial tours where a trainee visits different departments over a 12-month or two-year period of induction don't provide this all-important stretch experience which talented newcomers relish.

First supervision

Supervising people for the first time is usually the second important development event chronologically. This might be in a support role at the top of work level 1, or as a full accountable level 2 manager. The young manager quickly learns that it is often people, not technical issues, that are the most difficult. Accountability for people is a critical learning, which should both remain and continue throughout a long career. This is often a neglected area in the work experience of young graduates, such as marketers and financiers, which shows up as a shortcoming later in their careers.

Turnarounds

Turnarounds represent another excellent source of testing both technical ability and what has been learnt today. It requires naked leadership. This is typically a pressure situation, a task with a tight deadline and with staff who could be negative and demotivated. Credibility has to be learnt quickly. Diagnostic skills and ability to quickly sort out key priorities are needed before results can start to be achieved. Such jobs are likely to be at least level 2 or level 3. This is the type of situation that might justify a lateral development move within a level of accountability.

Start-ups

Starting something from scratch is a taxing learning process. It challenges what until now has been taken for granted. Areas of conviction, or of lack of certainty, are probed. This is a particular challenge and depending on the balance of the tasks would probably be at least level 3.

Projects

Projects and taskforces require many of the qualities needed in a turnaround situation. But in addition they may call for evidence of teamwork skills and ability to influence others, especially if the individual is the project leader. One of the major challenges of project work is managing a temporary group of people who have different full-time bosses. Project leadership can start at level 2 (more will be written about project accountabilities per work level in Chapter 10).

Change in scope

This often occurs as one crosses from operational to strategic accountabilities, ie from level 3 and level 4. A top executive's career usually involves a number of changes in scale and scope. As McCall points out, the key learnings come from 'first time' components, such as managing multiple functions for the first time (general management) or being responsible for the bottom line of a unit for the first time.

Line to staff switch

It has already been shown how a stint in the corporate centre is seen as a positive move in the Unilever corporate culture, which has a critical impact on the career development scheme. Lessons here often involve greater exposure to strategy and the top managers of the business, better understanding of the rich balance of the business, a feel for the culture and how to influence powerful people in the field without formal authority.

The value-added role of the centre probably starts from level 3, which involves accountability for contributions to policy and strategy. This indicates that the most worthwhile transfers to the centre should occur from level 3 and above.

Learning or results

One of the key considerations of leadership development is the maximization of learning and development opportunities. This is where the tracking concept can become so powerful. If one is trying to develop a Track 5 or Track 7 leader then sometimes they may not be the best person to obtain immediate results, as an investment in a job where individual learning will be very high is the better decision in the long-term interests of the company. A culture that is obsessed with 'the now, action and results' will tend to chew up its management rather than develop them. It will typically be a high-pay, high-churn company, a buyer not a developer of talent.

BOUNDARY MOVES

During work on the development of managers who could work effectively in international roles at level 5 during 2002 and 2003, it emerged from field work and interviews that 'boundary moves' are critical in development and learning on the job for these managers.

A 'boundary move' is a job change that takes the incumbent outside his or her level of comfort. This stimulates learning and personal development, assuming the individual has the capacity to gain from the experience. The challenge is to stretch the talented manager without snapping the chain of learning and confidence building associated with the move.

Typical boundary moves are the crossing from one function to another, a move to another country, to a project (from line to support), to the head office from the field or vice versa, or a move to a higher level of accountability. As has already been demonstrated, most grading and rank systems confuse status and accountability, so in practice it is often not clear when a real increase in accountability has occurred.

For most people, one boundary move at a time is a big enough challenge. For high-flyers heading to the upper echelons of a large complex organization with at least six levels of accountability, two boundary moves at a time can be managed. For the very best, potential CEOs of level 7+ organizations, maybe three boundary moves at once is digestible, but this is generally not recommended.

The military services tend to orchestrate career building experiences more carefully then most organizations. Their major problem is managing and balancing the differing demands of war and peace, which cause their structures to concertina back and forth, between excessive stretch and over-supply.

One international company I worked with recently identified 10 such boundary moves as key contributing experiences for potential country managers. These reflected in large measure the type of 'developmental experiences' advocated by Morgan McCall.

ANGLING FOR HEALTHY SALMON

Helen Handfield-Jones (2000) believes that job experience drives executive talent and outlines four key steps:

> First – The way a job is structured with both headroom and elbow room.
> Second – High potential people should move through a series of challenging jobs.
> Third – The job should provide a range of challenges.
> Fourth – Learn from highly skilled colleagues as well as superiors.

I have endeavoured to demonstrate how leadership development is best served by the holistic decision-making accountability approach to building a healthy organization.

Firstly, it ensures that the key roles in the organization have an accountable purpose aligned to the strategy and objectives of the business. This in turn makes for challenging and demanding roles whose natural by-product affords scope for learning and development.

Secondly, having established the stepping-stones of accountability, the next task is to identify who should occupy these roles. Analysing an individual's contribution against the framework of Accountability competencies can facilitate this.

Thirdly, having established a person's capacity for promotion one should consider the track which could be unfolding in front of this individual. This will help enable superiors to judge the pace at which he or she should be promoted over a 15-year period to ensure appropriate development.

The challenge, as Csikszentmihalyi (1991) has explained, is to maintain an individual in psychological flow 'in balance', neither overstretched nor underused. In other words, to stay on track. This can be pictured as shown in Figure 8.11.

Fourthly, the challenge for top management is to identify the appropriate developmental experiences aligned to key phases in a person's career, which optimize learning and development opportunities. Appropriate progress through the work levels simplifies this process and should help identify whether a 'start-up' or 'turnaround' experience, for example, is called for to ensure the best results for both the individual and the organization.

By following these four steps top management will ensure that their salmon are swimming downstream. They will not need to resort to

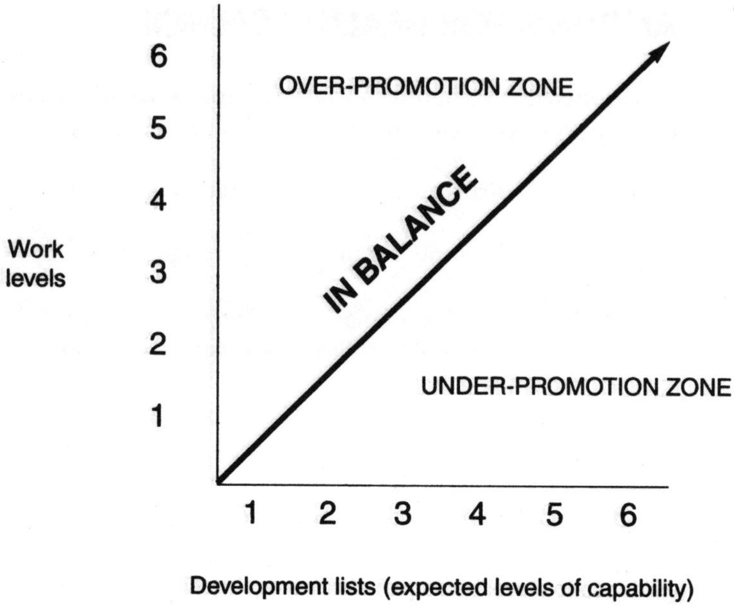

Figure 8.11 *Model of managerial balance (optimizing challenge and capability)*

crass culling schemes akin to throwing a stick of gelignite into the management development pool. But, as every good angler knows, catching prize fish is never straightforward. In 1997 Stephen Perkins reminded us: 'The next century will be the age of the multinational employee. Every successful major business will invest heavily in the development of a distinctive international cadre of executives. This group will be among the premium capital any organization would wish to have access to.'

There are plenty of anglers on the bank, and sometimes even though the salmon has been hooked, it manages to wriggle free and slip away. Tracking and landing your salmon takes skill, know-how and patience.

Step 10

Identify the career and learning tracks across the accountable decision-making levels, which successful managers in your organization have followed in the past. Use these as a basis for current learning and career mapping.

SUMMARY

This chapter has provided more evidence of the contribution that DMA can make in the field of leadership development and career planning. Evidence was provided of how careers have evolved in one global organization. It also demonstrated how an individual's development could be tracked over time and how reasonable predictions could be made about likely future developments up to 15 years ahead, provided the appropriate developmental experiences (as spelt out by the research of McCall *et al*) and boundary moves are carefully mapped out.

9

Mobilizing change

Communication is often the most neglected element of organizational change. Tesco and Unilever both put tremendous effort into mobilizing change. Most of this chapter will focus on Unilever, which implemented the changes to structure, job evaluation, salaries, benefits, appraisal, skills identification and training and competencies simultaneously in about 100 countries. This was an enormous change programme that had to be planned with great precision. It was orchestrated by a professional and reputable HR function, although not without some difficulty, as will be explained.

Tesco, on the other hand, implemented the changes in a more staggered fashion, affecting about 10 countries. Although the scale was not so great in Tesco, the planning was equally meticulous. Line management was more directly involved in the work levelling in Tesco working in close partnership with HR. Both companies relied on projects with full-time leaders, Tesco probably the more extensively. The up-front commitment in both companies was huge. For example, Unilever expenditure on communications and mobilization materials ran into seven figures.

This chapter will touch on resistance to change and will outline a five-phase model which was designed to help mobilize change and implement DMA in a global setting. The extensive commitment to consultation and training together with the range and variety of communication materials will be explained. I will also comment upon how the type of change affects the communication process. Since not everything was an unqualified success I will also refer to the lessons learnt on this journey. Finally, the effort to evaluate the implementation process in Unilever will be described.

RESISTANCE TO CHANGE

The increasing pace of change is commonplace today. But dealing with it is still a challenge. Many recognize intellectually the need for transformation but find it difficult to overcome the emotional barriers that arise. Sometimes change is stimulating but more often it is a feared, even traumatic experience because of lack of leadership, sensitivity to people and attention to their needs for communication.

Experience in Unilever was no exception. The resistance to change was widespread. And although communication is the lubricant of change we made our fair share of mistakes along the way. We recognized in due course that we needed to take people through five critical communication phases to ensure a degree of comfort and commitment in implementing the most complex series of HR changes we had ever taken at one time. Discontinuous organization change is an important determinant of organization adaptation. Responding to regulatory, economic, competitive and/or technological shifts through more efficiently pushing the same organization systems and processes just does not work, as Solow, Dertouzos and Lester demonstrated in 1989. Tushman, Newman and Romanelle (1986) had already pointed out that organizations might need to manage through periods of incremental as well as revolutionary change. The change that we were trying to communicate with the introduction of DMA and the associated changes in remuneration and appraisal were to different degrees both evolutionary and revolutionary changes. As will be seen below, this helped complicate the communication task.

COMMITMENT AT THE TOP

An essential element of successful organization change is support from the top of the organization. The chairmen agreed in principle but, given the importance of the proposed change, insisted that this issue be fully discussed by the full executive board. An entire day was set aside to discuss this issue and the board of 14 people was broken into three working syndicates. This was quite significant because it was only the second time in recent memory that the board had worked on any issue in syndicate form.

With the wisdom of hindsight, not enough thought was given to the make-up of the three syndicate groupings. It transpired that the most enthusiastic supporters of the new approach were in one syndicate; fortunately this syndicate included the retiring Chairman and the Chairman Elect. The other two syndicates were more of a mixed bag, which made the task of persuasion more challenging.

At Tesco the CEO was committed from the outset. He set the agenda for change.

THE HR FUNCTION

Dave Ulrich (1997) has written that the next agenda for competitiveness and issues such as globalization, appropriate technology, profitability through growth and capacity for change all have at their core the management and, in particular, the leadership of human resources. He goes on to identify four distinct roles that Human Resource staff much assume in order to lead transition: strategic partner, administrative expert, employee champion and change agent.

The role of change agent

Recognizing the central and critical role that the HR function would have to play in helping to manage this change process, we very early in the piece started to share our thinking with the HR community in Unilever. This process started with a presentation to the top HR executives. I think it is fair to say that we underestimated the degree of persuasion needed for this group, which, although not resistant to change, was more defensive than expected.

As with any reasonably sized group, there were a number of different attitudes encountered. During the first presentation of our initial ideas one or two felt they were fundamentally flawed. Some questioned whether the new language definitions and terminology that we were using were not 'modern and exciting enough'. It was suggested that the work levels would only be valid and appropriate if a corresponding hierarchy of processes accompanied them. An attractive thought, but when we arranged a separate meeting to identify these processes no solution was found and no model seemed to be available.

When confronted with completely new concepts, some members of this group tended to resist their acceptance without some form of modification. It was interesting to note that a number of these senior executives had developed their careers in industrial relations in Europe during the 1970s. This had been a time when successful 'solutions' invariably involved the politics of compromise. They were conditioned to be flexible and avoid the intransigence (or intellectual rigour) of the 'right solution'. They were not entirely comfortable with the discipline of a model that offered little room for manoeuvre on matters of substance. This was quite a challenge since we were communicating a model that had been tested and validated by extensive fieldwork (which is not that common for HR in business). This was not just a tentative theory or initial proposal for discussion. We were trying to sell our exciting conclusions, and achieve understanding of the new ideas. We were not seeking approval or ratification of the substance of these ideas. Their validity was not open to the type of political tinkering favoured by midnight debates in smoke-filled rooms. For example, if five work levels were found from analysis to accommodate a particular business unit then a discussion that perhaps it might be easier to sell six rather than five was really rather meaningless and unhelpful, whereas a discussion to understand why five and not four or six levels was appropriate and beneficial. We were trying to deliver the latter while some of our colleagues were focused on the former.

It was also clear that some individuals were concerned that critical areas of expertise might be taken away from them, and this clearly created some anxiety. The new approach was being proposed to replace the existing job evaluation scheme. But many of the top HR directors, including myself, had been trained in understanding and applying this job evaluation system, which for most line managers remained a mysterious 'black box'. The whole purpose of the changes being advocated was to arrive at a more transparent and simple system, which could be understood and applied by line management themselves.

Understandably, some HR directors were concerned that a source of their professional power was being eroded and, understandably, this made them uncomfortable. For a variety of reasons it was clear that the HR community was both anxious and apprehensive about the impact of the changes being proposed. They wondered whether they could manage the programme being advocated in the time frame available. Thus we were confronted with a more negative to neutral atmosphere than expected from the key individuals whom we would need to convince and reassure before they would be on side and ready to lead the change process.

Empowering the HR community

The plan was to empower the HR managers across the organization, of whom there were about 1,000 in total, to become the key catalysts and counsellors of change, which nevertheless was to be fronted and led by line management. Galvanizing this professional group was one of the major challenges we confronted. An analysis of key stakeholders' attitudes is critically important to shape and guide subsequent action.

Some of the reactions were predictable and were largely anticipated. Others were not. Very early on in the project we arranged a major meeting with a group of managers who led a key regional HR network. The main reason for this meeting was that we were aware of the fact that this group of managers knew that key projects had been running for some time focusing on potential change in the area of remuneration, job evaluation and appraisal. We had assumed that this group would be interested and hungry to be brought up to date with the latest developments and thinking preparatory to planning together the next phases of implementation. In fact when we started to present the progress to date on an inevitable path of change there was strong resistance to the very idea of change. These managers were not expecting change, it appeared, and felt that the existing policies and systems were 'just fine'. This was surprising, as there had been a number of groups, both of line managers and HR managers, who during the previous couple of years had advocated strongly the need for change. This reaction forced us to do some fundamental rethinking about the communication process, which will be covered in more detail – see Figure 9.1 below.

CONSULTATION WITH LINE MANAGEMENT

In the early stages of the project we had been involved in extensive consultation with line managers, particularly the chief executives of business units and their HR staff. By and large, line management were less defensive than those in HR. I think it is fair to say that the latter were concerned with the great burden that they could see which they would have to carry in addition to an already busy work schedule. But it was also about this time that the words of Machiavelli began to ring in our ears:

> There is nothing more difficult to undertake than changing the way things are done. You will have resistance from those who stand to lose as a result of the proposed changes and only luke-warm support from those who are likely to gain.

Influence of the audience's work levels on the consultation process

It was also well into the consultation process that we tumbled to a fundamental lesson which should have been apparent from the application of the very logic of accountability that we were trying to sell. We were consulting equally with managers in levels 2 and 3 and those in level 4 and above. Moreover, the topics, which were being canvassed with both groups, were identical. After some time it was very clear that asking managers in levels 2 and 3 for fundamentally new ideas to improve existing systems was of limited value. They tended to be uncomfortable with this type of consultation. We often got the response, 'Why is this taking so long?' These managers were more comfortable with a more concrete treatment of the issues. We realized that we needed to spell out why there was a need to change, what would be the key features of the new system and, most importantly, how they would be able to implement it.

On the other hand, managers in the strategic levels of accountability were more comfortable with an unstructured discussion in which not all the solutions were being presented in a finished state. This of course made sense because the very nature of their jobs was associated with boundary reconfiguration. They were comfortable with macro issues and of course made many helpful suggestions and gave a number of critical insights, which led to improvement in the ideas under consideration.

For example, initially we were referring to 'core' and 'support' jobs. It was pointed out that this could be confused with the need to sell businesses that were not part of the core strategy. Therefore the use of the word 'core' could imply that 'support' jobs were unimportant and superfluous, which was the exact opposite of the message we were trying to put across. We therefore changed the term to 'line' job, which did not have negative baggage.

We learnt that it was very important to tailor the content of the consultation process to the needs and abilities of the audience. For example, managers in levels 2 and 3 wanted to learn about the new system and how to implement it. They were not comfortable with a discussion of possible solutions.

THE COMMUNICATION MODEL

In digesting the lessons that we were learning as we progressed along the path of project and concept design we were greatly assisted by Towers Perrin London-based communications consultants, Jessica McNicholas and Jenny Robinson. The model draws heavily on the work of several notable writers such as Elizabeth Kubler-Ross on bereavement, Irvine Janis on persuasion and Hovland on proximity and communication studies.

In 1990 Warren Bennis outlined a number of pressures that militate against effective leadership:

- general inertia and resistance;
- mountains of entrenched bureaucracy;
- short-term business pressure;
- corporate politics;
- inadequate information flows.

Recently, Guy Charlton (2000) posed the question that we were struggling with at the time. 'Can the organizational leopard change its spots?' He concluded, as we had done, that if we can show people how to change and in the process point out the personal benefits and reasons for change to them, then the choice and the consequences proceed more smoothly.

It seemed clear from a number of sources that there were five critical phases in the change process, which needed to be understood in order to design and deliver effective communication. The result of this analysis was the Towers Perrin Five-Phase Change Model set out in Figure 9.1.

The model teaches us that:

- Communication needs to match the phase in which the audience sits. The easiest and most reliable indicator of the audience's postion is obtained through listening to concerns and questions. The questions nearly always correlate to a phase:
  - Why? Phase 1;
  - What? Phase 2;
  - How, for me? Phase 3;
  - How for others? Phase 4;
  - How to improve? Phase 5.

- Communication can achieve, at maximum, two to three phases of movement through the model – so 'one hit' of communication will not persuade people to change.

- Faster progress through the model is achieved through intimate media. Remote media will achieve, at most, a one-phase shift. For example: individual, face-to-face meetings are the most intimate, distribution e-mails are the reverse.

- Although the model is drawn as linear, people's emotions and progress through it are often iterative (back and forth) – communication needs to take account of this by ensuring that those doing the communicating are at least one phase ahead of their audience, emotionally and intellectually.

- To achieve change it is *not* necessary to have all audiences at phase 5. The critical strategic decision is to identify which audiences need to have reached phase 3 and beyond ('hearts and minds') to achieve critical mass change.

The mobilization process was as follows.

Phase 1

The first phase was establishing why it was necessary to change. When first confronted with the possibility of change, the most common response was denial. In fact if people were in **denial**, as we

	Phase I	Phase II	Phase III	Phase IV	Phase V
CHANGE PROCESS	ASSESSING WHAT NEEDS TO CHANGE	PROPOSING CHANGE	IMPLEMENTING CHANGE	USING NEW APPROACH	SEEKING WAYS TO IMPROVE
TYPICAL REACTION	Denial	Resistance	Adaptation	Acceptance	Commitment
INDIVIDUAL REACTIONS	The way we do it now works. Why change?	That's wrong! We can solve this another way. This will disrupt our business	I understand what is changing and how it will affect me. I do, however, remain to be convinced	I see how the system is beginning to work	There are still ways to improve
INFORMATION NEEDED TO PROGRESS	WHY	WHAT	HOW	HOW	HOW

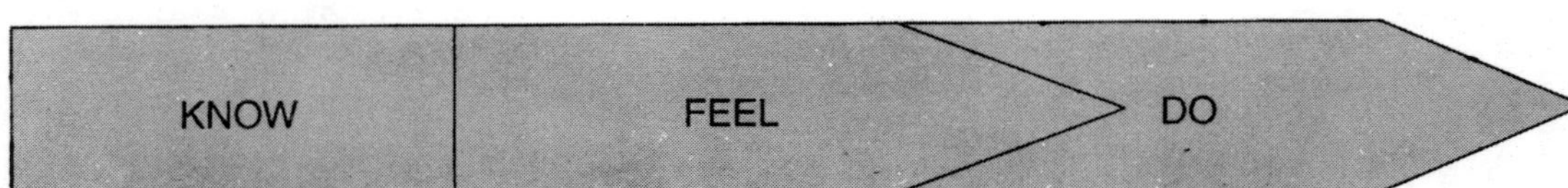

Figure 9.1 *Five-phase change model*

had encountered, while we were assuming that they might be in Phase 2 or 3 ready to accept and digest new information, then the communication would clearly fail and the appropriate action that was expected to follow would be blocked. In order to move people from the first phase it's important to give the background to the fundamental reasons driving the change. In a business organization it is critical that these are seen to fit with the business strategy. At the time Unilever, for example, was reorganizing on a worldwide scale under the umbrella heading 'Delivering Outstanding Performance'. Given this context, the changes being proposed in remuneration, job evaluation and appraisal were packaged as 'The Integrated HR Approach to Achieving Outstanding Business Performance'. Much of the communication and information required in the first phase is more cerebral than emotional.

Phase 2

The second critical phase occurs when specific new ideas are being canvassed as part of the change proposal. The typical reaction is often **resistance**. At this stage there is an acceptance that perhaps change should occur but the common reaction is a negative response to the first ideas on the agenda. As the model demonstrates, the movement now is more from the reasons for change towards establishing what principles, policies and practices are being put forward for consideration.. During this phase we are often confronted with gut reaction or how people feel about what is being proposed. It's important that the information provided is simple, succinct and states clearly what the new ideas are. The communication vehicle being used must anticipate that some emotional appeals may be necessary, in contrast to the earlier phase where a lot of the initial communication was based on less emotional appeal.

Phase 3

The third phase in the change and communication process is good news. By Phase 3, **adaptation**, individuals have accepted the need for change and are now focusing on how they will be affected by it and/or how they can implement the new change. However, there are still likely to be critical areas where they remain to be convinced of its appropriateness. The theme of communication is now trying to establish *how* the new changes can be put into action and much of the discussion focuses on debate about *how* the implementation process can be managed. For as Winnie the Pooh once said: 'it's not the **what** I'm having trouble with, it's the **how**'. When Phase 3 has been reached the communication process is more satisfying as the back of the resistance is now broken. But that is not to say that the next two phases are plain sailing!

Phase 4

The fourth phase represents the period when the change has been successfully implemented and the first stages of evaluation are probably taking place. Thus the changes have been **accepted** even though it is not clear yet how successful the whole process has been and indeed whether the stated objectives have been met. Nevertheless, the focus of this phase is on action and it's during this period that much of the personal communication with individuals occurs.

Phase 5

In the fifth phase, **commitment** is the osmosis process during which the new ideas and systems have started to become embedded in the organization. With the experience of implementation and a more complete understanding of how the new systems are working, the stage of continuous improvement is reached. There comes a time, of course, when it is felt that the existing system can no longer be meaningfully improved and at that point we are on the verge of a new Five-Phase Change Process where a totally new process is going to be required as the only means of effective improvement.

When this Five-Phase Change Model was first presented to our HR colleagues one of the younger wits in the audience neatly summed up the degree of challenge we were facing. 'The problem with some of our managers is that they are still in Phase 5 of the previous systems!'

TYPES OF ORGANIZATIONAL CHANGE

Nadler and Tushman (1990) highlighted four types of organizational change (see Figure 9.2) of two kinds:

- *Strategic and incremental changes*. The fundamental aim of such change is to enhance the effectiveness of the whole organization, but within the general framework of strategy. Such changes are

	Incremental	Strategic
Anticipatory	Tuning	Reorientation
Reactive	Adaptation	Re-creation

Figure 9.2 *Types of organizational change*

incremental and have an impact on the total system of the organization and fundamentally redefine the organization or change its basic framework strategic.

- *Reactive and anticipatory changes.* These are changes that are made in direct response to some external event. They are often forced on to the organization and are therefore reactive. Examples would be the change process that Ford and IBM went through following their problems in the early 1990s. Anticipatory changes occur when the leaders in the organization believe that change and anticipation of events still to come will generate greater competitive advantage. GE is the classic example of a business engaged in anticipatory changes.

Change that is both incremental and anticipatory is called **tuning**. Incremental change, which is initiated reactively, is called **adaptation**. Strategic change that is initiated in anticipation of future events is **reorientation** while that which is prompted by immediate demands is **re-creation**.

One of the problems with the changes in the Integrated HR Project in Unilever was that the organization changes and new approach to evaluating responsibilities required for the acceptance of the DMA logic and work levels were Reorientation. But those related to pay and appraisal were Tuning changes.

Reorientations are more difficult and the more risky. They are usually initiated ahead of the competition and in advance of environmental pressures. This requires top executives with vision. A major challenge occurred when we were asked, 'Who has introduced work levels before on a global scale?' The answer that no one had and that therefore we were leading was clearly not comforting to some of the directors as they looked over the abyss of leadership.

Nadler and Tushman point out that 'given organization and individual inertia re-orientations cannot be initiated or implemented without sustained action by the organization's leadership'. Indeed, as Vancil (1987) had earlier noted, reorientations are frequently driven by new leadership, often brought in from outside the organization. One of the fortuitous elements of the reorganization in 1996 was the passing of the baton to the new Chairman, Niall Fitzgerald. Although he was not an external appointment, he was a source of new momentum for change in the business. We used this opportunity to launch a series of newsletters, which initially featured the new chairman endorsing the new approach.

Figures 9.1 and 9.2, outlined above, graphically illustrate the complexity of communicating change on a global scale. On the one hand the receivers' attitudes, values and emotions during the change process have to be anticipated and managed. On the other, this process becomes ever more complex when the nature of organizational change is different for the respective elements of the change project.

COMMUNICATION MATERIALS

Paul Strebel (1996) has pointed out that in Fortune 1,000 companies the success rate for organizational change management is well below 50 per cent and may be as low as 20 per cent. He goes on to say that personal commitment to an organization comes from an understanding of the following questions:

- What am I supposed to do for the organization?
- What help will I get to do the job?
- How and when will my performance be evaluated, and what form will the feedback take?
- What will I be paid, and how will pay relate to my performance evaluation?

The Integrated HR Project was attempting to answer these questions.

During the process of change the identification of the appropriate communication materials is a prerequisite for success. The culture of an organization will shape the appropriate forms and channels of communication to be employed. For example, Unilever prides itself on being a 'multilocal-multinational'. Historically the 500 business units or local companies are considered to be the fundamental building blocks of the organization. This has generated a feeling in the business of decentralized autonomy and independence. Given this environment, it would be wholly inappropriate to arrange for mandated communications from the corporate centre. It was essential in order to harness the advantages of a corporate initiative that scope was built into the communication process for local interpretation and variation.

Core materials

The first key step was to identify what were the core materials that needed to be communicated to answer the questions highlighted by Strebel. For example, in order to have a successful basis to international management development and assessment of accountability it was important that the new model was not diluted. It was therefore not possible for a local company to operate with six or seven work levels when it had been established that what was required across the concern was up to five. Similarly, the key principles of the reward and appraisal policies were also established. Once these central tenets had been agreed scope was built in for local companies or regions to 'top and tail' the material to suit their local circumstances. As a result the corporate centre prepared key material covering the philosophy of the overall approach to be adopted. Statements of policy and principle together with the underlying manuals, for example, set out the work levels and the redefined competencies aligned to work levels. The overall approach to performance appraisal (to be relaunched as the Personal Development Plan – PDP) was to be standard in format. In order to ensure that these basic messages were transmitted quickly and consistently a series of training workshops were designed and run around the world. These were aimed at both the HR network and key line managers.

Presentation kits

Since this communication process was going to be led by the line it was important that presentation kits were made available which covered the core text to be communicated. These presentation packs, containing core presentation slides, videos and frequently asked questions, were then added to by local units in order to achieve a local flavour. For example, in Latin America regional management decided to translate the key manuals into Spanish and Portuguese. In South Africa the change programme was run under the heading of 'Achieving Excellence' which was part of a reorganization and transformation that was taking place in the country at that time.

Similarly, although the remuneration principles had been agreed for the concern as a whole, nevertheless it was very clear that the market rate required for management in Shanghai was totally different from that in São Paulo. Thus local countries were free to establish the competitive remuneration profiles in their respective markets while at the same time respecting the overall approach designed for the benefit of Unilever as a whole. It was important that the essential components were not devalued in any way since this would have militated against the fundamental objectives, which were to facilitate the concern's global performance in the areas of organization design, personal accountability, reward, individual development and career planning.

In a globally networked company such as Unilever, where it is believed that the success of the organization is built upon the international movement of key management, it is absolutely essential that there is a consistent bedrock of policies and systems that facilitates this overall process. In a global company that is run along conglomerate lines, where interchange between the businesses and/or countries is not an ongoing requirement, then arguably there would be no need to establish global policies and systems in the areas of pay and performance.

Information requirements

A large global project such as the Integrated Approach to HR Management can take some time to implement. Often, as was the case in Unilever, individual pilot studies commence the rollout process and it is very important to ensure that the rest of the organization both learns from these early experiences and is kept abreast of ongoing developments. To meet this need, working together throughout with the communication consultants from Towers Perrin, we produced a number of newsletters and articles, which were sent to key members of the HR community and line managers who were interested in being kept up to date.

In order to signal the involvement and strong support from the top of the organization, in the first newsletter that was sent out in March 1996, just after the largest reorganization in Unilever's history had been announced, we deliberately took the opportunity to lead with the main article featuring the new Chairman Elect. He clearly and unequivocally spelt out why he believed in the work-level approach and what benefits he foresaw it could add to enhancing the performance of the new reorganization that had just been announced. Through this series of newsletters we were able to announce other key steps concerning the rollout and the target date (April 1998) by which time every business unit within Unilever was expected to be on the new system.

Although at the time over 70,000 Unilever employees were on e-mail around the world, the intranet system was not universally applicable owing to telecommunication problems in some parts of the world. Thus we were not able to use the intranet and Web sites as much as we would have liked. Certainly anybody contemplating changes of this magnitude today would ideally make use of electronic communication as much as possible. This would obviate the need perhaps to have a series of newsletters and articles as was required two or three years ago. Such is the pace of change! As I now work with other organizations these are options we have to keep exploring.

Cost

There is no doubt that there is a great tendency to shortcut on the costs of communication and training. We found that to do the job effectively the money spent on communication materials ran into seven figures. This did not take into account the time that management spent on this project in communicating and counselling both groups of managers and individuals.

TRAINING

A major effort underpinning all of these activities was the amount of training that was required. Once the total project was authorized we immediately began running workshops. These were aimed initially at the senior members of the HR network and our plan was to cover the top 20 per cent so that they would be totally conversant with the five phases of communication and could then similarly train managers in their own units.

The next key groups we targeted were the CEOs of various business groups, research laboratories and heads of key departments in the corporate centre. Again it was important that they had an opportunity to understand the background to the series of changes so that they could convincingly lead the communications with their own teams. Secondly, we were keen to consult with this group since, as I have already indicated, we found that they often had important suggestions, refinements and improvements to the changes that we were planning to put in place. As the implementation was being completed we made a major investment in a series of interactive CD ROMs, which were available to any individual who was keen to study the new approach in more detail. These involved jobs in key parts of the organization where the individual could go through a learning process of the CD ROM case study trying to establish the correct work levels. We had felt very keenly the need to stimulate the osmosis process of understanding so that we could move strongly into Phase 4 of the communication programme and prepare for Phase 5. Obviously continuous improvement would be that much more effective the more people understood the full process.

Tesco's approach to mobilizing change was different but equally impressive. The main difference was the multi-phasing of the project and the greater direct involvement of line management. The project, or programme in Tesco language, was known as 'One Team Rewards', and was led by a main board member (Michael Wemms until he retired in mid-2000, and then Philip Clarke) with Clare Chapman, the HR Director, as programme champion. The programme board consisted principally of senior line managers representing key constituencies in the business. It meet weekly and closely supervised and advised a number of project teams. The key, full-time, project team leaders were Richard Dodd (One Team Rewards), Conway Daw (communications), Maya Brown (rewards), Helen O'Keefe (benefits) , Naveed Ahmed (systems) and Nicola Steele (work levels and organization).

Nine implementation teams were set up representing key domains in the business. They were led by a line manager on a full-time basis. They and their teams were then extensively trained by Nicola Steele and myself in work levels, for example, so that they, under guidance, could then work-level their parts of the business up to the main board. These teams worked in parallel on a 16-week Activity Plan, which culminated in 'Read-across (consistency) meetings' prior to sign-off at board level.

Conway Daw and his team designed communications material, Nicola Steele produced a Work Level workbook and Maya Brown a Managing Pay booklet. They also set up a 'work room' on the company intranet which could be accessed by the project team members.

LESSONS LEARNT

As already indicated, in pioneering the application of the DMA model we made a number of mistakes along the way. As I now work with other organizations, I try to ensure I use this learning process to avoid making the same mistakes again.

Robust model

Anybody setting out on a major HR change needs to ensure that the underlying conceptual framework is sound. As already indicated in Chapter 6, many people make the mistake of launching into broadbanding of money without having thought through the underlying paradigm required.

One company, which broadbanded money in 2000, in fact set its pay bands right through the middle of the real levels of accountability. This was confirmed by a DMA analysis in 2002. In the meantime the staff had become very disenchanted with the lack of transparency, logic and equity in the new system. By 2003 this demotivation was widespread, with predictable pressure for regradings, which saw a surge in grade-drift and cost to the tune of 14 per cent. Business growth was less than 25 per cent of that figure during the same period.

In Tesco the One Team Rewards Project started as a broadbanding project. But Clare Chapman, the HR Director, and Richard Dodd, the project manager, first saw the need for a conceptual framework and recognized the potential of DMA. If the underlying paradigm is lacking or faulty then no amount of excellent communication and training will avoid the obvious problems that will quickly emerge within a year or two of implementation. We spent a lot of time obtaining the empiricaldata, which proved that the model of accountability was robust and resilient. This is important because the framework continues to be challenged by line managers when they find that their organization is sub-optimal according to the DMA principles. Their logical response is to challenge whether this 'theoretical model' really fits the pragmatic requirements and challenges of their business. By having a sound empirical base it is relatively straightforward to establish and identify where the shortcomings are in sub-optimal organizations.

Don't underestimate the resistance to change

It is a platitude today to say that people resist change. Being aware of this, we consciously targeted the HR function initially to lead this process since it harboured the designated agents of change in the organization. But even the designated shock troops were not beyond more than a few tremors of uncertainty themselves. While line managers applauded the aim to do away with the black box of job evaluation and develop more open and user-friendly systems of reward and leadership development, this caused anxiety in the HR community. What would happen to their expert jobs? Would they lose influence and status in this 'brave new world'? Would all this talk of delegation to the line erode established HR career paths? And since there was no precedent elsewhere of the successful introduction of DMA on a global scale, they were sailing into uncharted waters. Hence change that excited the few unnerved the many.

Looking back, it is clear that we did not pay enough attention early enough (in Unilever) to the HR network's concerns about the impact of DMA upon its own profession. In Tesco the HR function became the pilot group for the testing of the Activity Plan, which led to important learnings and modifications of the original plan as the learning points were taken on board. I have subsequently applied this lesson when working with other organizations in 2002 and 2003.

Don't short-change on full-time project members

Both Tesco and Unilever committed considerable full-time resources to their respective mobilization programmes. On balance, Unilever nearly cut it too fine, which placed great pressure on non-project managers. The price was more variation in the quality of implementation.

The Tesco project culture is impressive and once they mobilized their teams the work-rate, commitment and results were most effective. At the time of writing, their efforts have not had time to be evaluated but that will naturally form part of the Group's annual company-wide employee survey.

But resourcing projects of this nature requires good budget discipline, a realistic assessment of the workload involved, careful planning of deadlines and flexibility coupled with project discipline to meet deadlines. Tesco seems to be better than most in these areas. Their approach to programmes and projects is covered more fully in the next chapter.

Importance of communication model

The distilling of the communication model into the five phases of development was vital in sharpening the effectiveness of our training and communication process. We also found from experience that it was not wise to skip any of the phases of the model. It seems that if you skip stages then you place unnecessary pressure and risk on the communication process. We found it was necessary to continually 'start at the beginning' and assume **denial** and **resistance**.

It is very tempting, when faced with the time pressures of implementation, to jump into Phase 3 of the model. Our experience suggests that this is always a mistake if the aim is to win hearts and minds. People need to know why the change is occurring and very quickly seek personal assurance as to the likely impact upon themselves. The longer there is uncertainty about the individual consequences of the macro changes being introduced, the greater is the period of potential resistance, which puts great strain on the entire communication process.

Because of the reorganization in 1996 we effectively lost a year during implementation. This had some advantages but the major disadvantage was the fact that the period of uncertainty for individuals was extended longer than had been planned. This was not ideal.

Know when to stress the benefits

As one moves through Phases 1 and 2 of the communication model it is important to think through the compelling proposition for those receiving the message. There is always a comfortable tendency to treat the audience as a unitary body whereas it is pluralistic, with many different interests and concerns. Some may feel they are losers, not winners, as a result of the change. In the Unilever 'big bang' approach there was good news for young, high-performing managers with potential to ascend the work levels – about 30 per cent of the total population. Much thought was given to the remaining 70 per cent. This was a key reason why the new approach to appraisal with its emphasis on skill development was introduced at the same time. This was potentially good news for everyone.

In Tesco's phased approach it was important to dispel fears about the next phases by anticipating concerns (eg having an answer ready for the question, 'How will I progress through the work levels in future'?).

One of the major obstacles to changing a job evaluation system is the issue of fewer administrative promotions. It is a very emotional concern for many individuals. Even the most macho superiors are unnerved, it seems, by this 'problem' and tend to revert to Phase 1 behaviour: 'Is the grading system really broke and do we really need this solution?'

The most frequently asked question on the workshops we ran in both Tesco and Unilever was 'But how will I get promoted now?' and 'How will I motivate my staff now there are fewer promotions?'

It is necessary to change the nature of the personal development debate and communicate clearly that real promotion is about increased accountability and not the fiddling of an outdated system. Administrative promotions are popular because they offer more status and more money.

There are inevitably some problems with those who resent those of lesser status (ie of a lower grade in the old currency) being stationed in the same level of accountability. The answers have been outlined in Chapters 6 and 7. Administrative promotions are largely about money. Pay increases are possible within a work level, and the anchor rates approach of Tesco avoids the trap of turning the pay ranges into 'promotions'. The distinction between skills and competencies clarifies when someone should move within a work level (and maybe have a pay increase) and when it is time to move to the next work level – a real promotion.

Status loss is mainly psychological but it is very real. I do not know of any culture that does not value status in some guise or another. Sensitivity about such realities as titles and benefits is very important in this context. It is important not to duck these issues and risk devaluing the new approach. Openness and transparency are vital for the building of trust and confidence during the change process.

Shape consultation to target audience

As has been outlined in the section on Consultation above, the substance of the message has to be tailored to the level and quality of the audience to ensure the most productive response.

Those in operational work levels are not generally at ease with unstructured discussions on the establishment of policy or strategy. The discussion is more fruitful if the focus is upon the *how* and delivery rather than the *what* stages of design. I well remember one individual whose first response to every new idea was, 'It will not work in my country', but who could never give any facts or reasons to explain why not. Unwittingly, we had taken him out of his operational depth into the deeper currents of strategy.

We learnt, the hard way, that it is very important to have the right content and level of issues for discussion for the right audience in order to get the most constructive outcomes. We initiated some discussion with strategic managers in Latin America, which exceeded our expectations once we had the subject material pitched at the right level. Meetings scheduled for three hours took more like five and laid the foundation for important learning elsewhere in the organization.

Know the tipping point for change

Malcolm Gladwell (2000) has popularized the idea of the tipping point for change. The trick is knowing when sufficient critical mass has been achieved for it to drive the desired change. In this context it amounts to identifying the handful of leaders in the organization who will 'turn the herd'.

As already indicated, one of the somewhat surprising features of our work was the defensiveness we experienced from the HR community. If that was the bad news, at least the good news was that the number of people required to shift the herd was remarkably few. Probably fewer than 10 (1 per cent) real enthusiasts, who were convinced of the need for change and had the ability to communicate this to their colleagues, were critical in establishing successful momentum and finally successful implementation.

There were three key people in Unilever who influenced North America deciding to go first and pilot the project at the beginning of 1997, namely Jim McCall, Keith Rowland and the late Kathie Cunningham. In South Africa two individuals, Gavin Neath and John Harvey, were the driving forces; in Latin America the key catalysts were Christine Horsfield and Brian Mahoney; in Europe a key player was Guy de Herde (later also influential in Arabia); while in Australasia it was Ian MacDonald.

Key players in Tesco early on were Richard Dodd, Maya Brown, Ann Hazelden and Nicola Steele. Similar roles have been played by

Mike Cutt, Rob Barnett and Guy Eccles at B&Q, George Battersby, Malcolm Saffin, Penny Stoker and Maryann Barnacle at Amersham, Karen Millar, Trista Bennetts, Mark Thomas at Marks & Spencer, Shaunagh Dawes and Katie Peters at Somerfield, and Commander Lee Dawson in the Royal Navy.

Now, when I am setting up a project, I deliberately seek out 'evangelists', just 1 of whom is worth 10 normal project members. I wouldn't have believed in advance that such a small number of individuals could have such a far-reaching ripple effect across their respective organizations. This was a key learning point.

Involve line management

Both Tesco and Unilever ensured that line management led what were essentially changes to HR policy and systems. They invested a lot of effort in convincing the work level 5+ managers of both the need for change and the need for them to lead it. This was easier in Tesco as about 90 per cent of this group were in the UK and part of a ready-made forum, the 'retail council', which met together every three months or so. It was involved in all the key stages of the proposed changes and some of its members were on the programme board.

The involvement of line management in leading the implementation projects has already been described in this chapter. In fact, if the line does not lead the change process, no matter how good the HR network may be, mobilization will probably not occur.

Use pilot studies

Both Tesco and Unilever tested their implementation ideas via pilot studies. Tesco first carried out a 'behind-the-desk' study in a major head office department.

This led to refinement of the mobilization plan, which was then tested in full on the HR function. This led to further learnings which were incorporated in the 16-week Activity Plan rollout. For example, more time was built in.

Unilever first implemented in North America, a year ahead of the overall implementation plan. Three months later South Africa implemented. These two pilots also afforded valuable lessons which were subsequently applied in the global rollout. Amersham, Marks & Spencer and Kingfisher similarly tested the ideas in pilot studies.

EVALUATION

The changes that started in January 1997 in North America, and in South Africa in April 1997, were implemented across the whole of Unilever in April 1998. The next key step was to evaluate how well this project had been implemented and whether the original objectives had been met. We decided to do this as part of the annual audit programme in the latter half of 1998. The auditors had access to all of the original material that went to the board and were able to identify the reasons for making the change in the first place and the various objectives and constraints that had been set in the interim. I then met with 10 of the leading auditors from around the world and ran a workshop outlining in more detail what the introduction of work levels should have achieved, the kinds of problems that some units had encountered, and some of the shortcomings that might be present if implementation had not gone smoothly or effectively.

This audit was conducted between October and December 1998 across 31 units in 28 countries covering approximately 6,000 managers in 10 business groups (out of 12) and in 4 corporate functions. Perhaps predictably at that stage, the report concluded: 'It is too early after the implementation of work levels in 1998 to establish whether many of the desired key benefits have been achieved (for example flatter structures, longer job tenure, increased international mobility).' But notwithstanding any of above, the following recommendations where included:

> The work level principles can be used as a conceptual aid to companies who are setting up a new organization, or for assisting the integration of acquisitions into the Concern. The specific problems of over layering should be identified and where possible, organizational changes should be identified and implemented to achieve compliance with the work level principles.

It was also noted that 'communication of work levels and pay scales (within work levels) has in general been open and has been completed in all but a few companies where there are special situations' (for example, Zaire), and that authorization procedures had been defined and followed. 'There is total consistency in the procedures for work levels 4 and 5. In operating companies work level 3 determinations are normally approved by Company Chairmen. At work level 2 there is less consistency. In all cases reviewed however, the HR Director was involved in the evaluation.'

The key recommendation was: 'It is fundamental to the long term success of work levels that a system is established which will provide a basis for Corporate HR Group together with Business Groups to regularly analyse, monitor and control progress to ensure consistency of application of policy across Business Groups, and Còrporate functions. In addition Corporate HR Group should make resource available for identifying inconsistencies and exceptions and to advise Business Groups on how these should be managed.'

Thus, although this evaluation was completed within six months of implementation, it was clearly accepted that the introduction had gone well. There were, however, signs that the normal pressures within the business could militate against the ongoing effectiveness of the programme unless key databases and information processes were installed together with expertise that could resolve problems and issues.

The message in the communication context is that it is difficult to introduce a change of this magnitude and equally difficult to maintain the momentum to ensure that the full benefits are obtained. Arguably this is the main challenge of any significant change process.

At the time of writing, Tesco has just implemented DMA. It is too soon to evaluate the results. However, the company does conduct an extensive annual attitude survey (Viewpoint) which will provide valuable feedback on the acceptance of One Team Rewards.

Step 11

To ensure successful mobilization of organization-wide change:

- ***Appoint and train project team(s) led by line managers:***
  - ***with full-time resources, not less than work level 3;***
  - ***with clear budgets and deadlines.***
- ***Ensure professional communication advice and material is on hand;***
- ***Have suitably briefed senior line management lead, communicate and own the change.***

SUMMARY

Unilever put an enormous amount of effort and thought into mobilizing the change required to implement the approach outlined in this book. Tesco, implementing from 2001, similarly attached great importance to mobilizing the change effort. Conway Daw was appointed full time to this task towards the end of 1999

Given the size of the task confronting these companies, and the tight time scales, not everything was perfect. But the amount of time, money and commitment was probably unprecedented for a change to HR systems and practice in both companies. Even so, much vigilance is required to ensure that the osmosis process of understanding and extension into continuous improvement – **Phase 5** – is achieved.

10

The future.com

A number of themes currently dominate concerns about global business trends at the outset of the 21st century. Some preoccupy those in business, such as the imperative for increasing growth and the unforeseen advent of the Internet. Others preoccupy those outside business. There is concern about the disappearance of jobs, the impact of technology and capitalism's insensitivity to the worsening social and economic imbalances between the haves (increasingly educated and skilled knowledge workers) and the have-nots.

THE CHALLENGE OF TOMORROW

The purpose of this chapter is to examine the resilience of the decision-making accountability (DMA) model in the face of these emerging developments. It might be argued that so far this book has focused on the developments of today and yesterday. But what of tomorrow? Plotting the events and patterns of the past is not too difficult. Predicting the future is a different proposition, as Bill Gates (1996) has observed: 'People often over estimate what will happen in the next two years and under estimate what will happen in the next 10.'

Is the logic and power of DMA relevant to the fast-moving virtual world of the Internet and cyberspace? How will accountability be plotted in these new organizations of clicks and mortar? Will work life-spans in global enterprises be governed by existing or new patterns of development? Will the principles of accountability withstand the relentless speed and shifting forces of technological change and invention? Or is personal and organizational accountability already destined for the industrial museums of the 20th century along with the concept of the job?

I will argue that DMA is equally important to companies chasing growth and/or e-business opportunities. The message for bricks and mortar and clicks and mortar is the same. Furthermore, I will suggest a new idea of 'growth per accountability level' as a powerful new approach to personal and organizational health in the 21st century.

THE GROWTH IMPERATIVE

Growth is back on the agenda. During the 1960s many cash-rich companies frittered away earlier gains in a spate of ill-conceived diversifications. Growth, any sort of growth, was the orthodoxy of the day. Consumer goods companies plunged into sporting goods, breweries bought supermarkets, and automobile companies bought computer companies and so on. As these companies weathered with difficulty the less benign 1970s, this approach to growth was redressed in the 1980s. Peters and Waterman (1982) advised companies to 'stick to the knitting'. Companies were exhorted to return to their core business. Many of the diversifications of the 1960s became divestments in the 1980s as boards struggled to return their businesses to profitability.

The buoyant 1990s began with a scramble for new markets around the world following the collapse of communism. With sensible investment new growth was readily available. Some of it was relatively straightforward to acquire. For example, West German companies had easy pickings in the former East Germany. Seemingly huge, tantalizing markets in Russia and China lured many companies to invest in those countries. But the upsurge in company results often masked shortcomings in the existing strategy and organization. The good business results in the 1990s were also accompanied by a decade of good news on the equity markets. By the turn of the century most of these opportunities had been exploited but shareholders and analysts have hungry expectations, and the explosive market growth of dot.com start-ups has merely whetted their appetites for more of the same. The pursuit of growth is *de rigueur* today. Stock markets have ruthlessly taken money out of so-called low- or non-growth companies. Thus inherently sound and well-run companies such as Procter & Gamble, Coca-Cola and Cadbury have seen their market values plummet at times during this period.

The economic history of trade cycles demonstrates that periods of boom are followed by harsh corrections. One philosophical reaction to the growth of the 1950s and 1960s was Schumacher's 'small is beautiful'. More recently, Kennedy has echoed Malthus' concerns about the impact of population growth on the world's available resources. Today, many of the world's CEOs are obsessed with obtaining sustainable profitable growth. In 1999 Unilever's historical growth targets were doubled. At the same time their key competitor Procter & Gamble embarked on an identical strategy. It is a moot point whether they can both succeed. P&G has already shed one CEO in this attempted dash for growth.

ACCOUNTABILITY FOR GROWTH

Be that as it may, the current advice on how to up performance in the growth stakes is set out by Baghai, Coley and White (1999). Their analysis is as follows; it is important to:

> distinguish between the embryonic, emergent and mature phases on a business's life cycle. We refer to these stages as the 3 horizons of growth.
>
> Horizon 1 Encompasses the businesses that are the heart of the organization. In successful businesses these account for the lion's share of profit and cash flow.
>
> Horizon 2 Comprises businesses on the rise: fast moving, entrepreneurial ventures in which a concept is taking root or growth is accelerating. Though substantial profits may be four or five years away.
>
> Horizon 3 Contains the seeds of tomorrow's businesses – they are real activities and investments. Should they prove successful, they will be expected to reach Horizon 1 levels of profitability.

Defining the three horizons

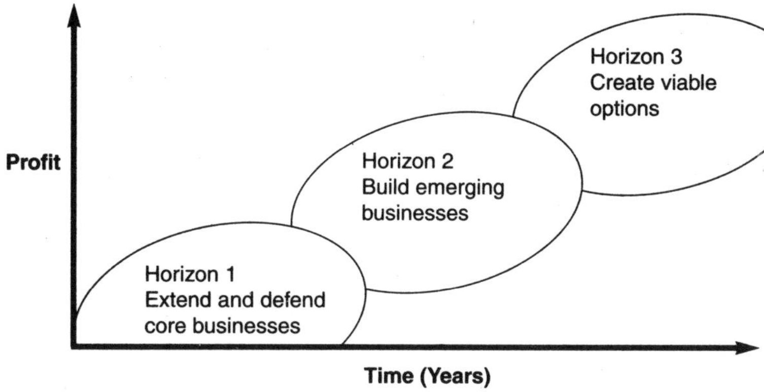

Source: *The Alchemy of Growth*, P5

> Initiatives in the 3 Horizons pay off over different time frames. The goal of managing the 3 Horizons, by contrast, is to develop many businesses in parallel without regard to their stage of maturity. The 3 Horizons must be managed concurrently, not sequentially.

The decision-making accountability model dovetails very neatly for those companies pursuing the three horizons of growth. Those primarily accountable for achieving the ongoing business would be in the operational levels 1–3. Their work is essentially ensuring that existing assets perform better, while those in the strategic levels, 4–6, would be held accountable primarily for nursing emerging fast-moving ventures outlined as horizon 2. Finally, those in the governance levels would be expected to 'create viable options for embryonic ventures in horizon 3', such as exploiting e-commerce opportunities. At the same time, they would hold the lower levels accountable for concurrently pursuing horizons 1 and 2.

The DMA model helps to define appropriate resources to build horizons 2 and 3. For example, in the mid-1990s Unilever made a strategic decision to enter Vietnam. The plan was to rapidly build a fully fledged standalone business, which would grow to work level 5. Although at the beginning the resource infrastructure did not warrant level 5, a work level 5 manager was appointed who was capable of quickly realizing the corporate growth objective.

On the other hand, I was recently working in a business where the board had put a 'horizon 3' initiative in place. But because no one on the board had knowledge of the horizon 3 markets, the venture was suffering from neglect and absentee management and was in danger of withering on the vine as the staff in the lower levels became increasingly disenchanted with the lack of direction – a clear case where those at the relevant levels of accountability were failing to manage their three horizons concurrently.

The DMA model can help sharpen accountability for a multi-layered growth strategy at all levels in the organization. It will therefore deliver more than today's fashionable attempts to build an enterprise culture, 'whatever that is', as John Hunt of the London Business School trenchantly observed in 1999.

THE IMPACT OF THE INTERNET

The arrival of the Internet is both the most exciting and most frightening business development on the cusp of the 21st century. It was unheralded, and arrived at blistering speed. Furthermore, the pace of development continues to accelerate. This is opening up exciting new business opportunities with potentially frightening consequences. Writing as recently as 1999, Baghai and colleagues did not even contemplate the possibility that a horizon 3 dot.com initiative could quickly cannibalize their horizon 1 and 2 businesses. CEOs have never been confronted before with such stark choices yet without any established business models or 'rules of the game' to guide them. They are being relentlessly confronted by what Downes, Chunka and Negropente (1998) describe as the law of disruption – namely that while technology changes exponentially, social, political and economic systems change only incrementally. Furthermore, these CEOs know that the prevailing conventional wisdom insists that they must lead in this situation, not follow, to have any chance of survival, let alone success in this marketplace battle.

In April 2000, the Global Organization and Management Council of the Conference Board met in Washington to discuss the organization design implications of e-business developments. The uncomfortable conclusion was that there are as yet are no clear or proven solutions. Each of the global corporations present was experimenting with various business-to-business (B2B) and business-to-customer (B2C) configurations. It was clear that there is still considerable confusion between e-commerce (dealing with the Internet, digital communications and IT applications that facilitate buying or selling processes) and e-business (optimizing an organization's performance through the adopting of digital technology and the use of the Internet or intranet as the primary communications media). Dot.com businesses such as Amazon or a manufacturing company such as DELL are examples of e-business leaders.

The Council also identified that this is an area of new but unavoidable conflict for CEOs. This was the thrust of an analysis presented by consultants from the Delta organization. Their latest thinking was summarized in their publication Dot-Combat (2000). Two of the principal sources of conflict are development of new channels and potential investments in technologies, start-up ventures and revenue generators that may cannibalize the value of past investments and assets, and customer and supplier relationships. For example, in 1999 Proctor & Gamble set up an Internet cosmetics business for new products (Reflect.com) for direct transactions with consumers, which did not delight their largest customer, Wal-Mart.

Another problem identified that e-businesses have to move much faster than the core business yet current governance procedures have been designed for the latter, not the former. There are also difficult decisions to be made about reward and management strategies between the different business formats.

Finally, CEOs are being confronted with new leadership choices. In 1990 Chris Lorenz wrote about how BP's top three executives were trying to change from the traditional command and control style to a more empowering, consensus style of leadership. Most enlightened CEOs tried to travel down this path during the 1990s. But consensus takes time. Business leaders are used to taking decisions based on objective analysis and careful deliberation, drawing upon years of accumulated know-how and experience. But the exigencies of e-business require quick, autocratic decisions based largely on ignorance. The style and results of this decision-making process are bound to generate conflict and turf wars among executive colleagues, and the consensus of this Washington meeting was that most CEOs are not comfortable or skilful in resolving such conflict.

BETWEEN A ROCK AND A HARD PLACE

These twin objectives of growth and establishing e-commerce and e-businesses are potentially self-cancelling. Driven by a desire to satisfy stock market pressures (and enrich themselves) most CEOs are signing up to the aggressive growth objectives, which are likely to be undermined by e-commerce and IT developments. But is there anything in the latter which conflicts with the principles of decision-making accountability? My contention is that there is not. More than that, DMA will clarify emerging areas of conflict and uncertainty and help resolve them.

It has already been established above that the onus for developing dot.com initiatives lies squarely upon the chief executive. The establishment of any new venture is subject to common principles of accountability even if the organizational format is a journey into uncharted territory. In December 1999 I helped to draw up an accountability profile of a new role in Unilever for a head of e-novation – See Figure 10.1. The role was pitched at level 5 to be effective, but short-sighted company politics was driving for an appointment at a lower level, defeating the objective of the exercise.

Apart from establishing the highest level of accountability, the other critical decision is to correctly identify the frontline, or lowest level of accountability. As indicated previously in this book (Chapter 4), the frontline is not always at level 1. Many start-up dot.com ventures can enjoy a very flat structure if the frontline is at the second or third level of accountability. This could happen in a highly creative start-up. This, for example, would appear to the case with recent dot.com ventures of scientists emanating from Cambridge University in the UK.

On the other hand, recent interviews with incumbents in the Tesco.com direct shopping venture in the UK, currently the largest Internet grocery shopping business in the world, identified the front-line as clearly at level 1, while the top job was among the company's strategic echelon. Evidence to date therefore confirms unequivocally that electronic accountabilities, whether existing, growing or totally new, can be accurately identified and mapped by the DMA approach. Furthermore, it can help avoid the pitfalls of confusing new organizational forms with the demands for clear accountability.

A JOBLESS WORLD

At a European HR conference in Monaco (3 April 1996), William Bridges surprised his audience when sketching a future without jobs. 'Jobs will disappear, but not accountability for work.' His presentation was based on his book *Job Shift*, published in 1996. Bridges' thesis is as follows. The job, with defined fixed boundaries, is a product of the

Senior Vice-President – Unilever E-Novation Centre

Principal Objective of Role
To identify appropriate leading-edge *e*-commerce and *e*-business methods and technologies and promote their use within Unilever to enable the Concern to exploit new e-commerce business opportunities and to improve the efficiency and effectiveness of all its business processes to world-class levels.

Reports To
Unilever Chief Information Officer.

Organisation
Will lead a small team of *e*-business experts who will support in the fulfilment of this principal objective.

Principal Customers
Unilever Business Managers (particularly those involved in new *e*-commerce business ventures). Global Process Owners and their teams.

Main Responsibilities

- To keep fully abreast of all major external developments in *e*-commerce methods and technologies, and to identify those which may be appropriate within Unilever's various business processes (to be Unilever's leading-edge 'window on the *e*-commerce world');
- To educate Unilever's Business Managers, Global Process Owners and their teams in the opportunities offered by such developments, and to stimulate enthusiasm for exploiting them;
- To work with Business Managers, Global Process Owners and their teams to:
  establish controlled pilot tests of the new methods and technologies;
  if successful, roll them out across all Operating Companies and/or Business Groups.
- To establish and maintain an E-novation funnel of new *e*-business projects, to ensure that:
  there is a constant stream of such projects, at the various stages of completion;
  such projects are well controlled and monitored;
  appropriate resources are devoted to each project;
  there is no duplication or fragmentation of effort.
- To identify appropriate partner companies to work with Unilever where this would be of benefit to both parties (e.g. where neither Unilever nor the potential partner has all the skills and competencies needed to exploit the opportunities available).

Ideal Candidate Profile

- Broad knowledge of business processes and organisation
- Knowledge and experience of I.T.
- Well networked in Unilever
- Some knowledge and experience of *e*-commerce and *e*-business
- Fast learner
- Strategic and innovative thinker
- Good adaptive and influencing skills
- Proven record of making things happen
- Courageous with high self-confidence and integrity

Figure 10.1 *Job description*

Industrial Revolution. The shift to jobs emerged in the 1780s in England. It spread into other industrialized countries in the 19th century to package work in their burgeoning factories and bureaucracies.

Prior to that time, people worked on clusters of tasks, assignments and projects in a variety of locations that they could walk to, on a schedule set by the sun, the weather and the availability of work (for example, the harvest). People *did* jobs; they did not *have* a job. In the rapidly changing world of the 21st century jobs are fixed solutions to elastic problems. Fixed job solutions made sense in the slowing-moving factories and offices of the pre-electronic era. Technology and the onset of the knowledge age in the 1990s demand fluid, reactive work from increasingly informed and skilled individuals. Charles Handy's concept of the portfolio career plugs into this vision. The Internet has made these insights dramatically tangible. Bridges argues that the job is proving to be part of the problem, not the solution, because it increasingly inhibits flexibility and a speedy response to the threats and opportunities of a rapidly changing market. Jobs tend to inhibit change. They reinforce work and its demarcations rather than the needs of the customer. Trade unions are struggling with this development. Too many are still obsessed with job protection.

In 1997 John Yurkutat noted that 'The job is not dead, but it is rapidly being deconstructed into its basic components.' Bridges may be exaggerating to make a point. Clearly jobs are not dead (yet) and arguably not all will disappear, especially in the service industries. It is hard to visualize hospitals and all retail outlets, for example, becoming totally jobless although (in the case of the retail industry) the nature of service and its format is starting to be deconstructed by the Internet. But the human need and desire for social interaction should not be underestimated in this process. I well recall a workshop in Brussels during 1976 when Charles Handy predicted that by the end of the 20th century fewer people would commute into London because they would work from home in village communities and therefore British Rail had overestimated traffic flows as a result. It has not happened yet.

But notwithstanding some modification of Bridges' thesis, the trend is unmistakable, as Ed Lawler reaffirmed in 1990 'More and more individuals do not have stable work activities that can be described as jobs. Instead, they have roles and general areas of responsibility that they flexibly perform.'

Bridges, Handy and Lawler have signalled that we are returning to a work format which, although increasingly disembodied in terms of time and space, is akin to work patterns prior to the Industrial Revolution. Work boundaries are increasingly fluid and permeable and work practices changeable and flexible. More and more people work on assignments, projects and 'pieces of work'. Full-time employment for more than one employer is becoming more common, as is change of employment. Handy had already predicted in 1984 that 'Less than half of the workforce in the industrial world will be in "proper" full time jobs in organizations by the beginning of the 21st century.'

Clearly these developments impact organization design. Bridges believes this will lead to project-oriented structures, which he reminds us was first suggested by Melvin Anshen in 1969. He cites 'totally project organized' Oticon, the Danish hearing-aid manufacturer, as the prototype of the future. 'Although the average corporation has not yet abandoned traditional vertical hierarchies in favour of project clusters, time has only served to underscore the logic of Anshen's insight. In fields where rapidly changing technology, fashion or work demands, projects have already become the norm' (1996). (Bridges seems to suggest here that projects don't require accountability, but ironically the conference he addressed in 1996 also featured the CEO of Oticon, Lars Kolind, who clearly saw himself as accountable for the organization's success.) Other writers have also detected this need for more fluid organizational forms and various terms have been coined along the way. The first to address this issue in the 1980s was Professor Miles at Berkeley University in southern California, with his concept of network organizations (such as Benetton). Other descriptions include clusters (Quinn Mills), flotillas (Peter Drucker) and shamrocks (Charles Handy).

THE ORGANIZATION OF PROJECTS

If work in future is going to be more and more dominated by project work and assignments, the need to accurately define different types and levels of projects is critical. Experience to date suggests that this is frequently an area of uncertainty and wasted resources clouded by organizational politics and lack of clear accountability.

Many parts of Unilever are project-rich organizations such as the research laboratories and the corporate centre. Yet time and again the management of projects is ineffective. In one major study of the Financial Controller's Department in the corporate centre during 1996 it was found that 'projects' occupied a dominant place in the culture of the department. There seemed to be about 80 separate activities labelled projects. There was no accepted definition or nomenclature for organizing projects and no mechanism for setting priorities. The distinction between the work stemming from the department's normal objectives and additional work was not clear. Resourcing was accordingly somewhat haphazard and the result was overload, constantly changing priorities and frustration for the members of the department.

I similarly found in 1998/99 that another corporate department was unable to meet project deadlines and seemed to be totally constipated by blurred accountabilities and duplication of work as a result of people unable to operate effectively in the right levels of accountability.

The laser of the DMA model also identified gaps and overlap in the research laboratories. There wasn't really a clear difference between projects at the various work levels. For example, leading a project at level 2 is a very different proposition from leading a global project at, say, level 5. In the latter part of the 1990s a number of these major projects seemed to be slipping off the rails, with little corporate learning taking place in the process.

Tesco also changed project management in different parts of the business.

Problems of definition

Although these companies spent a lot on project training around the world, it was surprising to find that there was no tight definition of specific project accountabilities, other than the unhelpful offerings such as 'something you do that has an end point' compared to a process which is 'ongoing, repetitive or operational in nature and does not have an end point' (which is no doubt news to the customers of the processes!). Or a project is a 'non-routine, non-repetitive, one of a kind undertaking normally with a discrete time, financial and technical performance goals'.

These were definitions taken from in-house training material. They do not make clear the difference between a task of ongoing work and a project (which in future could be the permanent ongoing format of work). The governance, strategy and operational accountability are not clear. Projects are clearly not limited to only the operational domain. The definitions do not tackle the critical issues about resourcing: for example, how to manage the fact that team members are temporary resources whose bosses are elsewhere in the organization and over whom the project leader/manager has limited authority.

The roles of steering committees, project sponsors, project managers, project champions and project leaders are not always clear and vary depending on which part of the organization you happen to be working in.

By and large, financing of projects was not the major problem, but not surprisingly, given the lack of standard disciplines, performance against time frames and budgets was not brilliant. Nor was there significant shared learning from project failures in the past. The fact that this scenario is probably widespread is rather disconcerting if work is tending more towards assignments, projects and 'pieces of work' in the future.

PROJECTS AND DMA

Application of DMA logic helps clarify the organization of projects. The key is to first clarify the difference between work, tasks, and projects and then align these with work levels.

Work, tasks and projects

Work

Work is activity with a purpose. It calls for judgement and discretion when making decisions to solve problems that arise when carrying out specific tasks within a defined time period.

Task

A task is a commitment to produce a designated outcome. The outcome might be a product or a service, specified in terms of quantity, quality, time and cost.

Tasks are part and parcel of normal work, which are sanctioned by an individual's boss. They stem from the nature of work in a given role and tend to be regular and repetitious. They differ from a *process*, which is a continuous operation or treatment without an end point. They therefore do not require special arrangements outside the normal lines of management accountability.

Tasks can vary according to their technical context and level of accountability:

- Tasks at work level 1 are clearly defined, with concrete outcomes specified and known in advance. Task completion may require mastery of defined techniques.
- At work level 2, tasks are less specified and call for more judgement based on defined know-how or expertise.
- By work level 3, task complexity is greater as the key linkages and interactions between separate tasks have to be managed as a coherent whole.
- Tasks at the strategic work levels, 4 and above, are increasingly less defined and spelt out in advance of the activity in question. They emerge from the needs of business strategy, company objectives, policies, culture and principles. Furthermore, their organizational reach becomes increasingly wider and critical to the performance of the total business.

Project

A project is a form of work, which is a special type of task, with particular characteristics. It is beyond the normal or ongoing duties: a unique, non-routine, non-repetitive, temporary undertaking with discrete goals, which typically involve more than one person, cutting across organizational and functional boundaries.

A project therefore requires interdependent work between individuals who:

1. have different permanent bosses,
2. are led for the duration of the project by a fully accountable but temporary boss (the project 'team leader'),
3. who in turn is answerable to a 'project owner'.

Project accountabilities

Projects require authorization of plans, capital, people, resources and time frames. Since projects can vary from local to global in extent, these authorization steps involve special arrangements centred upon the activities of *leadership*, *ownership* and *sanctioning*.

Project leader

This is a temporary appointment responsible for managing and leading the project team for the duration of the project. The project leader is responsible for planning, organizing, staffing (including power of veto), directing and controlling activities to meet time, cost and performance objectives. If necessary, he or she can initiate transfers of members from the project and is expected to make the case for additional resources when necessary.

The project leader would normally be one work level higher than members of the project team.

Project owner

The project owner would be expected to initiate a project, typically as part of normal work at a strategic level of accountability in response to an identified opportunity in the market or a gap in resource or service delivery. Nevertheless, there can be occasions when project ownership is assigned from above.

The project owner would make the case for the project, gather high-level support, define the initial terms of reference and negotiate the corresponding resources, time and performance parameters. The project owner has power to appoint (and dismiss) the project leader(s) and therefore needs to be at least one work level higher.

The project owner is accountable to the sanctioning body (typically a steering committee) for the overall coherence of the project (especially if there is more than one project leader), the recommending and maintaining of professional and technical standards of excellence, the achieving of key performance indicators, and the management of external bodies and third parties. The project owner would be expected to draw attention to major deviations from plan, together with the implications.

Project sponsor

For strategic projects (work level 4 and above) having impact on more than one country, business unit or function, the sanctioning body will typically need to be a corporate steering committee, where the project sponsor is the chairperson representing the key corporate interests likely to be affected by the project.

The sponsor is accountable for ensuring that the project proposal can deliver its aims in a way that is beneficial to the company and fits into the current strategic plans and priorities. The sponsor would also be accountable for assessing issues such as project overload and potential conflicts of interest and dissipation of resources, bearing in mind priorities in relation to work elsewhere in the organization.

A key role of the sponsor is managing the corporate governance process and facilitating a smooth ride for the project in the allocation of key resources, the clearing of organizational obstacles and the modification of corporate priorities, policy and strategy as appropriate.

The project sponsor sanctions the appointment of the project owner and can stop or extend the remit of the original project.

Implications

The project sponsor needs to be a higher work level than the project owner, and preferably a higher work level than the members of the steering committee. There is a clear spine of accountability through *project leader*, *project owner* and *project sponsor*, who should each be in a different work level to ensure genuine empowerment and effectiveness.

The work level of the project is driven by that of the project owner, who is accountable for technical and professional problem solving of the project. This does not mean that the project owner must personally carry out the problem solving or even be the ultimate expert on the project, but it does mean that the project owner must identify, cajole and ensure that the right technical solutions are found and successfully applied.

Given the overall integrating skills required of a project owner, the minimum level of accountability should be work level 3.

Alignment of projects and work levels

Work level 1

As should be apparent from the above, there are no projects at work level 1. The work level of a project is driven by the project leader who needs to be at least work level 2 to manage people and budgets.

Special, non-routine work at level 1 is task related, which involves mastery or acquisition of techniques. Work level 1 staff may be members of projects, led by someone in work level 2 or above.

Work level 2 projects

These are the least complex projects where work level 1 staff from different sections are drawn together to help produce a solution that is not in the current 'routines', databases or training manuals. Projects of this type are likely to have few members, a limited budget and a short time frame (up to about six months), and are often part of a bigger project.

In the case of a discrete, one-off project it is even feasible that the project manager may not have a programme manager. In this case the project manager could also be the 'project owner'.

The executive sponsor can be at work level 3, if there was no connection to a wider programme.

The following accountabilities are those of a work level 2 'project owner':

1. Nature of work – to meet the needs of a specific client, or technical problem in one functional or business area such as a department. Although therefore the project is focusing on the needs of one situation or problem, the work may require the coordination of a number of work level 1 technicians

2. Resource complexity – the main resource is the project team and the budget items are likely to be dominated by people-related expenses. Capital expenditure is therefore limited and technical resources are not significant.

3. Problem solving – a significant amount of technical know-how combined with general skills needed to manage a group of individuals. The former will require diagnostic ability while the latter will call more for judgement and the ability to set and manage priorities.

4. Change – the focus is upon improving efficiencies of designated equipment, services or processes within an existing infrastructure of resources.

5. Natural work team – likely to be peers of the project managers across the department or function affected by the project.

6. External interaction – defined third parties as affected by, or suppliers of, the relevant equipment, service or process under examination.

7. Time frame – up to about six months, in a retail environment for example.

Work level 3 projects

These are more complex projects, which need to integrate the work of subordinates in work levels 1 and 2 covering different systems and services, which together deliver a complete solution. The answer, although concrete, is not in the company's existing sets of routines or databases.

Work level 3 projects are applicable to more than one functional or business area. They may also involve sub-projects at work level 2 which would have project 'leaders' with the project 'owner' at work level 3 and the 'sponsor' at work level 4. A self-standing project that is not part of a programme (defined below) will be led by a work level 3 project manager, with a work level 4 executive sponsor.

The following are the accountabilities of a work level 3 'project owner':

1. Nature of work – to meet the needs of more than one section of the business. The critical objective is to integrate the system and service needs of level 1 and 2 situations to ensure that a complete solution is forthcoming.

2. Resource complexity – the capital and personnel needs of the project can be significant and require careful management over a time frame of at least a year, and is expected to have a noticeable impact on the annual customer and operations plans.

3. Problem solving – involves identifying patterns and key linkages in the performance of the project resources and the solutions being prototyped, to ensure that the project objective is being achieved within the benchmark parameters.

4. Change – to ensure that the outcome of the project leads to a more effective solution in meeting the shortcomings which have led to the setting up of the project in the first place. This may require making changes as a result of introducing technologies, systems or solutions that have worked well elsewhere. Thus work level 3 projects start to impinge on culture and previously defined ways of doing things.

5. Natural work team – peers include the top operational managers across the organization, such as factory managers, distribution centre managers, senior buyers and the like.

6. External interaction – the project manager must manage third parties who may be supplying or demanding the new solution as the means of improved service or business performance.

7. Time frame – at least a year.

Alignment of programmes and work levels

Programmes operate at a strategic level in this model and have their own independent infrastructure of operational projects. They stem from the strategy and needs of the business. They are set up to find a solution, which is not apparent at the outset. A programme director is now the 'project owner', with a sponsor who would normally be the leader of a corporate function, geography, or line of business impacted by the programme.

The 'project owner' (programme director in this case) would be work level 4, with the sponsor at work level 5 or above.

Work level 4 programmes

Programmes are likely to be international, whereas independent lower-level projects are likely to be more local in scope. Work level 4 programmes move into the area of breakthrough solutions. It is not enough merely to find a concrete solution that already exists somewhere else, whether within the organization or externally. The thrust now is to discover new applications and solutions that are based upon new technology, and new applications of know-how, which have the potential to change employee and/or customer values and behaviour. Prototype solutions have to be found and tested which may not already exist in concrete form.

The following are the accountabilities of a work level 4 programme manager:

1. Nature of work – to initiate new solutions to identify problems in line with the programme objectives, the terms of reference for which may well have been recommended by the programme manager in the first place.

2. Resources – the programme is likely to consist of a number of projects, which need to be coordinated to ensure overall cohesion of effort and results. The planning and negotiation of resources, such as technology, people, budgets and deadlines, is complex and critical for the overall success of the programme.

3. Problem solving – the establishment of the programme is typically in response to a gap in existing resources or service delivery or the recognition of a new market opportunity. This may have been first recognized by the programme manager and/or presented as a problem for resolution. The programme calls for an ability to mentally model and conceptualize tomorrow's solutions and to manage others to put these potential solutions into practice.

4. Change – meeting the programme objective will call for an ability to initiate change and ensure that it is implemented. The change can entail concrete applications, such as new technology, or softer challenges, such as managing the impact on values and culture.

5. Natural work team – the network of contacts will be predominantly national, but increasingly international such as functional heads in other continents in large multinational organizations.

6. External interaction – one of the challenges of the programme manager is to identify the external sources of major change such as technology suppliers, and to manage the interface of external providers of programme resource.

7. Time frame – at least two years.

Work level 5 programmes

These programmes would be international, group-wide, have a 'project owner' in work level 5 and ideally a main board sponsor. The programme manager at work level 5 is likely to be running sub-programmes as part of the overall corporate agenda. These programmes would be moving into the upper reaches of breakthrough solutions, which would entail industry or global innovation and leadership.

The following are the accountabilities of a work level 5 programme manager:

1. Nature of work – programmes at this level are concerned with boundary reconfigurations of existing or potential businesses, geography and functions.

2. Resource complexity – the management of a complex infrastructure of programmes and projects is required. The resource demands are very significant and would be decided upon at main board level. It is doubtful whether work level 1 staff would be capable of contributing to the projects required as part of this programme. The allocation of resources among competing sub-programmes and projects becomes increasingly critical to the success of the programme.

3. Problem solving – the intensity of the problem solving is driven by the complex interconnectedness of the key elements of the company (business lines, geographical possibilities, technological advances such as the Internet and functional developments) and the fact that the programme objectives may be spelt out in abstract mission statements. Assessing the initial and ongoing viability of the programme is a major challenge.

4. Change – the challenge is to find totally new solutions which are in line with the strategic direction of the business, eg how to be the no. 1 retailer in country x, the region, such as CEE, or the world. This includes defining the areas and possibilities for innovation, while drawing upon research and major innovations elsewhere to ensure that the company stays at the forefront of best practice in change management.

5. Natural work team – colleagues at work level 5 or higher across the entire company.

6. External interaction – activities here are driven by the desire to eclipse all competition. This entails finding ways of managing the external environment in line with the organization's values and identifying the means to achieve market leadership.

7. Time frame – at least three years.

In summary, projects are operational (junior project managers being in work level 2, project managers in work level 3), while programmes are strategic (programme directors typically being in work levels 4).

THE ROLE OF TECHNOLOGY

Technological changes are very important but their impact is prone to be overstated or misunderstood. For example, in 1958 Leavitt and Whisler wrote their now famous article concerning 'Management in the 1980s' which introduced the term Information Technology. Subsequently they have been frequently misquoted for predicting that IT would wipe out middle management. In fact what they wrote was that 'IT is likely to have its greatest impact on middle and top management' and that 'There will be many fewer middle managers'.

Impact on middle management

The major insight of the article was the prediction of 'a radical reorganization of middle management with certain classes of jobs moving down in status and compensation while others move up'. They also noted that 'The jobs of today's hourly workers tend to be highly programmed' (ie level 1 accountability). 'Conversely the jobs at the top are largely unprogrammed. They are "Think" jobs – hard to define and describe operationally' (ie strategic levels). 'Jobs in the big middle area tend to be programmed in part but with varying amounts of room for judgement and autonomy' (ie levels 2 and 3). Leavitt and Whisler also concluded that 'Not all middle management jobs would be affected by the new technology.'

Since then, IT has removed jobs principally at the first level of accountability. This is entirely predictable since work at this level is prescribable and programmable. Therefore by definition it can be automated. Jobs in the next two levels might disappear because their subordinates have gone or real-time Internet or intranet links have shrunk geography and reduced the need for travel and/or face-to-face meetings. But judgemental, thinking work for work level 2 and above cannot be actively replicated by a machine. 'So far,' according to Bill Gates (1996), 'every prediction about major advances in artificial intelligence has proved to be over optimistic. Today even simple learning tasks are well beyond the world's most capable computer. When computers appear to be intelligent, it's because they have been specially programmed to handle some specific tasks in a straight forward way – even Deep Blue, an IBM machine developed specifically to play chess... As long as computers are being programmed for special tasks they aren't learning – and if they aren't learning, they pose no threat to humans.'

IT has removed drudgery at level 1, mainly in the developed world where the cost of labour can make the investment in technology worthwhile. In the 1970s and 1980s we saw much work in factories and warehouses automated. In the 1990s this trend migrated to offices and retail outlets where checkout counters' work was also largely automated, with point of sale data being fed back into the supply chain for replenishment of products. More recently we have seen bank branch networks decimated by Internet banking, and now e-procurement on B2B and B2C transactions is becoming widespread across the globe. Customers in some retailers are already checking out their purchases themselves with hand-held terminals. Technology, the handmaiden of speed and convenience, marches relentlessly forward. But these developments are not entirely removing the need for critical middle management vertebrae in the spine of accountability, except where those jobs were dedicated completely to the management of subordinates in level 1 whose jobs have been automated. It is very difficult if not impossible to empower people in level 1 by lifting their responsibilities to level 3. It is certainly not possible for a machine.

Advancing technology has always reconfigured work; this is not a new phenomenon. It probably began with the invention of writing about 5,000 years ago, which in turn was revolutionized by the invention of printing by Gutenberg in 1452. The next re-mapping of work occurred with the Industrial Revolution when the fixed and defined job appeared in the 1780s in England. Just as medieval monks and 18th-century cotton workers found their skills superseded by technology, so 20th-century workers and managers have found their jobs replaced or modified by Information Technology, the most extreme manifestation of which is currently the Internet.

Impact on the organization

Each of these radical technological changes affected the organization of work. Although it is not yet clear what final formats will survive the Internet, it is already clear that the concept of centralization and decentralization have been virtually obliterated as an axis along which companies should organize. In the first 70 years of the 20th century centralization was seen as the means of control. This was the result of the command and control models set up in the 1870s. Decentralization was at first an acknowledgement that time and geography placed limits on that control. Decentralization grew out of pragmatism. It was not an ideal initially. Even in 1970 I can recall waiting two or three months for a response to a question or proposal mailed to London from New Zealand. The key feature of decentralized units was the fact that they were disconnected from each other while being thinly wired to the centre. The growing size and complexity of international organizations in the last third of the 20th century demonstrated that the command and control model of centralization was becoming cumbersome and unworkable in a more rapidly changing world in which many employees were becoming more educated and capable of taking on a heavier decision-making burden.

Coupled with the findings of the behavioural scientists, decentralization started to become fashionable. It better fitted the logic of job enrichment and empowerment for better-educated employees. But the belief was one or the other, not both. As already indicated (in Chapter 2), confusion over this option led to rich structures, as businesses tended to do a bit of both. They tried to be both centralized and decentralized. It was fascinating at the end of the 1980s (as Unilever prepared its first pan-European organization) to observe managers grappling with this dilemma. The initial reaction was to go for one or the other option but in truth, for the first time, the optimal organization design involved a blend or mix of both centralization and decentralization, but not in the same functions. Consequently in the new regional configurations, the marketing and supply chain functions, for example, needed to be centralized to maximize efficiency and scale, whereas the sales function needed to be decentralized, maintaining a country focus. (Interestingly, by the end of the century developments in the trade had already made that part of the organization obsolete.)

As Malone and Laubacher pointed out in 1998: 'With the introduction of powerful computers and broad electronic networks – the economic equation changes. Because information can be shared instantly and inexpensively among many people in many locations, the value of centralized decision-making and expensive bureaucracies diminishes. Individuals can manage themselves co-ordinating their efforts with other independent parties. Small becomes good. The new co-ordination technologies enable us to return to the pre-industrial model of tiny, autonomous businesses. But there is one crucial difference: electronic networks enable those micro-businesses to tap into the global reservoirs of information, expertise and financing that used to be available only to large companies.'

Interconnectedness

The Internet connects individuals, micro and macro organizations. It does not recognize constraints of time, place or space. This is the latest challenge facing leaders of organizations. They can have centralization and connected decentralization simultaneously in real time. This has never been possible before and it has massive implications for organization development. In 1996 Gerhaard Schulmeyer from ABB estimated that European companies are still overstaffed by 20 per cent. This is probably a conservative figure for Europe allowing for the fact that it was a pre-Internet estimate.

Can the DMA principles cope with the new reality of interconnectedness and how can it help organize an appropriate response? The first strength of DMA is the fact that its principles apply equally well to both micro and macro businesses irrespective of the level of their front or top lines. A micro business could be 2/1 (with the top line at 2 and the frontline at 1) or 4/2 in configuration, whereas a macro global business could be 7/1, and so on. My focus here is the global business.

Interconnectedness poses two immediate problems. The first is the potential for information overload. It is therefore essential that those with strategic accountabilities remain in their correct level and do not get tempted to do the work of others, as this is now possible in a way it never was previously. Secondly, interconnectedness is providing severe strategic challenges even for businesses with a long-established brand and a successful strategy. For example, a well-established newspaper such as the *New York Times* has to decide whether to put free news on to the Internet. But historically the production and the selling of news was its very *raison d'être*. Will it be giving away its birthright? Will the electronic initiative cannibalize existing business? Will it generate conflict with existing customer channels? Will they lose consumers? What are the consequences for the existing brand?

What are the likely consequences of not going on the Internet? Is a new strategy required? These are tough questions and I suspect that the impact of Internet competition will see a few businesses lurch into oblivion unable to cope with the ambiguity of interconnectedness.

There will be increased ambiguity as a result of these developments. This will inevitably give rise to turf wars, conflict and uncertainty. It will be more critical than ever to clarify roles and accountabilities in this environment.

I already have evidence that the DMA model is a sound blueprint, which can provide clear answers in the face of new challenges from Web sites, intranets and the Internet. Work patterns and process flows will be different, calling for different skills, but the need for performance management and accountability will persist.

CAPITALISM'S LACK OF ACCOUNTABILITY

It was indicated at the beginning of this chapter that there is concern about some of the human and social side effects of the free market. One is the dehumanizing impact of the Internet on jobs and people's livelihoods. The second is a concern that free market capitalism is seen as an end in itself. Just as the cost saving pursuit of process re-engineers damaged individual and organizational health, so the endless pursuit of efficiency and growth ultimately floods the world with superfluous and wasteful goods. But most worrying of all is the fact that, despite the earlier reference to stakeholders, most mega-organizations are in fact not really accountable to anyone.

One of the best expositions of these ideas is Charles Handy's 1997 book *The Hungry Spirit*. He contends that the idea of the organization as shareholders' property is increasingly out of date. He suggests the idea of a company as a community in which employee citizens have a right to a fixed period of residence, justice, free speech, a share of the wealth and a right to be consulted about important decisions. He also feels that the legal structure of companies must change to recognize that key assets are increasingly the people. This makes sense as the knowledge age unfurls and more people-asset-rich companies such as Microsoft become the norm.

Faced with little enthusiasm for state ownership, no trust in the unbounded free market and confusion about the third way, Race Mathews (1999) has recently argued for a return to the idea of distributism favoured initially by Belloc and Chesterton. Distributism argues for ownership to be widely distributed rather than concentrated in the hands of the state or wealthy minorities.

The DMA solution set is consistent with these visions of the future. It presupposes that individuals contribute to their maximum ability, that their accountable work and capability are 'in flow' (see Chapter 8) and that the sum of the contributions of physically and psychologically healthy and satisfied individuals is a healthy organization, which contributes ultimately to a healthy community.

TIME-IN-ACCOUNTABILITY LEVEL – A NEW APPROACH

Ironically, in the early 1990s focus on high-flyers' short time-in-job in Unilever led to the introduction of DMA with its associated work levels. It was felt that the move to five management levels of accountability would remove the obsession with progress through 17 job classes of administrative 'promotions' which led to a change in job every one or two years, which in turn led to a dilution of key skills in the business. But by the late 1990s it was apparent that the concept of time-in-job was passé. It represented yesterday's rigidities and not today's realities or tomorrow's challenges.

The demands of the knowledge age are placing more emphasis on the person and the tasks he or she is capable of undertaking. And as I have tried to establish in this book, talented people seek challenge, learning, recognition (in some cases, power), a sense of achievement and good rewards. This can only be fully achieved where there is role clarity and accountability for resources and results. I have also demonstrated that simply paying lip service to teamwork and empowerment will not deliver these goals. Similarly, although project management is becoming increasingly common, loose, ill-conceived 'project organizations' are not the appropriate answer either.

So the job with fixed boundaries is disappearing. But work is not disappearing, nor is accountability for that work. Indeed, as already demonstrated, more businesses are more global than ever and competition is more intense. Accountability for results (increased profitable growth and more e-business success) has probably never been more high profile. The removal of under-performing CEOs is not uncommon these days. Stakeholders, particularly shareholders, increasingly demand high standards of performance, good results and complete transparency. These cannot be consistently delivered in a business that is over-managed, with role confusion and blurred accountabilities. Previous job evaluation systems or systems of rank did not help yesterday's organization avoid hierarchical bulge and they do not meet today's requirement for more fluid assignments and projects together with a greater need to focus on an individual's development, up-skilling and constant need for marketability. The DMA model does meet these demands.

The concept of time-in-accountability level (or in Unilever and Tesco, time-in-work level) fits best with expected future work patterns. It can move with the trend away from focus on the job. As shown in Chapter 8, time-in-work level can be a very powerful method for assessing an individual's development and progress while affording clear career planning perspectives. It was shown how carefully orchestrated boundary moves make a critical contribution to personal learning and leadership development. It is also clear that the best global companies will gain from having a dynamic network of managers with considerable international service. There seems to be an established myth abroad these days that believes that prior to 1980 everyone had a job for life and that today no one has a job for life.

It is possible to identify different skills per work level for a given profession or area of work. I have recently done this for the Global IT Infrastructure Organization in Unilever. One can also establish which different tasks, assignments or projects will lead to the acquisition of appropriate skills over what period of time, before the individual in question is ready and equipped to move to the next level of accountability. Chapter 8 illustrated indicative times that need to be spent in a given level, taking into account also an individual's potential, or track. The importance of 'dwell time' and diversity of experience in 'general management' levels 3 and 5 was also highlighted. Increasingly, this process will not be about jobs – it will be about mastery of techniques and technologies known and even unknown at this stage. This will call for continual training and exposure to change. The leadership challenge of tomorrow will be figuring out how to keep people on the crest of the wave of competence and learning for their respective level of accountability in a sea of uncertainty and technological advancement.

DMA, THE INDIVIDUAL AND SOCIAL CAPITAL

By now it should be clear that the thrust of DMA is the building of a healthy organization. But a healthy organization presupposes healthy individuals. Just as the free individual is the bedrock of democracy, so the empowered individual is the cornerstone of DMA.

In these days of possible over-reliance on the market, Putnam (2000) has singled out three forms of capital: 'Physical capital and human capital – tools and training that enhance individual productivity – and social capital, social networks that have value.' DMA takes as a given physical and human capital. It is also in the sphere of social capital: what Handy has called 'community' and Gifford 'civil society'. It presupposes a healthy, unfettered individual, competent and free to choose with a right to self-fulfilment (not to be confused with self-aggrandizement). It also takes as a given the imperative of collective effort, social networks and the 'sturdy norms of reciprocity' but not the enslaved collectivism of communism.

As noted in Chapter 1, behavioural scientists have established what drives individuals, especially knowledge workers: a worthwhile and challenging task, psychological space to meet that challenge or purpose within a supportive and enabling environment that recognizes and rewards achievement and individual worth. In short, a sense of purpose and worth. *DMA's contribution is ensuring HOW to achieve the equivalent of Putnam's well-connected individual in a well-connected society.* He also noted: 'Of all the domains in which I have traced the consequences of social capital, in none is the importance of social connectedness so well established as in the case of health and well being.'

In an organizational context, DMA is thus simultaneously the means of achieving a 'private good' and a 'public good'. It liberates the individual while ensuring that the organization does not ossify as a result of slowly strangling on the rope of a cluttered hierarchy of administrative promotions and obsession with control. Organizational capital is a subset of social capital.

IN SUMMARY

If one accepts that the model of the industrial era has served its time and that the technological demands of the knowledge era will generate different configurations of work such as 'doing jobs' rather than 'having a job', then it stands to reason that job evaluation and competency systems built around jobs alone will become increasingly irrelevant. In this sense the DMA model stands on the threshold of the brave new world well equipped to accommodate these changes. Thus Unilever's concern with time-in-job at the end of the 20th century should now be with time-in-work level at the beginning of the 21st century. The work-level analysis would suggest they should be wary of promotions above level 2 unless the manager in question has had about five years per work level, depending on their potential. When combined with developing skills and competencies per work level and the concept of tracking elaborated in Chapter 8, it can be seen that DMA is ahead of its time in being able to meet the challenges of at least the early part of this century.

For this reason it is now apparent that time-in-accountability level is the powerful new concept for leadership development and planning an individual's lifetime work patterns. As already illustrated, DMA is well attuned to the developing needs of e-business. Furthermore, without DMA these processes will become more random and haphazard as existing approaches are built around the central tenet of 'having a job' which is quickly becoming outmoded as a reliable basis for individual development and life-planning of work. It will also call for a radical rethink of reward practices and associated HR management concerns. In short, DMA arguably provides the most powerful basis for building a healthy organization in the 21st century – a revolutionary approach to people and management.

References

Abbeglen, J C and Stalk, G Jnr (1985) *Kaisha: The Japanese corporation*, Basic Books Inc, New York

Abosch, K S (1995) What employers want, what employees need, *Compensation and Benefits Review*, American Management Association, New York

Anshen, M (1969) The management of ideas, *Harvard Business Review*, July–August

Armstrong, M (2000) Feel the width, *People Management*, 3 February

Ashton, C (1999) *Strategic Compensation*, Business Intelligence Limited, London

Baghai, M, Coley, S and White, D (1999) *The Alchemy of Growth*, Orion Business Books, London

Bain, N and Band, A (1996) *Winning Ways Through Corporate Governance*, Macmillan Press Ltd, London

Bain, N and Mabey, B (1999) *The People Advantage: Improving Results Through Better Selection and Performance*, Macmillan Press, London

Baker, M (2003) Perot the younger, *Sunday Telegraph*, 7 December

Barkdull, C W (1963) Span of control: a method of evaluation, *Michigan Business Review*, Vol 15

Barnevik, P (1997) Inventing the Future, speech given to the International Industrial Conference, 29 September

Beaven, D (1982) What the ratios saw, *Management Today*, July

Bennis, W (1966) The coming death of bureaucracy, *Think Magazine*, IBM
Bennis, W (1989) The split brain at the top, *Across The Board*, September
Bennis, W (1990) *Why Leaders Can't Lead*, Jossey-Bass, San Francisco, CA
Billis, D (1984) *Welfare Bureaucracies*, Heineman Educational Books, London
Bloch, S and Whiteley, P (2003) *Complete Leadership*, Pearson Education, Harlow
Boam, R and Sparrow, P (1992) *Designing and Achieving Competency: A competency-based approach to developing people and organizations*, McGraw-Hill, London
Boehm, K and Phipps, L (1996) Flatness, *The McKinsey Quarterly*, no 3
Bose, P (2003) *Lessons from the Great Empire Builder: Alexander the Great's art of strategy*, Profile Books, London
Boyatzis, R (1982) *The Competent Manager*, Wiley, New York
Bridges, W (1996) *Job Shift: How to prosper in a world without jobs*, Nicholas Brearley, London
Brown, D (1998) Teamwork replaces the chain of command, *The Financial Times*, 19 August
Brown, D and Armstrong, M (1999) *Paying For Contribution*, Kogan Page, London
Brown, W (1971) *Organisation*, Heinemann, London
Brown, W and Jaques, E (1965) *The Glacier Papers*, Heinemann Educational Books, London
Bungay, S and McKinney, D (2003) Mission leadership, *Ashridge Journal*, Spring
Burns, T and Stalker, G M (1961) *The Management of Innovation*, Tavistock Publishers, London
Cadbury, D (1992) *Report on the Committee on the Financial Aspects of Corporate Governance*, London, 1 December
Campbell, A, Goold, M and Alexander, M (1995) The value of the parent company, *California Management Review*, **38** (1), Fall
Chambers, E G *et al* (1998) The war for talent, *McKinsey Quarterly*, no 3
Charlton, G (2000) *Human Habits of Highly Effective Organisations*,Van Schaik, Pretoria, South Africa
Child, J (1977) *Organisation: A guide to problems and practice*, Harper and Row, London
Child, J and Loveridge, R (1990) *Information Technology in European Services*, Blackwell, Oxford
Collins, J (2001) *From Good to Great: Why some companies make the leap and others do not*, HarperCollins, London
Collins, J C and Porras, J L (1994) *Built to Last: Successful habits of visionary companies*, Century, London
Crystal, G S (1991) *In Search of Excess: The overcompensation of American executives*, W W Norton, New York
Csikszentmihalyi, M C (1991) *Flow: The psychology of optimal experience*, Harper and Row, New York

Dale, E (1952) *Planning and Developing the American Organisation Structure*, American Management Association, New York

Davis, S M (1987) *Future Perfect*, Addison-Wesley Publishing Company, Massachusetts, MA

Davis, S M and Lawrence, P R (1977) *Matrix*, Addison-Wesley Publishing Company, Massachusetts, MA

de Geus, A (1997) *The Living Company*, Nicolas Brearley, London

Delta Consulting Group Inc (2000) *Dot-Combat Managing Conflict in the Strategic Enterprise*, New York

Dive, B J (1989) *Competitive Structures for the 90s*, Unilever Personnel Division, London

Dive, B J (2003) When is an organization too flat? *Across The Board*, July–August

Donkin, R (2001) *Blood Sweat and Tears: The evolution of work*, Texerre, New York

Downes, L, Chunka, M and Negropente M (1998) *Unleashing the Killer Digital Strategies for Market Dominance*, Harvard Business School Press, Boston, MA

Drucker, P F (1954) *The Practice of Management*, Harpers and Row, New York

Drucker, P F (1987) *The Frontiers of Management*, Heinemann, London

Drucker, P F (1988) Managing in the 90s: new roles – new rules, *Industry Week*, April

Drucker, P F (1988) The coming of the new organization, *Harvard Business Review*, January–February

Drucker, P F (1990) Lessons for Successful non-profit Governance, *Non-profit Management and Leadership*, **1** (1) Fall

Drucker, P F (1998) Management's new paradigms, *Forbes*, October

Evered, J F and Evered, J E (1989) *Shirt-Sleeves Management*, American Management Association, New York

Farnham, A (1999) Anti-hierarchy gurus fall flat on their faces, *Sunday Telelgraph*, London, 4 April

Felton, R F, Hodnut, A and Witt, V (1995) Building a stronger board, *The McKinsey Quarterly*, no 2

Fisch, G G (1963) Stretching the span of management, *Harvard Business Review*, September–October

Fitzgerald, N F W (1996) Talking on the level with Niall FitzGerald, *Work Levels Newsletter for Unilever Personnel*, no. 1, March

Follett, M P (1949) Lectures in business administration, in *Freedom and Co-ordination*, ed L Urwick, Management Publication Trust Ltd, London

French, W L and Bell, C H (1973) *Organisation Development: Behavioural science interventions for organisational improvement*, Prentice-Hall Inc, Englewood, NJ

Galbraith, J R (2000) *Designing The Global Corporation*, Jossey-Bass, San Francisco, CA

Ganguly, A (1999) *Business-driven Research & Development Managing Knowledge to Create Wealth*, Macmillan Press Ltd, London

Garratt, R (1996) *The Fish Rots from the Head: The crisis in our boardrooms*, HarperCollins, London

Garratt, R (2003) *Thin on Top: Why corporate governance matters and how to measure and improve board performance*, Nicholas Brealey, London

Gates, Bill (1996) *The Road Ahead*, Penguin Books, London

Gaugler, B and Thornton, G (1989) Number of assessment centre dimensions as a determinant of assessor accuracy, *Journal of Applied Psychology*, **74** (4), August

Gifford, P J (1998) *African Christianity Its Public Role*, Hurst & Company, London

Gladwell, M (2000) *The Tipping Point: How little things make a big difference*, Abacus, London

Goold, M and Campbell, A (1987) *The Role of the Centre in Managing Diversified Corporations*, Blackwell Publishers, Oxford

Graicunas, V A (1937) Relationship in organization, in *Papers on the Science of Aministration*, ed L Gulick and L Urwick, Columbia University, New York

Greenbury, R (1995) *Directors' Remuneration Report*, 17 July, London

Hamel, G and Prahalad, C K (1994) *Competing for the Future*, Harvard Business School, Boston, MA

Hampel, R (1988) *Committee on Corporate Governance: Final report*, London, January

Handfield-Jones, H (2000) How executives grow, *McKinsey Quarterly*, no 1

Handy, C B (1976) *Understanding Organizations*, Penguin Books, London

Handy, C B (1984) *The Future of Work: A guide to a changing society*, Basil Blackwell Ltd, Oxford

Handy, C B (1990) *The Age of Unreason*, Harrow Books, London

Handy, C B (1997) *The Hungry Spirit*, Hutchison, London

Harman, D A (1996) Leaders can't do without them. How come they get such little respect?, *Across The Board*, February

Harvey, B (1996) Corporate governance and non-execs, *Financial Times*, 3 May

Hayes, R H, Wheelwright, S C and Clark, K B (1988) *Dynamic Manufacturing: Creating the learning organization*, The Free Press, London

Herzberg, F (1968) One more time: how do you motivate employees?, *Harvard Business Review*, January–February

Higgs, A and Rowland, D (undated) All pigs are equal?, *Management Education and Development*, **23**, part 4, 199, 349-62

Hilmer, F G (1989) Real jobs for real managers, *The McKinsey Quarterly*, Summer

Hilmer F G and Donaldson I (1996) *Management Redeemed*, The Free Press, Sydney, Australia

Hofrichter, D (1993) Broadbanding: second generation approach, *Compensation and Benefits Review*, September–October

Hollenbeck, G P and McCall, M W Jnr (1998) Leadership development: contemporary practices, in *Evolving Practices in Human Resource*

Management: Responses to a changing world of work, ed A I Kraut and A K Korman, Jossey-Bass, San Francisco

Jackson, L (1989) Turning airport managers into high flyers, *Personnel Management*, **21** (10)

Janger, A R (1960) Analysing the span of control, *Management Record*, 22

Janger, A R (1989) *Measuring Structures Comparative Benchmarks for Management Structure*, The Conference Board, New York

Jaques, E (1951) *The Changing Culture of a Factory*, Tavistock Publications, London

Jaques, E (1956) *Measurement of Responsibility*, Tavistock Publications, London

Jaques, E (1961) *Equitable Payment*, Heinemann Educational Books, London

Jaques, E (1964) *Time Span Handbook*, Heinemann Educational Books, London

Jaques, E (1976) *A General Theory of Bureaucracy*, Gregg Revivals, London

Jaques, E (1989) The CEOs Guide to Constructive Structure and Leadership, *Requisite Organization*, Cason Hall and Co, Arlington, VA

Jaques, E and Cason, K (1994) *Human Capability: A Study of Individual Potential and its Application*, Cason and Hall and Co, Arlington, VA

Johnston, M (1995) *Managing in the Next Millennium*, Butterworth & Heinemann, Oxford

Kane, D E (1985) Organisational effectiveness notes, *Resizing The Business*, General Electric, Fairfield, CT

Katzenbach, J R (1997) The myth of the top management team, *Harvard Business Review*, November–December

Katzenbach, J R (1998) *Teams at the Top*, Harvard Business Press, Boston, MA

Katzenbach, J R and Smith, D K (1992) Why teams matter, *The McKinsey Quarterly*, no 3

Katzenbach, J R and Smith, D K (1994) *The Wisdom of Teams: Creating the high-performance organisation*, McGraw-Hill, Boston, MA

Kearns, D T and Nadler, D A (1992) *Prophets in the Dark: How Xerox reinvented itself and beat back the Japanese*, Harper Business, New York

Klatt, B, Murphy, S and Irvine, D (1999) *Accountability: Practical tools for focusing on clarity, commitment and results*, Kogan Page, London

Klemp, G O (1998) *Leadership Competencies: Putting it all together*, Cambria Consulting, Boston, MA

Kraines, G A (2001) *Accountability Leadership: How to strengthen productivity through sound management leadership*, Career Press, Franklin Lakes, NJ

Kramer R J (1995) *Organizing for Global Competitiveness: The business unit design*, The Conference Board, New York

Krause, D G (2002) *Sun Tzu: The art of war for executives*, Nicholas Brealey, London

Kubler-Ross, E (1969) *On Death and Dying*, Macmillan, New York

Kumar, K R (1994) Focus on processes, speech given to the 'Process Organization' Conference, University of California, 30 November

Lawler, C (2000) Pay strategy: new thinking for the new millennium, *AMA Compensation and Benefits Review*, January–February

Lawler, E E III (1990) *Strategic Pay, Aligning Organizational Strategies and Pay Systems*, Jossey-Bass, San Francisco, CA

Lawrence, P R and Lorsch, J W (1986) *Organisation and Environment: Managing differentiation and integration*, Harvard Business School Press, Boston, MA

Leavitt, H J and Whisler, T L (1958) Management in the 1980s, *Harvard Business Review*, November–December

Lorenz, C (1990) A cultural revolution that sets out to supplant hierarchy with informality, *Financial Times*, London, 30 March

McBeath, G and Rands, D N (1964) *Salary Administration*, Business Publications Ltd, London

McCall, M Jnr (1998) *High Fliers: Developing the next generation of leaders*, Harvard Business School Press, Boston, MA

McCall, M Jnr and Hollenbeck, G P (2002) *The Lessons of International Experience Developing Global Executives*, Harvard Business School Press, Boston, MA

McCall, M Jnr, Lombardo, M M and Morrison, A M (1988) *The Lessons of Experience*, Lexington Books, New York

McClelland, D C, Atkinson, J W, Clark, R A and Lowell, E L (1953) *The Achievement Motive*, Appleton-Crofts, New York

McIntyre Brown, A (1997) The pay bandwagon, *Management Today*, August

Malone, T N and Laubacher, R J (1998) The dawn of the e-lance economy, *Harvard Business Review*, September–October

Mant, A (1997) *Intelligent Leadership*, Allen and Unwin, St Leonards, NSW, Australia

Mathews, R (1999) *Jobs of Our Own: Building a stakeholder society, alternatives to the market and the state*, Pluto Press, NSW, Australia, and Comerford and Miller, Kent

Micklethwait, J and Wooldridge, A (1996) *The Witch Doctors: Making sense of the management gurus*, Random House International, New York

Mintzberg, H (1989) *Mintzberg on Management*, The Free Press, New York

Moss Kanter, R (1985) *The Change Masters*, Unwin, London

Nadler, D A and Tushman, M L (1990) Beyond the charismatic leader: leadership and organisational change, *California Management Review*, **32** (2), Winter

Nohria, NN (1995) Mary Parker Follett's view on power, the giving of orders and authority: an alternative to hierarchy on a utopian ideology, in *Mary Parker Follett Prophet of Management*, ed P Graham, Harvard Business School Press, Boston, MA

O'Neill, Baroness O (2002) *A Question of Trust*, Reith Lectures, BBC London

Ouchi, W G (1982) *Theory Z*, First Avon Printing Company, New York

Page, C and Wilson, M with Kolb, D (1994) *Management Competencies in New Zealand: On the inside looking in?* Ministry of Commerce, Wellington, NZ

Pascale, R and Athos, A (1981) *The Art of Japanese Management*, Victor Gollancz, London

Pascale, R T (1990) *Managing on the Edge: How successful companies use conflict to stay ahead*, Penguin Books, London

Patterson, T T (1972) *Job Evaluation*, Business Books Ltd, London

Perkins, S J (1997) *Internationalization: The people dimension*, Kogan Page, London

Peters, T (1988) *Thriving on Chaos*, Alfred A Knopf, New York

Peters, T J and Waterman, R H Jnr (1982) *In Search of Excellence*, Harper and Row, New York

Petersen, D and Hilkirk, J (1991) *Teamwork: New management ideas for the 90s*, Victor Gollanz, London

Porter, M E (1980) Competitive Strategy: Techniques for Analysing Industries and Competition, Free Press, New York

Porter, M E (1997) Business Strategy Masterclass, IPD Conference, Harrogate

Putnam, R D (2000) *Bowling Alone: The collapse and revival of American community*, Simon and Schuster, New York

Quinn, J B (1992) *Intelligent Enterprise: A knowledge and service based paradigm for industry*, Free Press, New York

Quinn, J B, Baruch, J G and Zien, K A (1996) Software-based innovation, *Sloan Management Review*, Summer

Rao, S L (1997) White collar jobs, snip, snip, snip?, *India Today*, 8 September

Reich, R B (1992) *The Work of Nations: Preparing ourselves for 21st Century capitalism*, Vintage Books, New York

Retief, D and Stamp, G (1996) Towards a culture free identification of working capacity: the career path appreciation, in *Towards Culture: Free Identification of Leadership Potential*, ed J Venter et al, Knowledge Resources, Brunel University, London

Roes, R R (1979) *The Effectiveness of Company Organisation Structures*, Unilever Personnel Division, London

Rowbottom, R and Billis D (1987) *Organisation Design: The work level approach*, Gower, London

Rudis, E V (2003) *The CEO Challenge 2003: Top marketplace and management issues*, The Conference Board, New York

Semler, R (1994) *Maverick: The success story behind the world's most unusual workplace*, Arrow Books, London

Smith, A (1996) Flexible reward: is it really happening?, *People and Performance*, Hay Group, London, Spring

Solow, R, Dertouzos, M and Lester, R (1989) *Made in America*, MIT Press, Cambridge, MA

Sparrow, P (1998) Too good to be true, *People Management*, 5 December

Stalk, G Jnr (1988) Time – the next source of competitive advantage, *The Harvard Business Review*, July–August

Stamp, G and Stamp, C (1993) Well being at work: aligning purposes, people, strategies and structures, *The International Journal of Career Management*, **5** (3)

Stewart, A M (1994) *Empowering People*, Pitman Publishing, London

Stieglitz, H (1962) Optimising span of control, *Management Record*, **24**

Strassman, P A (1985) *Information Pay-Off: The transformation of work in the electronic age*, The Free Press, New York

Strebel, P (1996) Why do employees resist change?, *Harvard Business Review*, May–June

Thayer, A (2001) *Life of Beethoven*, rev E Forbes and ed I Curtis, Folio Society, London

Thompson, J (1967) *Organisations in Action*, McGraw Hill, New York

Toffler, A (1970) *Future Shock*, Pan Books, London

Tomasko, R M (1987) *Downsizing: Reshaping the corporation for the future*, AMACOM, New York

Towers Perrin UK (1997) *Learning From the Past, Changing For the Future: A research study of pay and reward challenges in Europe*, London, March

Tushman, M L, Newman, W and Romanelle, E (1986) Managing the unsteady pace of organizational evolution, *California Management Review*, Fall

Ulrich, D (1997) *Human Resource Champions: The next agenda for adding value and delivering results*, Harvard Business School Press, Boston, MA

Urwick, L F (1956) The manager's span of control, *Harvard Business Review*, May–June

Vancil, R (1987) *Passing the Baton*, Harvard Business School Press, Cambridge, MA

Van Fleet, D (1974) Span of control: a review and restatement, *Akron Business Review*, Winter

Van Fleet, D and Bodeian, A G (1977) A history of the span of management, *Academy of Management Review*, July

Von Clausewitch, C (1968) *On War*, tr J J Graham, Barnes and Noble, New York

Watson and Wyatt (1999) *Human Resources Review*, UK, February–March

Wheelwright, S C and Clark, K B (1995) *Leading Product Development: The senior manager's guide to creating and shaping the enterprise*, Free Press, New York

Wilson, T B (1994) *Innovative Reward Systems for the Changing Workplace*, McGraw-Hill, New York

Wind, J R and Main, J (1998) *Driving Change: How the best companies are preparing for the 21st Century*, Kogan Page, London

Yurkutat, J (1997) Is the 'end of jobs' the end of pay surveys too?, *AMA Compensation and Benefits Review*, July–August

Index